Ideology and Political Theory

A Study with Special Reference to the Disintegration of the Soviet Union

Ideology and Political Theory

A Study with Special Reference to the Disintegration of the Soviet Union

By

Kundan Kumar

2003

DISCOVERY PUBLISHING HOUSE
NEW DELHI-110002

First Published-2003

ISBN 81-7141-638-1

Published by

DISCOVERY PUBLISHING HOUSE
4831/24, Ansari Road, Prahlad Street,
Darya Ganj, New Delhi-110002 (India)
Phone: 3279245 • Fax: 91-11-3253475
E-mail:dphtemp@indiatimes.com

Printed at :

Arora Offset Press, Delhi

CONTENTS

PREFACE

The present book is organised into five chapters, each of which seeks to analyse a particular aspect of the communist ideology since its inception from the days of Karl Marx. To start with, the concept of ideology has been delineated in the context of historical perspectives especially stressing the interpretation given by several philosophers in the light of their experience during the period they lived in. The significance of Marxism lies in its claim that earlier philosophers had interpreted the world differently, its object was to create a new one. In order to analyse Marxism in historical perspective, all relevant strands in the development of the main theme have been briefly discussed as precursors in the wake of which the socialist thought ran its course.

However, philosophers remained engrossed with the conflicting claims of different ideologies each of which posed as a panacea for human problems. In the international gathering in 1955, they almost unanimously endorsed the view that there should not be any ideological conflicts in a free society and an ideological accord was the demand of the day. In brief, ideological conflicts should be replaced by consensus on ideological matters.

Ideologies do not arise in a vacuum nor remain mere subjects of speculation among the philosophers. They provide theories to a state system and are very much concerned with the structure of political power in society. Even in the days of Greek civilization ideology provided guidelines to the people as to how their normal forms of government if not pursued by altruistic motives and guided by noble sentiments could get perverted and give rise to tyrannies of various types.

Usually it is a political party that acts as the most important carrier and interpreter of ideology. In the book under reference, the Communist Party of Soviet Union has been analysed with particular reference to what extent it failed in its mission to educate people on whose support they wanted to survive. All these background developments form the subject matter of Chapter II.

The main theme of the essay, which is Soviet ideology, its origin, evolution and culmination, is designed to highlight the compulsions of circumstances that caused its emergence in the Soviet Union and led to its disintegration in 1991. Marxism, as Plamentz pointed out, could not have been produced in the dark ages nor could the steam engine, each of which required a certain social environment. Ideology like science is limited by the environment in which it is produced. In studying the emergence of ideologies we have not to go by the formulations of theoretical predictions but by the spirit of the forces that go to shape a society. According to Marxist interpretation, Russia, because of its industrial backwardness could not be a fertile ground for the growth of Communist ideology, but the basic idea was that Russian society of those days was most exploited economically and most conservative from the point of view of religion. These facts have been stated in detail in Chapter-III.

It may be recalled that during the First World War the allied forces as a matter of strategy had entered Russia probably on the invitation of the Tsar. During the Communist Revolution in 1917, the presence of the Western troops in the Soviet Union was used by Western powers against the new Soviet State. This added to the strength of counter revolutionaries who with their activities impeded the pace and development of the Communist revolution. The Soviet Union had not forgotten this bitter fact of history and continued to seek an opportunity to retaliate. The Marxist supporters found in the post-war period which gave them the opportunity to form a bloc extending over the whole of Central and East Europe. These developments have been discussed in detail in Chapter IV.

Finally, to face new challenges particularly in its efforts to assert its superiority over other systems the communist ideology had to spread its wings over a number of other allied spheres but it failed to resist the onward march of mankind towards achieving the cherished goal of freedom. The details have been stated to show how the process of disintegration had started much earlier than expected and how it resulted in complete collapse which at one time was considered to be a new religion for the mankind. The Nobel Laureate, Norman Angel once remarked that communism would succeed to the extent it became a religion and it would meet the fate of some of these religions which were imposed by a small sect over others for very dubious reasons. The scope of these issues has been widely covered in Chapter V.

It should be kept in view that the developments in the Soviet world since 1989 have had a tremendous impact on the entire global system. Gorbachev after assuming power in 1985 never believed that the end of the Soviet Union was so inevitable and imminent. So he tried his hand with Glasnost and Perestroika but the system had been so incorrigible that he had to remain a passive witness to the transition from one system to another. Meanwhile the fall of Socialist regime in Eastern Europe and the re-unification of Germany brought the disintegration of the USSR to the world view as a fact to which all had to be reconciled.

ACKNOWLEDGEMENTS

In the preparation of the thesis, under submission, the learned guidance that I received from my supervisor Dr. Nisar-ul-Haq, Reader in the Department of Political Science, Jamia Millia Islamia, has been a source of constant inspiration to me. The keen interest he took in the day-to-day progress of my research helped me to get it expedited without in any way affecting the work qualitatively. I will ever remain grateful for all that he did for me during the period I spent at Jamia. It is with a sense of great humility that I express my deep indebtedness to Professor S.J.R.Bilgrami, Dean of Social Science, Professor Z.M. Khan, Head of the Department of Political Science, Professor Z.A. Nizami, Professor of Political Science and till recently Director of the Academic Staff College and Professor Mohd. Mujtaba Khan, Department of Political Science for their encouragement, valuable suggestions and above all their readiness to help me in procuring the material from different sources which otherwise would not have been so easily available. In this context I cannot fail to express my gratitude to the other members of the faculty and fellow researchers who from time to time discussed the subject with me and gave their useful comments.

Among the libraries in which I had to work during the period of research, the Jamia Millia Islamia, Sapru House, Delhi University, Jawaharlal Nehru University, Nehru Memorial Museum and Library, Teen Murti House, Parliament House, have been the custodian of extremely useful material that I required from time to time to analyse the various aspects of the subject. I take this opportunity to thank the librarians and staff of these institutes for being extremely courteous to me during the period I spent in their association. Finally, the help I received from a number of other friends in extending their co-operation in several ways would ever remain an unforgettable experience of my life.

Kundan Kumar

INTRODUCTION

An ideology is a system of beliefs and ideas held in common by the members of a society either as a matter of experience or faith as inherited from its propagators. Ideology is the conversion of ideas into social levers, it is the commitment to the consequences of ideas. It not only sustains the society but also specifies a set of values that are more or less coherent. In political sphere it is regarded as a discourse in so far as it envisages guiding principles, practices and aspirations by which politically organised societies are to be governed. Complete individual loyalty to the ideology is demanded of those who accept it and it is essential and so imperative that the individual conduct is completely permeated by it. All adherence to the ideology are expected to be in complete agreement with each other.

The term ideology was coined in 1801 by Destutt de Tracy. Napolean Bonaparte referred to the "ideologues" as the mongers of metaphysical trash, and fixed the popular connotation of the term as visionary moonshine. Studies of "ideology" as a distinctive type of human thought have emerged only recently. Marx's penetrating mind for the first time made the concept of ideology part of a systematic doctrine. He analysed the dependence of our ideologies upon our environment and emphasized especially the importance of the socio-economic setting of ideologies.

There has been tremendous impact of ideology on political theorising. Marxism is an ideology and socialist regimes have based themselves on Marxism. Ideologies often assumed the role of a saviour when societies were in crisis. In periods of social turmoil and widespread public discontent people look around for ideas that would help them to understand the present realities. It promises for a better future. Certain ideologies thus appeal to the public mind not only for contemporary period but also in times to come.

Ideologies act as cementing bonds within a political system. They seek to bolster up a regime. Ideologies also play an important role in explaining political change. Political change is an essential element of political life. The speed and extent of change vary from system to system. Ideologies are the broad and comprehensive doctrines like liberalism, communism or fascism which having emerged in the past two hundred years acted as a peculiar and often decisive factor in contemporary politics. Our modern wars were ideological wars, our party conflicts were ideological conflicts. To understand the present and the past, we should have to understand the nature and effects of these ideologies; without it no study of modern politics, foreign or domestic, could make sense.

The Congress for Cultural Freedom, an association of Western intellectuals, met in National Museum of Technology and Science in Milan in mid-September 1955. Some 150 writers, politicians, public figures, journalists and university professors had gathered to discuss a theme which was on the agenda as the "future of freedom". The aim for setting up the conference was to liberate liberal and social thinking from unnecessary stratification and working out a common basis for formulating more realistic and more constructive ideas in regard to the free society.

Most of the participants endorsed the view that we were living in the twilight zone of ideology where acute ideological conflicts were at end. In their view there should not be any ideological conflicts in free society and "end of ideology" was a first requirement of the free society. They maintained that there must be an ideological accord in the society. Ideological conflicts should be replaced by consensus on ideological matters. Many other sociological and economic concepts emerged such as "convergence theory", "post capitalist society", "stages of economic growth", and "value-free social science". All these concepts were associated with the theory of the "end of ideology".

In the recent times, many far-reaching changes have taken place. The pace of the change in the world has accelerated. Marxian ideology which at one time had such tremendous impact that it divided the world into two ideological blocs. Now we see that Marxian ideology is waning. Developments in the socialist world especially after 1989 were so quick that political analysts and observers were completely confused and bewildered. The disintegration of the Soviet Union took place and many of East European countries opted for western democracy. Many factors were responsible for these sudden changes but the differences in ideologies were the main source of these changes.

Developments in the socialist world during the last few years particularly since 1989 have had a tremendous impact on the entire global system. As a matter of fact these developments were very quick. In spite of all the criticism of the Communist system and Marxist ideology, the critics did not visualise its total collapse. The change can be described as the fall of the Communist ideology. The process of change has been hailed by many in the west as an ideological victory of the capitalist model of democracy.

These regimes came to symbolise repression, censorship, ethnic chauvinism, militarism, red tape and economic backwardness. The failure of the economic content of communism, which, indeed was the most vital aspect of the Marxist-Leninist ideology, is believed to have been the bane of these societies as it wrought political degeneration leading to instability. Besides, in these societies there were some unique domestic, historical and political factors which also contributed to the rise of inimical forces to which the political-economic institutions fell prey in the final analysis. Gorbachev's policies of Perestroika and Glasnost did also contribute in bringing about the change.

Those countries that adhered to the Marxist-Leninist ideology differed with the west on socio-economic, political and cultural issues. Despite these ideological infirmities they claimed themselves to be more democratic. As it came to pass, the Marxist states crumbled under the dead weight of ideological inadequacies. The source of these contradictions in the Soviet

Union and other East European countries lay primarily in their differences in ideological thinking. The ideological dissimilarity with the west and its inability to absorb the shocks of the changing times led to the disintegration of the Soviet Union. Hence, with this backdrop the proposed study tends to examine the place of ideology in political theory and how far was ideology responsible for the disintegration of the Soviet Union.

The significance of the research under reference can be highlighted by stating the developments of contemporary events that have so rapidly overtaken the world and the measures that were adopted to face the challenges. At one time, ideology had a tremendous impact on political thinking. At the time of social turmoil and widespread public discontent, ideology played a very important role in giving people a direction in understanding the present and preparing for the future goal. But of late it has been realised that ideology had lost importance in so far as it could control the mass mind as their sole liberator from all social tyrannies. Now no ideologies can repeat the Marxist slogan that by accepting their philosophical tenets, 'the common man could not lose anything but chains'.

History is witness to the fact that Marxian ideology had its sway for a considerable long time. It stood as a scientific philosophy, revolutionary programme, progressive movement and the socio-economic, political, cultural and moral basis of more than a thousand million people. During the course of its journey, it successfully faced many challenges from within and without. It guided many revolutionary movements of this ideology which had divided the world into two blocs—the capitalist and the socialist. But these days Marxism as an ideology has been labeled as an outdated ideology which is unable to deal with the complexities of the late 20th century. It arouses curiosity to find out how far this assumption is correct. Whether Marxism has really come to an end or not would be a fascinating area of a study.

The pace of change in the world has been accelerated. One of the major reasons for the collapse of the monolithic communist state apparatus was its inability to absorb shocks and change quickly both in technology and in politics. This in a way vindicates the assertion of the end of ideology theorists that there cannot be only one model of managing modern complex societies, but it is the synthesis of the few that could lead to the establishment of a stable society. It is true that the ideological division of the world led to a continuing debate between the different ideologies competing and supplementing, but the emphasis of the end of 'ideology theory' was to go beyond this specificity and look to the essential convergence rather than divergence between two modes of arrangement and social engineering. This is in mark contrast to other ideologies like polycentrism or the Marxist schools that emerged in the west and remained confined mainly in the east among the dissidents.

For Marx, reality had no structure outside the one imposed by the human productive activity. For him, man himself had no essence of nature but changed through interactions with his national and social environment. All thought was a reflection of the environment in which man found himself. He believed that man has been the slave of extraneous economic forces and religious philosophical and political illusions and asserted that man if he only had the scientific understanding of society could determine his circumstances. Rejecting the three great sources of theocratic traditions in the West, Greek philosophy, Judaism and Christianity, Marx asserted that in future man, the creator, would become the most potential weapon of social change. He believed "in the unity of theory and practice and said that it is not consciousness that determines life but life that determines consciousness." In other words, it is the material development in society which had created a false distinction between theory and practice and spirit and matter. Theory according to him was, hand-maiden of practical material interests; communist theory for Marx is not a mere description or explanation of the realities of human life and society or even prediction of what is to come but the necessary weapon for the demolition of class-society and a blueprint for establishing a new world based on the knowledge that man creates himself.

In this context a new idea may be added. Marx also had a theory of history. But with the fall of socialism, Marx's theory of economic basis of society which forms the corner-stone of his historical materialism too has proved to be a dialectical obsession. But then how are social formations to be explained? Is there any other reliable pattern of development to depend upon? Again what is the next higher society and with what regimes? The search in the matter is imperative as a social obligation.

Even some communist philosophers believe that a historical type movement as Marxism was, is such that in forward movement of progress, it does not occur twice. History has no example of reconstruction, once a historical type is lost. Though the remanents of feudalism survive even today, we can never conclude that reconstruction of European feudalism as a historical type has become possible. The slave-holding society of the Roman type that existed for a period of 300 years cannot reappear even if desired. There are some remanents of a historical type but it never confirms its recurrence.

Karl Jasper used the term 'axial time' which prepares the objective conditions for the reappearance of a historical time and this specific 'axial time', once passed never does come again. Therefore, the idea of reconstruction of Marxian socialism is basically anti historical and as such stands rejected by us without any hesitation. There is another view which suggests that the idea of reconstruction persists. Some give the back-to-Lenin concept, other give the back-to-Marx idea, in which they say that the 1917 Revolution was premature as the then Russia was an underdeveloped country with little capitalist growth. There are still others who hope to rebuild Marxian socialism following the teachings of Marx, Engels, Lenin and Stalin and occasionally by invoking even Mao.

There are some Communists who think on the above lines in a mood of penance that emanates from truth of faith to which they want to stick. If the struggle for socialism had not been abandoned after the downfall of the Paris Commune, why should one give it up now following the collapse of the Soviet Union? By asserting the historic fall of Marxian socialism we, however, would like to point out that the disintegration of the Paris Commune is not similar to that of the Soviet Union. Paris

Commune was suppressed but the Soviet Union suffered a fall from within. Whereas the Paris Commune succumbed to the forces of external factors, Soviet communism died of its own inner contradictions rendering its revival an unlikely possibility.

ABSTRACT

Ideology and Political Theory: A Study with Special Reference to the Disintegration of the Soviet Union

I. Theme and its Significance

This essay primarily seeks to analyse the role that ideology in general has played in the development of human consciousness to move incessantly towards making human society free from all inner contradictions thus imparting not only permanence to its perpetuation but also ensuring maximum human happiness to the people.

Historically speaking it started from the days of Thucidides and Aristotle who are regarded as pioneer thinkers in the realm of political speculation. But the earlier ideas were refreshed in each age by the philosophers of the day. Each ideology claimed to be perfect in offering solution of the problems that the generations faced keeping in mind the limitations in which each was formulated. Thomas Maine's Utopia was a chain in ideological link of the West.

In the wake of the barbaric practices that were witnessed in the post industrial era in the form of worst possible economic exploitation by those who controlled means of production over the have-nots, a new wave of resentment stirred the conscience of all thinking people. The credit goes to Karl Marx who is considered the prophet of the age as it is he who gave form to what remained a vision to his predecessors? The basic postulates of his philosophy immensely influenced the mass mind everywhere. As he said the philosophers earlier had interpreted the word differently, his mission was to create a new one. There hardly had been any philosopher who could wield so much influence as Marx did among the largest masses of the people all over the world. There was a time when it appeared that Marxism had come to stay but the history which has been a cruel master reacted in a different way uprooting the ideology from the country which was regarded as the Rome of Communism.

An attempt has been made in these pages to analyse the concept and its working and also what brought about its downfall. Ideologies do not emerge in a vacuum nor do they wither away in the atmosphere of disbelief or non-believing. Likewise, ideologies do not die but they get eclipsed. They may emerge soon if the conditions conducive for their birth and growth again challenge the status-quo and call for the reversion of the old systems in a renewed form bereft of the flaws which brought about their downfall.

Finally, this essay does not essentially attempt to trace the history of disintegration of the Soviet Union which was no doubt the culmination of the process which had started much earlier. It is essentially a survey of events that led to the dissolution of communism which ultimately broke the backbone of communist system. The breakdown of the system has been the result of the failure of the Communist ideology to bring about, as it predicted, a new way of thinking among the mass mind of the Soviet people who were made to accept this ideology as a creed. It is none of the business of the present researcher to speculate on what will happen in the future. There are numerous theories being set forth to promote different answers to this query. One of them suggests that communism has been a long and painful transition from capitalism to capitalism.

II. Ideology and its Role

Our modern age is predominantly an age of ideology. Ideology has always been and will continue to be an inevitable commitment of our earthly existence. But "Studies of ideology" as a distinctive type of human thought has emerged only very recently. This discipline maintains that philosophical thought or, more correctly, thought in general, is always the expression of a specific social situation. Every social group develops its own conceptual apparatus, certain peculiar methods and a specific style of thinking according to its position in society. These patterns of thought are ideologies.

The ideology strictly means a system of ideas elaborated in the light of certain conceptions of what ought to be. It designates a theory of social life which approaches the facts from the point of view of an ideal and interprets them, consciously or unconsciously, to prove the correctness of its analysis and to justify that ideal. Thus every ideological construction involves the projection of a certain ideal into the future, keeping in view its evaluation in the present and also its evolution in the past.

Ideologies consist of programmes for the future of the society, the community, the nation, the state or the world, together with quasi-scientific explanations of social facts so interpreted that the desired future state is covertly or overtly scheduled to come about either logically, morally or from the point of view of natural laws.

The French philosopher Antonie Destutt de Tracy (1754-1836) coined the term 'ideologie' in 1796. De Tracy was an aristocrat, sympathetic to the French Revolution (1789), but was imprisoned during the Terror. Tracy saw 'ideology' as a science of the human mind and he believed that his task was not simply explanatory; he wanted to develop a system of education which would produce better people.

The word 'ideology' quickly degenerated into a pejorative term, referring more to the object rather than to the form of study, a situation which largely remains today. The best known Marxist statement on ideology appears in 'The German Ideology', which Marx wrote with Friedrich Engels (1820-95) in the 1840s. In their view the class which had the means of material production at its disposal, had control at the same time over the means of mental production, so that thereby, generally speaking, the ideas of those who lacked the means of material production were subjected to it.

In the field of ideologies much of the work done belongs to the cumulative study of problems that existed from the days men learnt to line together in society. The study of ideology is associated with the growing conviction that human behaviour is largely non-rational or irrational. The work of Charles Darwin has much to do with the spread of such ideas. Since there is no break in the chain of descent between man and other animal species we need not assume that the behaviour of man is determined by forces radically different from those operating in the behaviour of animals. Since behaviour of animals is largely impulsive and instinctive, men began to assert, at the turn of the present century, that human beings too have instincts, and that human actions are in considerable proportion non-rational or non-logical.

Ideologies come in all colours—red, white, green and saffron (communist, racist, islamic, hindu etc.). National socialism in Germany was exclusively devoted to the cause of a master race. The Klu-Klux-Klan of America and the skinheads of neo-Nazis of modern Europe, the Muslim and Hindu fundamentalists of Afro-Asian countries are all testimony of the power that ideologies exercise over the minds of men. Ideologies move men to close their minds to all extranuous ideas and to follow their particular ideologies zealously and even blindly.

In the absence of leadership by well organised minorities, mass populations are rarely, if ever, capable of decisive action. Revolutions always depend, therefore on the initiative of an organised minority. Among the communists, this minority was the dictatorship of the proletariat: a new kind of regime based not on popular consent but on the revolutionary power of a small, well organised elite, the communist party.

Ideology is never an end in itself but the means to an end, which end is the over all progress of mankind. Different ideologies have devised different means to achieve this end, and no ideology is, or can be, absolutely applicable and relevant to all times, places and circumstances. Every ideology has a particular time and place. There is a tide in the affairs of men which when taken in its stride leads to good fortune and prosperity. No one can stop the march of an idea whose time has come and ideas that are out of time with ground reality are fated to die. Capitalism and communism had to wait till the industrial revolution before they could be fully developed into the powerful ideologies of their times.

III. Eclipse of Marxism

Communists in pre-Marxian days used to claim that the people in the West always talked in terms of creating a Utopia on the model of Thomas Maine's 'Utopia'. But Marx in his view developed socialism from a Utopia to a science. Nearly 150 years separated the English bourgeoisie revolution and the French revolution. Another 80 years passed before the emergence of the prototype of the first worker's state—the Paris commune, but the October Revolution of 1917 laid the first foundation of the world socialist system.

Another claim of the communists was that Marx was the sole protagonist of what is known in history as scientific socialism. They believed that under the new dispensation a new society would be created in which the structure of power would be recast and the system of private property would be abolished. The call to create a society in which there would be no poor or rich, nor the private property would be allowed to exploit the have-nots drew popular response. Marx advocated that even the early christians did not believe what was possible or practical. All his life Marx continued to elaborate the basic principles of his philosophy which was not only a pioneer effort to pose a problem in a most logical manner but which also sought to solve the problems which so far were considered insoluble. In brief Marxism declared itself to be the science of how to construct a society of social justice which remained a dream so far for all those who believed to be the reformists of the society.

However, due to the collapse of Marxian socialism, the Utopian nature of communism has become exposed. Also with the fall of socialism, Marx's theory of economic basis of society, which formed the cornerstone of his historical materialism too appeared to be irrelevant. The question often posed was whether the change could be described as the fall of communist ideology or the failure of the soviet style of state system. The general consensus among scholars has been that it was the soviet system as set up by the leaders in power in the light of their understanding of the communist philosophy that had met its doom. The ideology and the system could not be identified as two separate entities.

The concept of communism as understood and promoted by Stalin was called 'army barrack' socialism upholding repression', militarism and ethnic chauvinism. After Stalin, a new leadership emerged which tried to give it a new meaning but they could not go beyond a certain stage in making communism as an acceptable alternative by other countries which had the same problems of poverty and backwardness to deal with. Even communism after the second world war was enforced by the military regime of the Soviet Union, it was never adopted as a system by a popular vote. The Soviet leaders struggled to improve their system by various means. But in the world of competitive ideologies they could not make much headway. On the other hand, problems went on accelerating.

The failure of the economic contact of communism which was the most vital aspect of the Marxist ideology turned out to be the sole reason for creating instability and finally its collapse.

During the cold war period reforms were introduced in the Soviet Union because it had lost this war. During this period Marxism had lost all force as an ideology and communism as a political order and Soviet type of socialism as an economic system. Meanwhile the Soviet wings had spread all over East Europe and major parts of Asia. This economic-military over-extension weakened the ideological force leading to dilution of Soviet authority over its allies.

The collapse of the Soviet Union in December 1991 ended an important chapter of history. The momentous changes that took place between 1985 and 1991, the magnitude and swiftness of the transition from Communism to post-totalitarianism and from Soviet to post-Soviet government were unanticipated and yet have somehow become inevitable. During Gorbachev's time it was already clear that the slow evolution of the Soviet system had accelerated swiftly. For sometime greater contacts with outside world, contempt for tired and aging leaders, rising economic expectations and the decline in growth caused by the arms race had been awakening the desire for political change among the elites. In a society with no independent institution it was impossible to express these demands in a sustained and public way. But the hunger for change was there and sometimes it had to assert.

When Gorbachev came to assume power in 1985 he sought to introduce some reforms through perestroika but he made it clear that it was not to replace Soviet system. It was not in his mind to change the economic and social structure of communist society. The aim of reforms was to overcome economic stagnation and to make the Soviet Union more effective and competitive. Glasnost was another concept associated with his name. It stood for 'openness', to make public what has been hidden. It increased the opportunities for public analysis by making information more accessible, removing the ban on certain topics and providing opportunities to ask questions and offer any conceivable options for answers.

The situation in Soviet Union had deteriorated so much that these well meaning concepts could not cut much ice and what was needed now was radical transformation of the whole Soviet system based entirely on new tenets of liberalism. But the problem was to democratise the country which had for a generation been under totalitarian regime, such a system could not be transformed into a new set up over night. It appeared as if it would take if not a generation, at least a few years to change the complexion of the society. In fact the events in 1991 did not launch the country on the path of democracy but it was a turning point, a moment of discontinuity. However, the 19th annual session of the Soviet Communist Party gave the lead to the developments that resulted in the break-up of the Soviet system. It is at that conference that a decision was taken to allow contested elections in the coming year. This marked the end of the one-party system, the collapse of one party itself and finally the collapse of the Soviet Union.

No one in 1985 imagined that USSR was under threat of falling apart. The process of disintegration happened to be remarkably smooth. Compared with other European empire the Soviet Union fell apart with no blood shed. Eastern Europe was given up without a shot being fired. The republics of the Soviet Union broke away with only minimal resistance from Moscow which preferred to remain docile. If later there was conflict it was not between Russians and non-Russians but between other ethnic groups. That Russia adjusted to the loss of empire and she reacted to transition non-violently and without turning to xenophobia has been a remarkable event of the century.

IV. Contents of the Essay: Synoptic View

As regards the pattern of analysing the theme of research, the dissertation under submission has been organised into five chapters, each of which seeks to analyse a particular aspect of the communist ideology since its inception from the days of Karl Marx. To start with, the concept of ideology has been delineated in the context of historical perspectives especially stressing the interpretation given by several philosophers in the light of their experience during the period they lived in. The significance of marxism lies in its claim that earlier philosophers had interpreted the world differently, its object was to create a new one. In order to analyse Marxism in historical perspective, all relevant strands in the development of the main theme have been briefly discussed as precursors in the wake of which the socialist thought ran its course.

However, philosophers remained engrossed with the conflicting claims of different ideologies each of which posed as a panacea for human problems. In the international gathering in 1955 they almost unanimously endorsed the view that there should not be any ideological conflicts in a free society and an ideological accord was the demand of the day. In brief, ideological conflicts should be replaced by consensus on ideological matters.

Ideologies do not arise in a vacuum nor remain mere subjects of speculation among the philosophers. They provide theories to a state system and are very much concerned with the structure of political power in society. Even in the days of Greek civilization ideology provided guidelines to the people as to how their normal forms of government if not pursued by altruistic motives and guided by noble sentiments could get perverted and give rise to tyrannies of various types.

Usually it is a political party that acts as the most important carrier and interpreter of ideology. In the dissertation under reference, the Communist Party of Soviet Union has been analysed with particular reference to what extent it failed in its mission to educate people on whose support they wanted to survive. All these background developments form the subject matter of Chapter II.

The main theme of the essay, which is Soviet ideology, its origin, evolution and culmination, is designed to highlight the compulsions of circumstances that caused its emergence in the Soviet Union and led to its disintegration in 1991. Marxism, as Plamentz pointed out, could not have been produced in the dark ages nor could the steam engine each of which required a certain social environment. Ideology like science is limited by the environment in which it is produced. In studying the emergence of ideologies we have not to go by the formulations of theoretical predictions but by the spirit of the forces that go to shape a society. According to Marxist interpretation Russia, because of its industrial backwardness could not be a fertile ground for the growth of Communist ideology, but the basic idea was that Russian society of those days was most exploited economically and most conservative from the point of view of religion. These facts have been stated in detail in Chapter III.

It may be recalled that during the First World War the allied forces as a matter of strategy had entered Russia probably on the invitation of the Tsar. During the Communist Revolution in 1917, the presence of the western troops in the Soviet Union was used by western powers against the new Soviet State. This added to the strength of counter revolutionaries who with their activities impeded the pace and development of the communist revolution. The Soviet Union had not forgotten this bitter fact of history and continued to seek an opportunity to retaliate. The Marxist supporters found in the post-war period a catalytic situation which gave them the opportunity to form a bloc extending over the whole of Central and East Europe. These developments have been discussed in detail in chapter IV.

Finally, to face new challenges particularly in its efforts to assert its superiority over other systems the communist ideology had to spread its wings over a number of other allied spheres but it failed to resist the onward march of mankind towards achieving the cherished goal of freedom. The details have been stated to show how the process of disintegration had started much earlier than expected and how it resulted in complete collapse which at one time was considered to be a new religion for the mankind. The Nobel Laureate Norman Angel once remarked that communism would succeed to the extent it became a religion and it would meet the fate of some of these religions which were imposed by a small group of people over others for very dubious reasons. The scope of these issues has been widely covered in Chapter V.

It should be kept in view that the developments in the Soviet world since 1989 have had a tremendous impact on the entire global system. Gorbachev after assuming power in 1985 never believed that the end of the Soviet Union was so inevitable and imminent. So he tried his hand with Glasnost and Perestroika but the system had been so incorrigible that he had to remain a passive witness to the transition from one system to another. Meanwhile the fall of Socialist regime in Eastern Europe and the re-unification of Germany brought the disintegration of the USSR to the world view as a fact to which all had to be reconciled.

1

EVOLUTION OF THE CONCEPT

Our modern age is predominantly an age of ideology. Ideology has always been and will continue to be an inevitable commitment of our earthly existence. There has never been a time, when human behaviour, particularly political behaviour, has not been largely affected by the mental images, through which men have grown accustomed to perceive and judge the world around them. The emergence of the comprehensive doctrines like liberalism, fascism and communism, during the past two hundred years had been a decisive factor in moulding our thinking in contemporary politics. Without some understanding of the nature and effects of these ideologies, no study of modern politics, foreign or domestic, could possibly make sense.

"Studies of ideology" as a distinctive type of human thought has emerged only very recently. This discipline maintains that philosophical thought or, more correctly, thought in general is always the expression of a specific social situation. Every social group develops its own conceptual apparatus, certain peculiar methods and a specific style of thinking according to its position in a society. Every pattern of thought, every philosophical or other cultural product belongs to the specific social group in which it originates and with whose existence it is bound. These patterns of thought are ideologies. In America, "ideology" and "ideologue" are still taken by most of the thinkers as derogatory terms, and are used to condemn or stigmatize. But to understand their meaning in sociological analysis it is necessary to forget this connotation. The ideology strictly means a system of ideas elaborated in the light of certain conceptions of what ought to be. It designates a theory of social life which approaches the facts from the point of view of an ideal and interprets them, consciously or unconsciously, to prove the correctness of its analysis and to justify that ideal. Thus every ideological construction involves the projection of a certain ideal into the future, into the evaluation of the present and into the past.[1]

In order to have a clear perception of the concept of ideology it would be relevant to review a few definitions enunciated by some eminent social scientists. For instance, for Raymond Aron "....ideology....is a pseudo-systemic formulation of a total vision of the historical world" Daniel Bell on the other hand considers 'Ideology as the conversion of ideas into social levers', ...'It is the commitment of the consequence of ideas'.... For the ideologue, truth arises in action and meaning is given to experiences by the 'transforming moment'. Robert A Haber considers Ideology as an intellectual production describing the society. Joseph La Polambara is more specific when he says that Ideology....tends to specify a set of values that are more or less coherent and that seek to link given patterns of action to the achievement or maintenance of a future or existing, state of affairs.

Karl Mannheim in stressing the main aspects of ideology, says that the term 'ideology' in the 'sociology of knowledge' has no moral or denunciatory intent. It points rather to a research interest which leads to the raising of question when and where social structures come to express themselves in the structure of assertions, and in what sense the former concretely determine the latter.

Taking more views into account Talcott Parsons states that ideology is a system of ideas which is oriented to the evaluative integration of the collectivity, by interpretation of the empirical nature of the collectivity and of the situation in which it is placed, the processes by which it has developed to its given state, the goals to which its members are collectively oriented, and their relation to the future course of events. Edward Shils summarizes the concept of ideology under a few heads. Firstly, to him ideologies are characterized by a high degree of explicitness of formulations over a wide range of objects with which they deal. Secondly, complete individual subservience to the ideology is demanded of those who accept it, and it is regarded as essential and imperative that their conduct be completely permeated by it; and finally all adherents of the ideology are urgently expected to be in complete agreement with each other.[2]

Ideologies, thus consists of programmes for the future of the society, the community, the nation, the state or the world, together with quasi-scientific explanations of social facts, so interpreted that the desired future state is covertly or overtly scheduled to come about either logically, morally or from the point of view of natural laws. There is a fundamental difference in method and aim between the ideologists and the social scientists. The general method of science is to collect with the guidance of hypothesis as many relevant data as possible and discover what uniformities they hold. The essence of the scientific approach lies not so much in the contents of its specific conclusions as in the methods whereby the conclusions are reached and continually corrected. The true scientist regards his theories as hypothesis. He is constantly on the alert to analyze his own mental processes and to keep his own emotions from colouring his theories. The ideologist on the other hand, holds his theories as articles of faith, and habitually confuses his assumptions with his conclusions.

Scientific method tries to eliminate or minimise all errors or illusions, but ideology assuming itself to be scientific, consciously or unconsciously makes use of illusions or even errors. Science questions everything. Ideology takes its illusions for granted and declines to question them. Hence, it sees beyond what does not exist. Science bases its beliefs on the best available evidence; ideology bases its beliefs on selected facts, frequently on imaginary evidence which will support its socio-philosophic assumptions. Ideology employs only that evidence which ratifies the conclusion as its ideological principles. The ideologist, hoping to bring about a better world, is interested not in a scientific knowledge of truth, but in its political or philosophical idea which would bring about the desired ends. His ideology does not include social facts in their complex and kaleidoscopic relations, but constructs them, according to its ideal in a well prepared picture. Ideologies are therefore a synthesis of facts and assumptions arranged to support an ideal which is not always in accord with social facts but which nevertheless needs to create a new social order.

In the field of ideologies much of the work done belongs to the cumulative study of problems that existed as far back as Thucydides and Aristotle. The study of ideology is associated with the growing conviction that human behaviour is largely non-rational or irrational. The work of Charles Darwin has much to do with the spread of such ideas. Since there is no break in the chain of descent between man and other animal species we need not assume that the behaviour of man is determined by forces radically different from those operating in the behaviour of animals. Since the behaviour of animals is largely impulsive and instinctive, men began to assert, at the turn of present century, that human beings, too, have instincts, and that human actions are in considerable proportion non-rational or non-logical.[3]

The non-rational character of human social behaviour runs through the literature of American sociology and social psychology from Ward, Giddings, Baldwin, Cooley and Ross down to the present time. This notion of the non-rational, character of human behaviour from the views of Freud and his followers, who by disclosing the relativity of morals and thoughts helped to undermine the 18th and the 19th century idea that the man is a completely rational creature.[4]

Historically the concept was strengthened when religious, political and economic controversies made their impact on the average man's mind.[5] Such intellectual conflicts made men aware of the quality of their adversary's thinking. The discrepancy between objective reality and social conceptions had been noted long before by Marsilio of Padua and by Machiavelli. Bacon analyzed the ideals, the pre-conceptions, and illusions of the populace which stood in the way of scientific knowledge. In the 17th century, discrepancy in definition of ideologies were spoken of as synonymous with climates of opinion. In the 18th century men were beginning to realise that ideas have a setting. Montesquieu suggested that men's mentalities are conditioned by the systems surrounding them.[6]

Origin and Approach to Ideology

The French philosopher Antoine Destutt de Tracy (1754-1836) coined the term 'ideologie' in 1796. de Tracy was an aristocrat, sympathetic to the French Revolution (1789), but was imprisoned during the Terror. On release, he turned his attention to what had caused such barbarities, and the more general question of the way in which the values of epochs and societies differed significantly. de Tracy was a true rationalistic heir to the Enlightened. He saw 'ideology' as a science of the human mind. Moreover, like many others of the Institute National, which had replaced the Royal Academies after the Revolution, de Tracy believed his task was not simply explanatory. He wanted to improve people—to show which ideas were false, and to develop a system of education which would produce better people. This association of 'ideology' with science was short lived. The word 'ideology' quickly degenerated into a pejorative term, referring more to the object rather than to the form of study a situation which largely remains today.

The first major figure to use the term in this pejorative way was Napolean Bonaparte (1769-1821). Napolean had initially been sympathetic to de Tracy's work. However, after becoming emperor, he caricatured de Tracy's group as 'ideologues'. Napolean thus began a long line of critics who were to associate 'ideology' with traits such as simplistic analysis, divorced from reality, and an authoritarian desire to improve people's lives.

Ideology as a pejorative concept was particularly important in the work of Karl Marx (1818-83). Indeed, a notable political philosopher, John Plamenatz, has written that it was Marx 'more than anyone, who introduced the word into social and political theory, and he used it in all its important senses without troubling to make clear how they differ.'[7] Subsequently, Marxist approaches have dominated the methodological debates about 'ideology'.

The best known Marxist statement on ideology appears in 'The German Ideology', which Marx wrote with Friedrich Engels

(1820-95) in the 1840s: "The ideas of the ruling class are in every epoch the ruling ideas, i.e., the class which has the material force of society, is at the same time its ruling intellectual force. In their view the class which had the means of material production at its disposal, had control at the same time over the means of mental production, so that thereby, generally speaking, the ideas of those who lacked the means of material production were subject to it."[8]

Marx was critical of those who held that the role of ideas was crucial in history and in social life. He believed that social existence determined consciousness, and not the other way round. He thus adopted a materialist view of history, in which economic forces rather than great leaders or ideas led to progress. Marx made a distinction in capitalist society between a 'base' and 'superstructure'. The former referred to the basic organisation of the means of production, and the resulting class system. The superstructure referred more to individuals and to ideologies. These ideologies were not simply 'isms' but were reflected in any feature of society which served to defend the ruling class. Thus ideologies were the legal, political, religious, aesthetic or philosophic principles which reinforced capitalist society.[9]

Marx did not believe that his own views were 'ideology' seeing them as based on a scientific understanding of history and the inevitable triumph of the working class and socialism. However, it was Engels who sought to popularise the term 'scientific socialism' for Marx's work.[10] In elucidating his philosophy Marx was especially indebted to the German philosopher C.W.F. Hegel (1770-1831). However, it was Marx who first attributed the term ideology to such belief systems, though as with much of Marx, there was some notable variation in his usage. In particular, there was a tension between the pejorative sense of ideology as something which marked the interests of capitalist society, and a more general sense in which ideologies were seen as necessary part of the belief systems of all societies.

V.I.Lenin (1870-1924) too identified Marxism as a science, but he effectively accepted that ideology was a term which should not be restricted to capitalist, or pre-capitalist. In 'What

Is to Be Done?' (1902) Lenin argued for a socialist ideology which could help develop, working class consciousness beyond the 'economism' of immediate concerns. Lenin especially believed that such an ideology was important to prevent the working class from falling into trade union consciousness. He saw unions as premised on the existence of capitalism, particularly in the sense that their demands for better wages and conditions could best be achieved through a healthy capitalism. Moreover, unions threatened to divide the working class into a relatively well paid unionised group, and an impoverished proletariat, lacking the leadership of those who had been attracted by unions. In Lenin's words: "All those who talk about overrating the importance of ideology, about exaggerating the role of the conscious elements, etc., imagine that the labour movement pure and simple can elaborate, and will elaborate, an independent ideology for itself'... But this was in his views a profound mistake. Since there could be no talk of an independent ideology formulated by the working masses themselves in the process of their movement, the only choice was either bourgeois or socialist ideology."[11]

This socialist ideology was largely to be developed by an intelligentia, which clearly must have broken free from the power of capitalist conditioning. Exactly where this left the materialist conception of history and especially the primacy of base over super structure, was never made fully clear. However, it reflected a challenge to those Marxists who sought to delineate rigid materialist laws of history.

This development was taken even further in the works of the Italian communist Antonio-Gramsci (1891-1937). Gramsci rejected the cruder forms of materialism which reduced the 'superstructure' to 'base' factors. In his later writings he also became increasingly critical of Leninism, believing that it did not pay sufficient attention to the strength of civil society in liberal democracies—namely-non-governmental institutions and forms of social conditioning, such as education, or the mass media. Gramsci believed that the rule of one class over another was not simply an economic one, it depended on 'hegemony'—on cultural and ideological forces as well.[12] Gramsci was especially interested in the role of intellectuals, whom he divided into 'traditional' and 'organic'. The former considered themselves to be free of classes, and rational people like university academics, and ecclesiastics. Organic intellectuals were closely connected organisationally with the class structure. These were people like members of the communist party, or unions. For Gramsci these were the intellectuals most likely to help create a counter-hegemony, through their writings or their role in key institutions.[13]

Gramsci's work also had links with parts of the influential French structuralist school. A key figure here was the philosopher Louis Althusser (1918-90). Althusser, in keeping with the later Marx, held that there was no rigid relation between base and superstructure in developing the idea of the 'relative autonomy' of the superstructure. However, whereas Marx had recognised the importance of institutions such as the family, or religion, he had not seen them as part of the state. Althusser held that the state and its influential tentacles were now much diverse. He included within this Ideological State 'apparatus spheres' such as education and trade unions.[14]

Over a hundred years after Marx had written the main corpus of his work, many Marxists were using superstructural factors to explain why 'contradictions' in the base had not produced the much heralded downfall of capitalism. The growing band of Gramsciites, for example, argued that capitalist societies were characterized by a hegemonic ideological conformity, which minimized conflict. However, some Marxists remained committed to a more rigid analysis of the relationship between base and superstructure, even if there were new nuances in the argument. Abercrombie, Hill and Turner, for example, viewed ideology as mainly useful for uniting elites; subordinate groups were seen as divided, and were influenced more by economics than ideology. In recent years communism may have declined as a major form of world government, but it still lives on as an important basis of academic critiques of dominant ideologies.

Invaluable contribution in the realm of ideology was also made by George Sorel. The term "ideology" was not used by Sorel, but he talked about the "myth". The best ideology for the workers, according to Sorel, was to adopt the myth of the general strike, the belief that the millennium would arrive when the proletariat arose and by a swift universal strike overthrew all the established organs of the government. Nietzsche made a considerable contribution to the study of how men behave and more particularly to the study of the relation between their actual behaviour and their professed beliefs and systems of belief in their religions, ethics and philosophies.

Emile Durkheim made an attempt to eliminate the influence of ideology from the social sciences. He wanted that the social sciences must become positive, scientific and inductive. Metaphysical presuppositions must be eliminated and social ideas must be treated as illusory things. If an idea or ideal penetrates, social life irrespective of right or wrong idea it becomes a highly important social reality in the making of which a given idea plays a decisive role. Durkheim did not use the word "ideology" but used the term "doctrine". This helped us in understanding ideology sociologically. Doctrine does not grow from the study of reality, but is a logical support for pre-conceived ideas.[15]

Vilfredo Pareto developed a line of thought that bears significantly upon the problem of ideology. Human action was divided into two classes—logical and non-logical, according to Pareto. Logical action is directed both subjectively and objectively towards the end in view. All other actions are non-logical for they have only a subjectively logical end which does not correspond with men's real purpose. Pareto analyses the prime fallacy in that aspect of modern sociology and psychology which regards as logical movements, those social phenomena which are in part automatic or instinctive, but mostly non-logical and irrational. Such social phenomena involve sentiments and passions, social institutions in the process of development or decay, educational ideas, religions, superstitions and myths, which in their cumulative effort enable the individuals to make a distinction between actual and theoretical and between actual and illusory results.

In "Politics as a Profession", Max Weber described his analysis on ideology. According to Weber, the politician always needs to have faith not only in his own motives, but also in those of his adherents as it is by their collective efforts that he relies to achieve the end in view. In Weber's view politician's actions are not guided so much by the sense of conviction, as by responsibility. The politician, therefore, cannot reflect, as the man of ethical conviction should, all actions involving morally dangerous means but on the contrary take the burden upon himself and place his own soul at stake since he bears the responsibility for the success of his cause.

Karl Mannheim in "Ideology and Utopia", examines the pattern of ideas underlying social actions. The analysis of ideology, in his opinion, is out of the Marxian attempt to unmask their opponents. What an ideology attempts to do so is to explain the course of the world, to catch the primary factors to historical dynamics. Mannheim reaches to what he calls a non-evaluative conception of ideology. All knowledge is relational and hence knowledge is itself to be understood in terms of the relation of the possessor of knowledge to the particular historical and social context in which he is thinking.[16]

Max Learner in his "Ideas are Weapons" says that men of action have probably always looked upon ideas as weapons. It is only that men of thought have been driven to accept the position. It was a period when it was fashionable to regard ideas as epiphenomena, mere ghostly and ineffective adjuncts in material processes or as based, more or less on dishonest rationalisation of economic compulsions. Ideas have come back with a bang in our own time through their recognized influence on actions in the mass of ideologies and propaganda flooding the modern world. Learner's position does not imply any return of the old faith that the truth always triumphs. It only means that the validity of an idea is one condition of its permanent effectiveness. To be valid, an idea or ideology must read correctly its whole social and natural environment, must be cognizant of its own origin, direction and ultimate aim, and must be applied with action. If it fulfils these requirements, a rational programme has a good chance of conquering the irrational one condemned by its intrinsic character to reformulate its aim with each passing wind.[17]

By investigating the problem of ideologies by various social scientists we perceive that in the domain of social sciences or more broadly of the nomothethic sciences dealing with man and human societies, any hard and fast differentiation between non-evaluating empirically minded worker and a social worker is difficult to establish, not only in view of the methods of the one or the other, but above all because of the psychological attitude they adopt with regard to their respective functions. Eminent ideologists like Marx and his followers have developed scientific and empirical aspirations.[18] Dispassionate observers, when confronted with highly emotional problem of ideology, have found that those who are unreservedly committed to social actions devote their scientific talent to find some concrete result of their labours.

Ideology in Transition

In every society where conflicting interests exist, the dominant social ideology must provide within a single unified and apparently consistent belief system such justification for every separate interests. When specific groups in society perceive their own interests as being not in harmony with the dominant social ideology, i.e. when contradictions are discovered in the consistent system of beliefs, there arises a challenge to the dominant ideology.[19] In the ultimate analysis such perceptions of conflicting interests and contradictions are related for change brought about as a result of the objective processes of social development. The specific form of such conflict and its outcome are however settled in the arena of politics and depend upon how successfully the alienated interests are reunified within an alternative and apparently consistent belief system which includes all the specific interests whose support is politically required.[20]

In transition, a new ideology must develop in dialectical relationship with the existing ideology. A dominant social ideology seeks to reproduce itself in belief systems of successive generations. Such ideological conceptions are related to basic social activities the specific rules which order such activities and the structure of relations produced by the process of reproduction of such activities. These material social processes sustain the associated ideological conceptions which in turn are consistent with the conditions required for the continuation of the material processes. However, there are distinct and concrete processes by which such beliefs themselves are reproduced over successive generations, through religious rituals and practices, relations within the family, schools and educational systems, the media of communication, art, culture etc. When new ideologies make their appearance, new and discordent interests would emerge in society in course of changes in material structures and processes. In course of time the new forces would disrupt the old ones creating parallel institutional processes.

During transition from feudalism to capitalism contradictions were discovered in the older dominant ideology of Catholicism and a new religious ideology of Protestantism was created. This disrupted the older ideological institutions of the catholic church and created new institutions providing in a new way the respective activities and domains of the individual, the church and the state. This should also be stated that after the transition, the new established capitalist process required for its reproduction a new dominant ideology, liberalism which sought to force the sphere of economic activity from all primordial or communal fetters. It enabled the sphere of economic activity to operate among free and equal individuals and restricted the domain of the state to the functions of a neutral guarantor of the rules governing these activities.

Liberal ideology can hold sway when the capitalist process of production truly operates within a free and unfettered labour and capital market and then demonstrate the apparent consistency of its ideological principles. Where the capitalist process comes to dominate the production economy with the aid and support to the open, forcible and discriminatory intervention of the state, the consistency of liberal principles cannot be so demonstrated. Capitalist economy in crisis reflects a crisis of liberal ideology as well, so that one gets the phenomenon of a multiplicity of ways of thinking. In this way ideological principles can be investigated and its development can be traced.

Science and Ideology

The counter-position of science and ideology, therefore needs to be clarified. Characterization of a set of beliefs as ideology implies the demonstration that those beliefs are non scientific and that they represent rationalization. It implies the incorporation into the system of beliefs of solutions already conceived outside the supposedly theoretical argument of certain group occupying a specific position in two social structures. We also know that the total stock of reasonably reliable concrete scientific knowledge which we now possess is quite inadequate to exclusively guide all practical activity which we find necessary to undertake even in everyday life. Hence, non scientific beliefs of some sort appear to be unavailable.

The problem is to tie the creation of knowledge to purposeful human activity. Purpose cannot be determined solely by scientific knowledge. In any given historical situation, purpose will be found to be determined by interest ideology. On the other hand, the scientific analysis of processes of change in the natural and social order i.e., their objectification in theoretical terms, will reveal to us the range of objective possibilities, the potential for change in given circumstances. This theoretical activity—the production of theoretical knowledge—is itself not independent of purpose. For purpose of facts and the choice of problems, the formulations of problems, the assignment of priorities among alternative fields of research, purpose thereby influences methods, procedures and techniques by creation of scientific knowledge.

The actualization of the objective possibilities revealed in theory is also the task of keeping this dialectical relationship in mind where theoretical and political activity is not however, easily accomplished. The inadequacy of available scientific knowledge means the continued prevalence of non-scientific beliefs of some sort. It often means the utilisation, indeed exaggeration of such beliefs for political purposes. The task of consciously expanding the range of scientific thinking in popular belief systems of making the knowledge of science available and acceptable to wider sections of people, is a practical political task which can be taken up only by those classes that are conscious of their objective social strength in carrying forward the historical process of social development. Only a vision of purpose can assess alternative objective possibilities and use the knowledge of science for the actualisation in history of this potential, only purposive practice can shift the true from the false. The two challenges are inherent in the human and historical situation indeed, if man ever does come to possess complete and true knowledge, science would become irrelevant and history come to an end.[21]

Is Democracy an Ideology?

Democracy can be seen in many different forms. Common distinctions are between the more participatory forms envisaged by direct democracy, and the more limited, pluralist, representative liberal democracy. Is extensive popular participation necessary to true democracy or are the masses more a threat to the freedom and tolerance which many conservatives in particular see as crucial to democracy? Clearly the term democracy can encompass almost polar opposites.[22] Indeed, in some ways the twentieth century—especially the period since 1945-has seen a competition amongst almost all the main ideologies to monopolise the term democracy. In the pre-1989 Eastern European communist systems called themselves 'People's' Democracies.

Arguing that democracy and capitalism are not ideologies raises the distinction between what Martin Seliger calls the 'inclusive' and 'restrictive' conceptions of ideology.[23] The inclusive interpretation of ideology sees a broad body of thought as 'ideology' the best example of such an approach would be Karl Mannheim (1893-1947), whose book 'Ideology and Utopia' (1929) has been described by Seliger as 'the first and so far the last comprehensive elaboration of a theory of ideology'. Mannheim, who had worked with Lukacs, accepted Marx and Engels view that ideological thought was distorted, but he argued, that the reductionist use of 'ideology' could be turned against Marxism. If the 'dominant ideology' was the ideology of the ruling class, why was not the ideology of other social groups also a body of self-interested thought?[24] However, what Mannheim termed the total conception of ideology seemed to make all social thought 'ideological', thus losing any possible ability to distinguish it from other potentially useful concepts such as 'political culture' or 'socialisation'.

The 'restrictive' conception has been especially common among American academics, and accepts only certain types of belief system as an ideology, usually limiting the term to radical/ extremist forms like communism and fascism. The argument here often focuses on whether a set of beliefs is 'monist': namely, the extent to which it is held that there is a single fundamental truth, depending on 'rationalist' knowledge. Such monist ideologies involve a rejection of pluralism, tolerance and nuanced forms of arguments. A more specific argument put forward by Noel O'Sullivan holds that ideologies always involve a programmatic element.[25] Formal politics, in other words the maintenance of procedural conditions are not seen as programmatic. Democracy could thus be ruled out as an ideology on this approach.

However, there are dangers in necessarily associating an ideology with a specific programme. Lenin was fond of the Napoleonic maxim: 'On s'engage, et puis on voit' (we enter the struggle, and then see how the situation develops). Early Italian fascism managed to adopt contradictory programmes in quick succession. Later fascism often played down the need for programme, stressing instead the need for leadership and action. Moreover, a commitment to formal political procedural rules could be an important part of a programme in post communist states. Concepts such as the 'rule of law', or 'checks and balances' are clearly related to a view of human nature and to some knowledge of history. There would be something strange about a person who believed that the human race was universally and inherently good, and that no abuses of power had ever taken place, who also held that formal rules were required to prevent political exploitation.

This line of argument points to a way of envisaging ideologies which can include conservatism and liberalism, as well as Marxism and fascism, which does not also involve accepting that democracy is an ideology. An ideology must posses a certain set of attributes; in particular an ideology has an overt or implicit set of empirical and normative views about (i) human nature; (ii) the process of history; (iii) the socio-political structure. This is not to argue that there is necessarily a single view of each aspect, or that views are held with rigid local consistency. For example, socialists could disagree over whether human nature was inherently good, or something which was socially determined. However, a socialist could not hold that human beings were inherently and irretrievably greedy and aggressive. Or, to take another example, Marxists could disagree over the extent to which great individuals and ideas mattered in determining the course of history, but they could not adopt a purely 'high politics' or 'idealist' approach which saw such forces as the main motor of history.

Democracy Versus Nationalism

This approach also helps to explain why democracy is not an ideology but nationalism is. Is not nationalism consistent with a broad variety of forms of government, both dictatorial and democratic? Have there not been liberal nationalists, fascists nationalists, Marxist nationalists, and so on—indicating that nationalism, like democracy is compatible with many ideologies? However, there are crucial differences compared with democracy. These do not simply stem from the fact that recent years have seen in the west a contest among ideologies to monopolise the term 'democracy', whereas nationalism has been more a pariah term. Nor is the main point that some ideologies have adopted nationalism for instrumental rather than fundamental reasons. Thus those Marxists who have been sympathetic to nationalism have seen it in terms of a wider view of progress: nationalism was seen as a stage some societies needed to go through, rather than as an underlying principle of political organisation. The central point relates more to the basic threefold framework of an ideology. There is no fundamental democratic view on issues such as human nature, or the process of history. On the other hand, nationalists hold that there is something universally natural about people wanting to group into national units. They see history as the process of successful, and unsuccessful, nation-building and rivalry. Nationalists can differ about the implications of these concepts, but there is a core set of values around which disputes centre.

What Political Ideology is Not?

It also helps to set out what a political ideology is not. Following are some of the basic conditions which should be kept in mind in analysing the correct nature of the political ideology. A political ideology is primarily concerned with the temporal conditions. Bodies of thought mainly concerned with the divine are better termed religions though there clearly can be a gray area between religion and ideology. This occurs when a religion feels it necessary to take on a more specific temporal role—in the way that Islamic fundamentalism has done recently.

Secondly, a political ideology should not be confused with propaganda. 'Propaganda' is another concept which arouses much controversy. Within communist systems propaganda has sometimes been used in a positive way to refer to rational political education, whereas 'agitation' was the term used more to refer to simplistic appeals. On the other hand, 'propaganda' tends to have pejorative connotations in the West, often being associated with deception and manipulation. It therefore seems best to limit the term to deliberate attempts to gain political influence by focusing on a relatively limited and a simple set of issues.

Thirdly, a political ideology, and propaganda should not be confused with socialization. This refers to the process by which values are transmitted to members of society, in particular with a view to integrating them within the dominant value-system. Studies of socialization could look at a variety of social and political phenomena such as the family, school, or the media. For example, the way women are sometimes portrayed in adverts as objects of sexual lust, or as dutiful housewives, is part of sexual stereotyping. However, it is not ideology, as it is only a partial world view. It may also not be propaganda, as much of it is probably not deliberate, but reflects more the norms which socialization can produce.

Finally, a political ideology is not the same as political culture. This refers more to actual values, rather than the process by which these are disseminated. The value structure of a society, or sub-groups within a society, includes attitudes and opinions which are not necessarily conscious, or systematic, and which stem from many sources. Thus it is possible to talk of an American political culture, or a midwest subculture, but these are not ideologies. They are essentially massbased, though there is of course a relationship to ideology. 'The American way of life', 'log cabin to White House' and so on, are very much part of individualistic, entrepreneurial liberalism.

The leading social psychologist Michael Billig distinguishes between 'lived' and 'intellectual' ideologies. The former refers to the 'ideology' of, say, environmental activists concerned with their local community, rather than the grand philosophical theory of some ecologists.[26] This is perfectly understandable for a psychologist, whose primary task is not to set out and understand political philosophy, or the history of political thought. Psychologists are interested in questions like why a certain sort of person is attracted to ecologism. It is similarly understandable why sociologists focus on problems such as the type of social conditions which produce certain ideologies.

The foregoing discussion leads us to say in brief that a political ideology is a relatively coherent set of empirical and normative beliefs and thought, focusing on the problems of human nature, the process of history, and socio-political arrangements. It is usually related to a programme of more specific immediate and short run concerns. Depending on its relationship to the dominant value structure, an ideology can act as either a stabilizing or a radical force. Single thinkers may embody the core of an ideology, but to call a single person on 'ideologist' or 'ideologue', would normally be seen as pejorative. The term 'political philosopher' or 'political theorist', therefore, seems more appropriate for a thinker capable of developing a sophisticated level of debate. Political ideologies are essentially the product of collective thought. They are 'ideal types', not to be confused with specific movements, parties or regimes which may bear their name.

Out of this analyses a question arises: if a political ideology involves the study of many thinkers, movements, parties and regimes, is there not a problem concerning the very construction of an ideology? Fascism and ecologism serve as good examples here, as they are the ideologies which arguably raise the most fundamental issues about construction. One key problem in constructing fascist ideology is whether the focus should be mainly on individual fascists, or whether the emphasis should be on movements, and regime policies—the types of problem studied more by historians. Some individuals can provide a high level of thought, of interest to the academic political theorist, but it is not clear how, indeed these influenced movements and regimes.

Moreover, Italian fascism and German nazism had very different movement and regime phases. Fascism in its pre-power phase tended to be radical, for example it was more accommodating to these interests. Many would, therefore, consider a model of fascism which was not based primarily on concrete regime. Marxist viewed Fascism as an example of false consciousness, largely to be understood in terms of base influences. Such an analysis saw fascism as a product of capitalist crisis, as the, form of 'dictatorship of capital' necessary when economic crisis meant it was no longer possible to preserve 'bourgeois freedoms'. It should be added that it is not necessary to be a Marxist to hold that fascist ideology should be seen mainly in terms of its social rule. Functionalists too have seen it largely in terms of the attempt to end annomalies, or to prepare societies such as Germany, Italy and Japan for the strains which elites believed would stem from the wars necessary to ensure national greatness.

Many of these points recur, and others emerge, if we consider how to construct 'ecologism'. Should we study major individual thinkers, or actual green parties and movements? The latter are clearly very much an ideological 'melange', and to some extent likely to make compromises to attract support. This would probably be even more than true if a green movement ever gained national office or, should ecologism be understood primarily in terms of its social base?[27] An extensive sociological literature shows that the membership of western green movements tends to be young, educated and employed in the non-productive sector of the economy. But does this mean we should call ecologism a middle-class ideology, or an ideology of the young (as fascism is often termed)? Such class issues are a perfectly legitimate concern within sociology, but the futility of using them to understand ideology per se can be seen by considering the hypothetical case of a green party which became a major national party. This would inevitably have to attract a broad class and age base: would ecologism, therefore then become an 'all class' ideology?

These points raise important questions which cannot be answered simply. Indeed, they threaten to lead on to ever-more methodical debates. Nevertheless, it is worth making true points related to fascism in conclusion here. First, studying 'practice' should not necessarily be seen as providing a truer insight than studying political ideas. Whilst what fascism actually did should never be forgotten (especially in view of its bestialities), the main fascist regimes were short lived, and went through turbulent times. Studies which focus primarily on movements and regimes should therefore not be seen as necessarily providing the key to 'real' fascism. Second, most recent historiography has shown that the relationship between fascism and business was complex, but that on balance fascism and business are more than vice-versa. Even among Marxists there are now major debates about the extent to which ideology can be reduced to interests, or about the relative autonomy of the state.

Ideological Trends

'Endism': On two occasions during the last thirty years, we have been told that the age of ideologies is coming to an end, that a form of pragmatic liberal- capitalism has won. At the turn of the 1960s, the American sociologist, Daniel Bell (1919-) wrote in even more sweeping terms of the 'end of history'. These arguments offer a useful starting point to a discussion of ideological trends in the twentieth century, because each involves a set of assumptions about how ideologies rise and fall, and thus cast further light on the question of approaches to ideology—as well as delineating trends. In his much-discussed book 'The End of Ideology' (1960), Bell celebrated the demise of radical ideologies, notably fascism and communism. He argued, "Few serious minds believe that one can set down 'blue prints' and through 'social engineering' bring about a new utopia of social harmony. At the same time, the older 'counter-beliefs' have lost their intellectual force as well. Few 'classic' liberals insist that the state should play no role in the economy, and few serious conservatives, at least in England and on the continent, believe that the Welfare State is the road to serfdom. In the western world, therefore, there is today a rough consensus among intellectuals on political issues, the chief being that the ideological age has ended."[28]

On the other hand, Bell and fellow academicians like Seymour Martin Lipset were celebrating the triumph of a socially concerned, liberal pragmatism. This was allegedly, being accompanied by the decline of what the influential French political theorist, George Sorel (1847-1922), had seen as political myths—namely, simple systems of thought and programme which could achieve emotive inspiration among a mass following. It could be argued that this end of ideology thesis was itself ideological.[29] It certainly seemed to echo the development of the 'totalitarian' model in the 1950s, which was covertly encouraged by the US government. This model sought to damn both the USSR and Nazi Germany as 'ideological' political systems, which had led to brutal dictatorships, and murderous world war. Nevertheless, the end of ideology thesis was not simply western triumph but it was based on a methodological view about how ideologies arose, and fell.[30] First, there was the belief that the spread of affluence had undermined the social conflicts on which radical ideologies were premised. In other words, ideologies were not something inherent in all societies as a means of social bonding or change, but rather something which emerged at times of strain or crisis.[31]

Second, there was the belief that ideologies such as communism and fascism had been a form of secular religion, requiring both faith and ultimately irrational styles of thought. These were seen as being undermined not only by the growth of popular education, but also by a growing intellectual awareness that such beliefs were 'irrational' or 'mythical'. In this context, a crucial figure was the Austrian 'emigre' Karl Popper. His post-1945 writings attempted to associate the scientific method with falsificationism: namely, a belief was rational, or scientific, if it was clear what was required to falsify it.[32] Ideologies were seen as ultimately unfalsifiable.[30] During the late 1960s the end-of-ideology thesis fell from favour. The apparent growing power of communism and radicalism in the third world, combined with dissent at home, seemed to damn the thesis to the intellectual dustbin.[33]

However, with the dramatic collapse of communist at the turn of the 1990s, 'endism' enjoyed a revival, most notably in the work of Fukuyama, who argued: "The twentieth century witnessed a series of contests between different ideologies for instance liberalism contended first with the remnants of absolutism, then Bolshevism and Fascism, and finally an updated

Marxism that threatened to lead to the ultimate apocalypse of nuclear war.[34]

Fukuyama looked around the world, and argued that there was a universal collapse of authoritarian government in favour of democracy. Like the earlier end-of-ideology debate, there was an element of western triumphalism, but there was also a methodological core. In the latter context, Fukuyama held (following Hegel and Marx) that there is an underlying pattern in the evolution of history, that there is an end state in which human society finally confirms to the underlying pattern of human nature, a quest for 'recognition' which requires the freedom only to be found in a liberal democratic capitalist society. Human nature is one of the three key factors which Fukuyama sees as directing history, and leading to the triumph, of liberal democracy. These three factors are (i) the struggle for what he calls 'recognition'; (ii) the logic of science's mastering over nature; and (iii) the absence of major contradictions in liberal democracy.

It is worth expanding the last point first, as it helps reflect the idealist aspects of Fukuyama's analysis. Fukuyama sees this as a direct refutation of the Marxist position—where the base determines the superstructure. He also sees it as a refutation of what he calls 'the Wall Street Journal School' of determinism—the belief that people are essentially rational, profit-maximising individuals who tend not to be swayed by great ideas such as freedom, or democracy. He accepts an idea going back to Lipset in the 1950s that economic development helps establish and stabilize democracy, but he sees the triumph of liberalism more in terms of ideologies than economics.

Fukuyama sees contradictions as helping to undermine twentieth century ideologies. In the context of other ideologies, he is presumably here thinking of things like communism's promise of democracy but practice of bureaucratic incompetence and shortages its inability to foster innovation and new thought. The last aspect leads on to Fukuyama's point about science's mastery of nature. By this Fukuyama seems in particular to mean the efficient and technocratic organization of production in capitalist economies give such societies a decisive military edge. Communism simply bankrupted itself and caused social discontent in its attempt to match and overtake western military technology.

Although many have endorsed the broad sweep of this analysis, it is important to note that Fukuyama's 'endism' is open to a variety of objections. For example, he has a one-sided reading of developments in the Third World and of international relations. Thus he neglects nuclear proliferation in a non-western world, much of which is becoming relatively poorer. His rose tinted view of the social tensions and inequalities within contemporary liberal democracies seems even more remarkable especially in the light of ethnic tensions highlighted by the 1992 American and German riots, and the economic was which dominated the 1992 American and British election campaigns, and helped Bill Clinton become the U.S. President. Reading Fukuyama should also produce a strong sense of "dejavu". Indeed, since the late nineteenth century there have been periodic bouts of 'endism', though the end which states celebrated have differed notably.

The End of Ideology and Deja Vu

Marx offered a form of 'endism' in the sense that he believed that there was a particular course to history, which would lead to the inevitable triumph of socialism. However, as Marxism has already been considered earlier, it is now relevant to note that the late nineteenth century saw a liberal triumphalism, proclaiming the victory of democracy and capitalism, which in the new context would play a decisive role in human affairs. However, by 1900 liberalism was coming under a two-pronged attack from both the left and the right, though there was also an element of symbiosis in this process. The rising forces of the left tended to see liberalism as both morally wrong, and damned by a series of problems and tensions. Liberal democracy, with its concomitant claims of equality before law, or rights, was viewed as a sham, hiding the interests of the rich and growing middle class (the bourgeosie). The reality of the capitalist freedom, according to socialists, was wealth inequalities which in turn caused all other difficulties. Ultimate power in democracies was seen as lying in the hands of the rich who controlled all avenues of power reducing the masses to the status of semi-slaves.

The conclusions drawn by socialists about this analysis of liberalism could vary notably. Most Marxists and some other socialists for example Sorel, believed that violence would be necessary to overthrow the (capitalist) state. Others, in particular the forerunners of modern social democracy like Bernstein, held that it was possible to achieve change through the legislative process. This meant that some liberal views, for example, about the neutrality of the state were accepted by this form of socialism. By 1900 most socialists were turning to the (Socialist) state as the vehicle to liberate the people. Here again, there was sometimes an element of symbiosis with liberalism, for 'new' liberals, such as L.T. Hobhouse (1864-1929), were putting forward arguments about why the power of the state could be expanded. In particular, activities which, could be seen as increasing individual autonomy and freedom, for example, extensive education provisions, were accepted by these new liberals. Even the most moderate socialists tended to view the state in broader terms than this, but the growth of statism within liberalism was to be an important point of linkage between the two ideologies. However, other socialists—especially anarchists and to a lesser extent syndicalists were hostile to any form of state, seeing it as promoting elitism and authority.

Authority was central to right-wing critique of liberalism, but there the fear was more that liberalism was undermining the authority necessary for social stability. From the time of the French Revolution, right wing critics, such as Joseph de Maistre (1753-1821), had argued that people had duties as well as rights. The 'masses' were largely ignorant and easily swayed and that social stability was ultimately founded upon consensual values which could not be created from scratch according to 'a priori' principles as man was ultimately neither rational, not perfectible. Even many liberals shared some of these suspicions of the masses, and the doctrine of popular sovereignty. This could lead to the 'tyranny of the majority' in John Stuart Mill's (1806-73) terms.

In the nineteenth century there was no necessary equation between liberalism and democracy, as the masses could be seen as a threat to individual rights, and rational government. By 1900 notably different forms of right-wing thought had emerged, in the way that there were different forms of socialism. A more reactionary strand, associated with thinkers like Charles Maurras (1868-1952), stressed traditional authority, and was usually monarchist and/or religious. As it was often tied to these particular interests, it found it difficult to exert mass appeal in a western world which was witnessing the onset of the universal franchise.

A moderate strand of the right, typified by Edmund Burke (1729-97), was more willing to encompass change, if it was really needed and could be achieved gradually. This moderate right was also willing to accept some aspects of liberalism, for example the rule of law, and more grudgingly the economic dynamism of liberalism. In the latter context there remained a hostility to radical 'laissez-faire' views, seeing its individualism as essentially a threat to social solidarity and its economic conception of life as alienating. By 1900 this more moderate right saw the ultimate bonds of society not so much in terms of economic interest, or in the religious and monarchial devotion of the reactionary right, as in nationalism, a force which at the turn of the nineteenth century had been associated more with the left through its critique of established authority and celebration of the 'sovereignty of the people' (a cry which inevitably raised the issue 'who are the people'?). This nationalism was often linked, especially in Europe, to welfare policies in a form of 'social imperialism', an attempt to attract the masses both through self-interest and myth. There was an element of this in America too, though the American dream was more individualistic, and usually isolationist.

Decline of Liberalism

During the inter-war years, liberalism seemed in terminal decline, particularly in Europe. Political parties based on its principles found themselves squeezed, losing members and supporters to left and right. The great slump which began in 1929 seemed to remove any final legitimacy for free-market production. Even in the citadel of capitalism, the USA, great public works were needed in the 'New Deal' to alleviate poverty and restore confidence. The great slump contrasted with a new age of Soviet planning, which began in the late 1920s, ten years after the revolution. The 1930s was the age of 'guided tours', when selected Westerners visited the USSR and returned (in the main) to sing the praises of what they believed was a full-employment, happy and prosperous 'New Civilisation'—to use the title of a book written by Beatrice and Sidney Webb (1858-1943 and 1859-1947), who had earlier done much to develop gradualist technocratic socialist theory.

Fascism, too, posed problems for liberalism. Interventionist economic policies in Italy and Germany during the 1920s and 1930s, apparently curing unemployment, seemed another confirmation of the death knell of 'laissez-faire'. More ominously, the emergence of mass, popular nationalism in economically developed countries did not fit easily within liberalism's view of 'history', leading to ever greater 'nationality'. In particular, it seemed to confirm the Sorelian idea that the masses were swayed by collective myths, rather than guided by individual rationality—a conclusion reached by many after the nationalist fervour of the First World War had subsided. The violence of fascism during its rise, too, raised issues about toleration and freedom which troubled liberalism (as did communist violence). Was it possible to tolerate the intolerent, to permit political movements which were based on ideologies which sought the overthrow of the liberal democratic system? Fascism was defeated by war, but in the initial post—1945 era communism seemed to have been strengthened.

Indeed, by the 1960s a growing number of peoples lived under communist rule. It is true that there were differences between communist systems, including a significant split between China and the USSR over both domestic policy and foreign interests. Nevertheless, communism was viewed by most commentators as an enduring force in world politics. Sympathetic commentators, and there were many in the west, often glossed over the problems of these countries, economic systems, their brutality and lack of civil rights, for example, the chaos of Mao Zedong's (1893-1976) 'Cultural Revolution'. Instead radical-chic students of the late 1960s waved Mao's 'little red book', chanted revolutionary slogans, plotted sittings and engaged in other forms of activity which would have led to their arrest in communist countries. More seriously, admiring comparisons were often made by commentators between capitalist and democratic developing countries such as contrasting China's apparent absence of gross poverty with India's starving, often begging, millions.

In the West, particularly in Europe, the first two decades after 1945 were characterized by an era of statism. This was the great age of Keynesian macro—and micro-economic policy, designed to level out the trade cycle, and ensure a prosperous full-employment economy. These truly were years of economic growth, which helped fund new welfare programmes and provide standards of living (judged in economic terms) undreamed of by nineteenth century socialists. Cars, televisions and a host of consumer goods became the play things of the masses. Pockets of poverty still existed, particularly in the more peasant based European countries and in the USA, but high levels of employment and statist policies funded by growth seemed to offer all the dreams of a new future.

For most western countries, the years immediately after 1945 were ones of relative stability and consensus. Against such a background, it is easy to see how Bell's 'end-of-ideology', thesis grew. Given the rise of statism in the west, and growing evidence of problems in communist systems, it is easy to see why another form of 'endism' became fashionable during the 1960s and 1970s, especially on the moderate left. This was called 'convergence theory', which held that communist systems would adopt more market oriented principles and pay greater attention to western freedoms, while western systems would become, if anything, more statist and welfare-oriented. This argument had various forms of methodological assumption. Usually it was argued that dynamic economies needed a level of freedom not found in communist systems. On the other hand, it was argued that democratic pressures in the west required a high degree of intervention to prevent gross inequalities and abuse of 'rights'.

In its most methodologically simple term, the argument was a form of 'I've seen the future and it works' (to adopt a famous western comment on the early USSR). This usually involved eulogizing social-democratic Sweden as a model of full-employment, prosperous, participatory society. Thirty years of, Sweden's social democratic consensus had broken down, and its much vaunted polity was characterized by features such as growing unemployment, and racism. Punitive marginal tax rates seemed to have encouraged evasion and been a disincentive to effort. Slowing economic growth helped lead a very high interest rates, which in themselves act as a brake on investment—and thus future growth. Sweden had gone from being a model to admire, to a case study of the problem of achieving growth in a high-tax and interventionist economy. Indeed, the social democrats, who dominated Swedish politics after the 1930s, lost power in the 1980s.

It could be argued that China had perhaps conformed to the convergence model in the economic, if not political sphere. However, by the 1990s the rest of the former communist bloc seemed characterized by a remarkable dual process. On the one hand it was adopting free-market principles and policies, such as privatization. On the other hand, former communist states seemed to be disintegrating in the face of ethnic rivalries and tensions. At present the latter tendencies seem distinctly stronger than the former, especially as it is hard to see how economic aspirations raised by the collapse of communism can be fulfilled in the short run, while it is easy to see how rapid economic change promotes a psychological need to achieve a sense of community through ethnicity.

In economic terms, former communist states are seen at times as more royalist than the king, for they are adopting radical free market policies at a time when there are growing doubts about them in the West. The Keynesian dominance of the immediate post war years in the west gave way in the 1970s and 1980s to the more 'laissez-faire' policies, which had been preached most notably by F.A. Hayek (1899-1992) and Milton Friedman for over twenty years. This was a time when New Right economic policies, including privatization and tax cuts, seemed to offer hope for rapid new growth. However, many Western economies have failed to achieve the growth rates hoped for, and a reaction to neo-liberal economic policies seems to be setting in. Some free market supporters argue that their policies were not really implemented in full, that administrations such as Ronald Reagan's and Margaret Thatcher's (let alone George Bush's and John Major's) were too influenced by pragmatism and electoral pressures. However, this raises major issues about whether a democracy could sustain the high levels of unemployment which such policies would almost certainly mean in the short run. It also raises questions about the acceptability of large interval differences in income and wealth.

The End of History and the Twenty First Century

The preceding discussion raises the issue what exactly is the relationship between democracy and capitalism, such as the one between the latter's concentration of power, and the former's promise of individual freedom; or between democracy's commitment to majority decisions, and the more liberal concept of natural rights. And what are the new radical challenges, glossed over in the above discussion, especially from ecologism or feminism?. In some ways, the ecologist's case could be read as stating that the triumph of capitalism is likely to lead to world destruction: how could mass industrialization be envisaged without destroying the world's ecosystem? Radical feminists can mock how 'democrats' concern themselves with issues like falling turnouts in elections, whilst ignoring patriarchy and the resulting male political domination. The last point illustrates the limitations of Fukuyama's definition of democracy, or rather his confusions about democracy. A minor example concerns the way he talks of America being a liberal democracy in the eighteenth century, and Britain being one by the mid-nineteenth century. Yet he also uses as a key defining aspect of democracy the existence of universal adult franchise (1920 in the USA; 1928 in Britain).

Fukuyama fails to see that some non-Western democracies, for example in Asia, are committed to democracy in the sense that their governments are accountable to their subjects and must maintain constitutional rather than personal rule. But this is not 'liberal' democracy. It is not founded on individualism, in the sense of rights, or on the dividing line between private and public which is central to western liberal democratic theory (if not always practice). Predictably, Fukuyama seems confused about whether countries like Singapore, even Japan, are democracies. Similarly, Fukuyama makes a serious mistake in using one word (capitalism) for many forms (American; Korean; Swedish; and so on). Fukuyama recognizes that there are differences, but seems to believe that western style capitalism and democracy will be the shape of the future. But is it that simple? Has not Islamic society resisted western 'capitalist' and democratic modes of socio-economic organization for centuries?

There are also more complex, controversial, philosophical points about democracy and capitalism. Friedrich Nietzche's (1844-1900) criticism of democracy, echoed by Martin Heidegger (1889-1976), was that the very nature of democracy, undermined a sense of 'recognition'. Was there not a levelling in democracy, in theory at least, which removed distinction and merit, which militated against leaders? Moreover if democracy truly was an end state, would there be any goals left worth fighting for, goals which historically had helped give people a sense of 'recognition' and purpose?

Modern Western Society is unlike any of the 'great' societies in history in that it stresses on the individual over the holistic group. Within it, relations between people and things (especially goods) seem more important than those between individuals. This point was made by Marx, and has since been picked up by others of very different political persuasions. Michael Polanyi in 'The Great Transformation' (1957) noted how exceptional the modern era is in the way that economies and the market are made sacrosanct. This raises the issue of how such a society is legitimized.

The market was initially supported in the West by the Protestant ethic, with its emphasis on profit as a reward for hard work, and other legitimizing aspects. However, markets are now increasingly seen essentially as efficient allocative mechanisms. The Hayekian 'epistemological' defence of the market makes little attempt to defend profit in terms of just reward; luck and other factors all play their part. Instead, the market is seen as a complex knowledge-mechanism. Attempts to 'plan' are now seen as inevitably leading to lower national income, bureaucracy, and 'infreedom'.

This problem of legitimation is stressed by Bell in his book 'The Cultural Contradictions of Capitalism' (1974), and others on both right and left have highlighted the moral void at the heart of modern liberalism. It is not necessary to be an ecologist to ask what happens if growth slows down, even stops. Looked at another way, it is not necessary to be a fascist to ask whether liberalism's individualist he-donist ethos makes it difficult for the West to fight a future major war or whether 'freedom' means the freedom of immigrants to move across national boundaries. It could be argued that these points miss the fact that the growing interdependence of market economies makes war less likely, or that mastery over nature and scientific accomplishment has opened up the prospect of ever-rising wealth. However, here the idealistic limits of the argument seem clear. Major problems continue to exist both within and between contemporary nations. The task at the end of the twentieth century, therefore, seems less the celebration of liberalism, than a careful consideration of both liberalism and other ideologies in order to understand what they have to say about the contemporary condition.[35]

Impact of Various Ideologies Down the Ages

Fredrick M. Watkins in his book "The Age of Ideology" tells us that all the major 'isms' of modern politics are secular rather than religious faiths. Their vision is not of a blissful life hereafter, but of a perfectible life on earth". That a perfect state is achievable here on this earth underlines all the secular ideologies. Therefore Watkins says that "the goals to which they (ideologies) address themselves are typically uptopian... Modern ideologies normally tend therefore to define their goal in unrealistically optimistic terms".[36] According to Watkins "over simplification is the primary characteristic of modern ideologies. This is their strength and also their weakness".[37] Because for every ideology there exists an anti-ideology and for the ideologies of liberalism, individualism, capitalism, democracy and secularism there exist the corresponding ideologies of Authoritarianism, Socialism, Communism, Dictatorship and Fundamentalism. Watkins says that "Ideological excess may also encourage the growth of anti-ideology." Plato also held that every government tends to perish by the excess of its basic principles.

Watkins believes that excessive inequality existed among the people and were responsible for both the French and the Communist revolutions. He says that it was the French Revolution's Declaration of the rights of man which outlawed at a single stroke the whole complex structure of special privileges and guaranteed the principle of equal rights for all," enshrined in its slogan of 'liberty, equality and fraternity'. Speaking of the Communist Revolution, Watkins noted that "Since economic inequality seemed to be the inevitable consequence of free competition, the proponents of equality naturally began to look on free market itself as the primary obstacle to human welfare." Aristotle believes that "the universal and chief cause of the revolutionary impulse was the desire for equality."

The other revolution which merits special mention is the rise of secular nation-states in opposition to the church. The reformation occurred in Europe as a result of the concentration of too much of power in the hands of a corrupt papacy and the priestly classes. The formation of the secular nation-state was a direct consequence of an overdose of religious authority.

The secular nation-state had evolved to such an extent in Europe that by the time of the formation of America, "the separation of church and state was a principle on which most Americans were soon able to agree." On the other hand, these days we are witnessing a revival of fundamentalist religious parties especially in Asia and Africa, which have developed as a backlash against what they perceive as a threat to their faith by the secular ideas of the nation-state. Too strong a development in either the secular or the religious dimensions causes a reaction in the opposite direction.

The formation of the state, whether theocratic or secular is based on the belief that individualism must not be allowed to tear apart the social fabric of the people. For this strong institutions are needed to repress the selfish and irrational impulses of individuals, and to inculcate civilised habits. The anti-establishment ideology of individualism must be countered by the conformist ideology of the social state. Supporters of the social state asserts that the essence of nationalism, after all is the belief that the interests of the nation are more important than the interests of any individual. But it was precisely this kind of a scenario that was predicted by George Orwell in his book in which the power of the state become so overbearing as to become unbearable. To every individual this would mean that he was constantly under the watchful eyes of the all powerful state where the 'Big Brother' was always watching. It was such conditions in Russia and Eastern Europe, where individual human rights had been reduced to farce that Mikhail Gorbachev stepped in to liberate the people from the clutches of a repressive state machinery. Ayn Rand had described such a super-state as a "super being embodied in no one in particular and everyone in general, except yourself."

Ideologies come in all colours—red, white, green and saffron (communist, racist, Islamic, Hindu etc.). National socialism in Germany was exclusively devoted to the cause of a master race. The Ku-Klux-Klan of America and the skinheads of neo-Nazis of modern Europe, the Muslim and Hindu fundamentalists of Afro-Asia are all testimony of the power that ideologies exercise over the minds of men. Ideologies move men to close their minds to all extraneous ideas and to follow their particular ideologies zealously and even blindly. Nietzsche says that "In individuals insanity is rare, but in groups, parties, nations and epochs, it is the rule." However, in the larger social setting it is always the chosen few, or the elite which lead or guide a movement, while the majority of the masses follow, blindly. In the absence of leadership by well organised minorities, mass populations are rarely, if ever, capable of decisive action. Revolutions regularly depend, therefore on the initiative of an organised minority." Among the communists, this minority was the "dictatorship of the proletariat': a new kind of regime based not on popular consent but on the revolutionary power of a small, well organised elite, the communist party".[38]

Ideology is never an end in itself but the means to an end, which end is the overall progress of mankind. Different ideologies have devised different means to achieve this end, and no one ideology is, or can be, absolutely applicable and relevant to all times, places and circumstances. Every particular idea or ideology has a particular time and place. There is a tide in the affairs of men which when taken in its stride leads to good fortune and prosperity. No one can stop the march of an idea whose time has come and ideas that are out of time with ground reality are fated to die. Capitalism and communism had to wait till the industrial revolution before they could be fully developed into the powerful ideologies of their times. But it also cannot be denied the rise of ideology was from the beginning associated with, and has at all times been much affected by the Industrial Revolution, and that 'The Industrial Revolution' itself owed much to the power of ideology. The fall of communism today is a sign of the times, that the factors that were ripe for the rise of communism and existed at the beginning of the century are no longer relevant. A Russian wife stated after the fall of communism that, "These rulers of ours who claim that the prime mover of history is the economic basis have shown by the whole of their own practice that real stuff of history is ideas. It is ideas that shape the minds of whole generations winning adherents, creating new forms of government, and society, rising triumphantly and then slowly dying away and disappearing". Great leaders are those who understand the indicators of the time and just happen to be at the right place at the right time, and seize the opportunity when it presents itself.

Ideology down the ages has been divided between two camps the liberals and the authoritarians, the radicals and the conservatives, the upper classes and the lower classes, the capitalists and the communists, the state and the church, the socialists and the individualists and the secularists and the fundamentalists. To many a philosopher speaking, the established order is a thesis, which inevitably produces its own anti-thesis, in the form of a new revolutionary class. Hence every state is in a situation of dynamic equilibrium. Any increase in one part of the state creates an imbalance in the other part. Balance is sought to be restored either by gradual changes, or else, if the imbalance is too great—by a revolutionary change. When the church or any other group representing a certain ideology later, authoritarianism or conservatism or capitalism or individualism, become too strong then the dice is loaded in favour of the anti-ideologies which soon give rise to a new set of ideologies such as communism and socialism. If on the other hand the secular state becomes too removed from religious concerns or the masses become unruly, liberty turns to anarchy, or if communism becomes too overbearing then reaction in the opposite direction is bound to occur. Aristotle stated that "political revolutions spring from disproportionate increase in any part of the state". Hence too great an inequality between any two opposing ideologies is a surefire recipe for a revolution or a change in power dynamics.

All ideologies are extremist in nature. To hold the central or the mean position is to be 'status quoist'. The extremist nature of ideologies created a polarity or a deviance from the mean which provides the direction to an ideology. To follow the direction indicated by an ideology fills its believers with a deep sense of purpose. The progressive nature of mankind ensures that the dialectic process of development is an on-going process. Every thesis has an antithesis, every ideology an anti-ideology. Mankind fluctuates between dialectically opposed doctrines depending on the given circumstances and the direction in which he seeks to move. Too much anarchy gives rise to an authoritarian ideology. Too much totalitarianism gives rise to a liberal ideology. Too much paganism gives rise to a religious revival, while religious decadence encourages paganism. Economic disparities encourage socialism while economic stagnation encourages the capitalist spirit. Rationalism is countered by romanticism. Hence ideologies provide a balancing function in a well ordered state, and any disproportionate increase in one part is balanced by an equal and opposite increase in another part. Over-centralization is countered by decentralization and vice versa. Hence the unity and integrity of mankind as a whole is preserved by a dynamic interplay of extremist and opposing ideologies.

The end of 20th century is witnessing a decline of the age of ideology and cold war which dominated the Western World since the dawn of the industrial age. The post industrial era has required us to go beyond the narrow ideologies which suddenly seem incapable of solving a host of contradictions which are cropping up the world over. Capitalism and communism are primarily economic ideologies based on a material view of the world. The current turmoil is a symptom of the obsession of the West with material advancement. Both ideologies have been overly concerned with the production, distribution and consumption of material goods. The governments have geared primarily for the protection and propagation of their respective economic systems. Materialism is the highest good of these purely economic doctrines where man himself is only secondary.

These economic doctrines in no way suggest how individual and societal development is to take place. Happiness, it is believed, follows automatically from material progress and the more one consumes the happier one becomes. Obviously this had not been the case. Man needs spiritual as well as material progress. In this context a brief review be taken of the implications of the great ideologies of capitalism and communism.

The problem with capitalism is that it results in a fragmentary view of the world. Each person is competing against the other, and all reality is viewed from their respective perspectives only. No one has an overall picture of progress, but all have self centered views of progress. This results in a lopsided development and not a planned, holistic approach to development. Planning is a socialist concept. 'Laissez faire' is against any planning, its rationale being that everything finds its own level in accordance with the law of supply and demand. Thus while we have a flourishing industry in soft drinks, cigarettes and cosmetics on one side, on the other we cannot even provide basic amenities of life to the common man. Why? Because the former is more profitable than the latter.

Our definition of profit motive has become so narrow that what is profitable for business is sacrificed for what is profitable for the individual. Everyone is so caught up with their own profit that nobody is interested in planning for the whole. Any state, if it is to survive and prosper, must have a powerful central planning body that look after the health of the state as a whole, and resolves conflicts between the parts on the principles of justice and not merely on the basis of their respective strengths in terms of money or power. Decentralization beyond a certain level, will result in the collapse of the centre and with it the state as a whole. Fissiparous tendencies will rent as under any organization if not firmly reigned in by a holistic approach to problems. Over centralization on the other hand will concentrate too much power in the centre at the expense of the states.

Today, big business and industrialists are pumping money into the government and lobbying to bring it about to their point of view. The government is fractured into pools of vested interests pulling in contrary ways. We have small warlords and big business tycoons, but no enlightened leaders. The rich plunder the environment and exploit the poor, increasing the gap between the very rich and the very poor. We have pools of riches in a sea of poverty. Those who believe that life is a jungle have even destroyed the jungle in which they compete for their personal gain. The company that produces lollipops is only interested that the maximum number of people should consume lollipops, whether they require them or not. No one cares about the whole organism, but only about lollipops, cold drinks, or cigarettes. Technology has become the biggest threat to the ecosystems and the environment, on which our very survival depends. But everyone is merrily chipping away even the last remnants of our ecology in the name of development, which is merely a cover up for private gain. And technology is the most potent tool in their hands, in their quest for political supremacy and to command the scanty resources of the world. There is nothing wrong with technology, provided it is put to a good end.

In capitalism, personal gain at the expenses of whole has become this end. What happens when healthy competition becomes a ruthless game of extermination, when work becomes exploitation and selfishness a virtue? Capitalism has no answers to such questions when the whole is threatened by the parts, it is the parts that must give way. For us, is not the highest ideal the greatest good of the greatest number; the good of the whole and not merely of a few parts? Greed has been developed into a coherent and powerful ideology over the past four centuries. Mercantalism, colonialism, Imperialism, Industrialisation and Privatisation have all in turn contributed to the crystallisation of the capitalist ideology of exploitation for private gain. In the name of liberty poor nations have been enslaved by the rich and man has been enslaved by money. According to the philosophy of consumerism the more things a man consumes the better off he is. The ultimate joy comes from possessions and money. You can buy anything with money: status, power, people, honour, justice—anything. Money is the new God to whom every one prays with folded hands and reverence. On whoever this God smiles, he is the most blessed. The richer one becomes the better it is. All else is folly.

It is obvious that the capitalist has a narrow view of life, which is personal gain, even at the expense of the state. The state, however has a broader view of life, which is the good of everybody. It is the duty of the state to maintain a balance between what is good for business and what is good for the people. Everything that is good for business may not be good for people. And only the state can enforce this. A state has a socialist outlook. Socialism in its higher and altruistic sense is a philosophy of cooperation, sharing, love, brotherhood of camaraderie.

While the capitalist thinks only of his own benefit, the socialist thinks of the greatest happiness of the greatest number. Yet over the years communism has become representative of state-control, totalitarianism and socio-economic stagnation, while capitalism has linked itself to democratic traditions, liberalism and progressive ideologies. This in part can also be attributed to the managerial revolution that took place within the fold of capitalism, which saw the transference of power from the capitalist to the professional manager. With the management and the labour being able to own shares in the parent organisation the distinction between owner and worker has also blurred, and the system has become closer to the Marxist ideals of collective ownership.

Russian Communism has exposed the unviability of the first course. The monolithic and absolutist structure of undiluted communism is intensely restrictive of growth, which proceeds by decentralisation and diversification. It is extremely difficult to move a monolithic structure in all its entirety, at once. It is a movement through parts, where a part spearheads and leads the whole and the whole follows the part. Within any organisation, it is the individual leaders who move the organisation. Also, growth to be all rounded, must be horizontal as much as vertical. And horizontal growth is a function of decentralisation. We must have numerous independent sources of economic activity in order to ensure diversity of goods and their quality.

Communism upholds mediocrity as the highest ideal. Absolutism is simply putting all your eggs in one basket—the Government's. Communism is a philosophy of the highest common factor. The ideal economy should lie somewhere between these two extremes. A monolith, the size of communist Russia, will stand as an example of unwieldiness down the ages. An organisation that is too large is very cumbersome and difficult to govern or move. The people begin to pass their own responsibility to the organisation and in fact look upon it as the cause of any inefficiency. Rather than helping to move the organisation they wait for the organisation to move them, and in fact resist any such attempts of the organisation. Initiative passes from the hands of the individual to the nameless organisation. Bureaucracy becomes unwieldy long and work proceeds at a snail's pace.

Bureaucracy, whenever it becomes a monolithic monster controlling the smallest of action of men, begins to strangle innovation and initiative for the sake of conformity. Capitalism is only relative to socialism. Absolute capitalism would be as disastrous as absolute communism. Ideology merely dictates what system is best under given circumstances. Currently while Russia is becoming more open and liberal, America is becoming conservative and protectionist. Circumstances dictate directions. Ideology is important in so far as it motivates people to become committed to its cause. And the avowed purpose of any ideology is to create the ideal state. The ideal state maintains a balance between centralization and decentralization, between liberty and control, between socialism and individualism, between progress and planning and entrepreneurship.

A state, in fact, goes through alternate cycles of centralisation and decentralisation, consolidation and expansion. The cycle may be viewed in its various stages (as Plato taught) as progressing from Monarchy through Aristocracy, Oligarchy, Democracy, Anarchy, Tyranny and then back to Monarchy; the art of Government is to understand which direction is dictated by conditions of the day: liberty or control. While a dose of liberty may prove to be a tonic to the beleaguerd nations of the erstwhile communist block, it may prove disastrous for the liberal America. In sum, individualistic societies need more of socialism and vice versa. It is absolutely relative. It is for the orchard to produce the best fruit and for the fruit to produce the best trees. The two are not mutually antagonistic but compatible.[39]

REFERENCES

1. William Albig, *Public Opinion*, New York, 1939, 12.
2. Definitions: Claim I. Waxman (ed.), *The End of Ideology Debate, Funk and Wagnalls*, New York 1968, pp. 3-4.
3. William James, *Principles of Psychology, 1890, and William Medougall, An Introduction to Social Psychology, 1908.*
4. W.H.McGovern, *From Luther to Hilter, Boston, 1941, Chapter IX.*
5. R.T.La, Piere, *Collective Behaviour, New York, 1938, 56 and 57.*
6. C.L.Becker, *The Heavenly City of the 18th Century Philosophers*, New Heaven, 1932, 5.
7. John Plamenatz, *Ideology*, Pall Mall, London, 1970, p.11.
8. Karl Marx and Friedrich Engels, *The German Ideology*, Lawrence and Wishart, London, 1974, p.64.
9. Karl Marx and Friedrich Engels, *Selected Works in One Volume*, Lawrence and Wishart, London, 1984, p.183.
10. Terrell Carver, *Marx's Social Theory*, Oxford University Press, Oxford, 1982, p. 44.
11. V.I.Lenin, *What Is to Be Done?* Progress, Moscow, 1973, pp. 39-40.
12. Georg Lukacs, *History and Class Consciousness*, Muslim Press, London, 1971.
13. Herbert Marcuse, *"One Dimensional Man,"* Routladge and Kegan Paul, London, 1964.
14. L. Althusser, *Lenin and Philosophy*, New Left Books, London,1971.
15. Emile Durkheim, *The Rules of Sociological Methods*, Chicago, 1937.
16. R.K.Merton, *Karl Mannheim and Sociology of Knowledge* (reprinted from the Journal of Liberal Religion, Winter, 1941), Merton gives citations of Mannheim's work.
17. Louis Wirth, *Introduction to Ideology and Utopia*, New York, 1938.
18. Joseph S. Roucek, *A History of the Concept of Ideology*.
19. Karl Marx, *Das Capital*, Vol. 1, p. 320.
20. N. Abercrombie, S. Hill and B.S. Turner, *The Dominant Ideology Thesis*, Allan and Unwin, London, 1980.
21. *Ibid.*
22. *Ibid.*

23. H. Seliger, *Ideology and Politics,* Allen and Unwin, London,1976, p. 13.
24. Karl Mannheim, *Ideology and Utopia,* Routledge and Kegan Paul, London, 1936.
25. N.O.'Sullivan (ed.), *The Structure of Modern Ideology,* Elgas, Aldershot, 1989, pp. 188ff. O'Sullinan is a disciple of Michael Oakeshott.
26. M.Billig, *Ideological Dilemmas,* Sage, London, 1988, pp. 25ff. Others have made similar distinctions, for example *Plamentae's Separation of Sophisticated' from Unsophisticated Ideologies, Op. Cit.,* p. 15.
27. It is important to underline that there have been many forms of Marxist Analysis of Fascism, even in inter-war-era. For example, see D. Beetham, *Marxists face Fascism,* Manchester University Press, Manchester, 1983.
28. D. Bell, *The End of Ideology,* Free Press, New York, 1962, pp. 402-3.
29. S.M. Lipset, *Political Man,* Heinmann, London, 1960.
30. For the classic statement of this work see Z.Brzezinski and C.J. Friedrich, *Totalitarianism, Dictatorship and Autocracy,* Praeger, New York, 1961.
31. Clifford Geertz, *Ideology as a Cultural System, in D. Apter (ed.) Ideology and Discontent,* Free Press, New York, 1964.
32. K. Popper, *The Open Society and Its Enemies,* Vol.2, Routledge and Kegan Paul, London, 1961.
33. For a later defence of the thesis, see D. Bell, *'The End of Ideology* Revised', (2 articles), *Government and Opposition,* 23, 1988.
34. F. Fukuyama, *'The End of History', The National Interest,* 16, 1989, p.3.; see also F. Fukuyama, *The End of History and the Last Man,* Hamish Hamilton, London, 1992.
35. Roger Eatwell and Anthony Wright(ed.), *Contemporary Political Ideologies,* Printer Publishers, London, 1993. *Article Ideologies: Approaches and Trends* by Roger Eatwell.
36. F.M.Watkins, *The Age of Ideology—Political Thought 1750 to the Present,* Prentice Hall of India, Pvt. Ltd., New Delhi (1968).
37. *Ibid.*
38. *Ibid.*
39. An Article by Ashim Gill, *Ideological Considerations—Impact of Various Ideologies Down the Ages,* The Hindustan Times, New Delhi, Feb. 17, 1996.

2

IMPACT OF IDEOLOGY ON THEORISING POLITICS

Political ideology is looked at as a set of political beliefs that characterise any group, government or the entire nation. Political ideologies are political ideas presented in a systematic and coherent pattern to achieve specific political goals through definite action programmes. These are methodically formulated and often related to philosophical systems. Their forms are often related to the distribution of political power which might mean both defence or change of the existing political structure and relationships.

According to Marx and Engels, ideology includes not only the theory of knowledge and politics but also metaphysics, ethics, religion and indeed any form of consciousness which expresses the basic attitude on commitments of a programmatic and rhetorical application of some philosophical system which arouses men to political action and may provide strategic guidance for that action.[1]

Ideology is a more specific term than ideas. It has in practice been employed with different emphasis. It is a pattern of ideas thrown up automatically by specific social circumstances. All societies generate their own ideologies. It is a total, all-embracing and systematic explanatory system and plan of political action. It is a set of ideas formulated into a precise political programme. It is a fervently held but impractical formula for a political utopia.[2]

Interest and Ideology

There is a close relationship between interest and ideology. Each seems to be influenced by the other. The interest may shape the ideology and be shaped by it. History is full of instances where the national interests were served by shaping ideology according to the goals. The annexation of India by Great Britain as its colony was described as educating, civilising and humanitarian mission while the real objective was economic exploitation of a backward country. Annexation was an act of imperialism in disguise but its humanitarian ideology was advanced in support of their expansionist policies. Similarly, when the U.S.A. annexed Philippines for trade and military purposes it explained imperialistic action as a humanitarian mission.

There also exists a close relationship between ideology and transition. In transition a new ideology must develop in dialectical relationship with the existing ideologies. A dominant social ideology seeks to reproduce itself in the belief systems of successive generations. Ideological conceptions are related to basic social activities and beliefs. However, there are distinct and concrete processes by which beliefs themselves are reproduced over successive generations, through religious rituals and practices, relations within the families, the educational system and the media of communications, art, and culture etc.[3]

In transition from feudalism to capitalism, contradictions were discovered in the dominant ideology of catholicism and a new religious ideology of protestantism was created disrupting the older ideological institutions of the catholic church and creating new institutions like the new national church, and secular schools etc. The capitalist process for its very survival requires for its reproduction a new dominant ideology—liberalism which frees the sphere of economic activity from all pre-communal fetters, enables the sphere of economic activity to operate among free and equal individuals.[4] Ideologies also often assume the role of a saviour when societies are in crisis. In periods of social turmoil and widespread public discontent, people look around for ideas that would keep and understand the present reality and hold the promise for a better future. Certain ideologies thus appear to be in public mind for certain periods. Further, ideologies differ in respect of their organisation of thought. Some like Marxist are much better organised while others are loosely presented. The classification of ideologies can also be made on the basis of their linkage with the political system. Ideologies can be either reactionary or revolutionary. The reformist types can be in the middle position. However, ideologies change societies and are also affected by social changes. This brings about new political realities which have to be accommodated with the passage of time.[5]

The theory of end of ideology is in itself an ideology. It suggests that ideological commitments have been fast evaporating with more and more economic prosperity in which some more political factors played their role. Daniel Bell is the most powerful exponent of this theory. Many other sociological and economic concepts emerged such as, single industrial society, stages of economic growth and value-free social science. All these concepts have been associated with the theory of end of ideology. In historical context the theory emphasizes that the aim of both capitalism and socialism is to establish an industrial society and both advocate two different ways to achieve this end. There is no difference between the economic structures of the capitalist and socialist societies. But the difference lies in the way in which its working effects changes in the evolution of the society.

Ideological position is vitally influenced by internal and international situations. It reflects a movement from one ideological position to another in a dynamic social situation. No ideology can ever remain static. Even in a country like the erstwhile Soviet Union, the official ideology faced occasional jolts. Stalin and Trotsky, clashed over ideological arguments concerning socialism in one country. The Sino-Soviet dispute could also be related to conflicting ideological position each held in the light of its own understanding and experiences.

Ideologies act as cementing bonds within a political system. They seek to bolster up a regime. The role of ideologies in liberal democracies is much less obtrusive compared to the explicitly stated and paraded ideologies of the socialist regimes. But it does not mean that western liberal democracies have a dearth of ideologies. In fact, the western liberal democracies have a pluralistic stance whereas the socialists lean more towards monolithic mobilization of the masses. All ideologies have the common purpose of mass mobilization in a political system.[6]

Man is endowed by nature with the precious capacity for thought and this process goes on endlessly creating a web of varied thoughts. In normal routine, materialistic correlations dominate the human thoughts. However, materialistic we may be in our ways of life, either by choice or by force of circumstances, we cannot help but formulate ideas, attitudes and beliefs about the society, in which we have to live for the greater part of our life. For the great bulk of mankind these thoughts cannot but make vague impressions perhaps barely consciously held. But for others even though a little enlightened, new ideas do not enter their consciousness clearly. They continue to behave that no high set of doctrines seems to provide a completely satisfying explanation of social relationships or guide to actions. Others enjoy the comfortable certainty of a tightly knit ideology.[7]

Political ideologies are also concerned with the locus and structure of political power in a society. They change the distribution of political power. They also legitimize the existing political set-up. Ideologies also explain political change which is an essential element of political life. The speed and the extent of change vary from system to system. Ball observed "political ideologies are a means of explaining political changes and assist in their acceptance."[8] Usually, it is a political party that acts as the most important carrier and interpreter of ideology. There has never been a time when human behaviour including political behaviour, has not been largely affected by the mental images or stereo-types, through which men have grown accustomed to perceive and judge the world around them. These are the ideologies reflecting broad and comprehensive doctrines like liberalism, communism and fascism, which have emerged in the past 200 years, are often decisive factors in contemporary politics. Our modern wars are ideological wars; our party conflicts are ideological conflicts. Without some understanding of the nature and effects of these ideologies, no study of modern politics, foreign or domestic, could make sense.[9]

Our modern ideologies are all based, in one way or another, on a belief that life here on earth is capable of being perfected by human knowledge and efforts. Since man is by nature an inventive animal, there have been significant improvement in human technology ever since the day when some cave men first began to chip flints into handy shapes. In the past 200 years with the advent of industrial revolution, revolutionary advances in science and technology have adorned life with telephones and automobiles and other unimaginable amenities and have gone a long way, towards routine man's perennial enemies like disease and starvation. These revelations could not have occurred without the aid and support of the ideological movement.

Industrialisation in the western world was also an ideological process. The industrial revolution itself owes much to the power of ideology. These were the sources of inspiration for a liberal and nationalist idea, it helped in increasing the pace of modernisation by overthrowing conservative forces of resistance. The industrialisation of the former USSR under Stalin widened the banner of communism and contributed in drastic modernisation of many under developed areas. Thus, when the impact of an ideology in the process of industrialisation is objectively viewed, we cannot escape the conclusion that political ideologies are clearly a factor to be reckoned with in contemporary politics.

A typical feature of modern ideologies is their militantly revolutionary character. The technological transformation of a society is a matter of evolutionary changes rather than of revolutionary leaps. In politics revolutionary changes are entirely possible. The characteristic function of modern ideologies has been to persuade people that to move forward, revolutionary attack should be launched against the established political order.[10]

Modern revolutionary movements have been regularly carried out in the name of the people. Revolutions regularly depend on the initiative of the organised minorities. Yet they all claim to act as representatives of the popular interest and try to the best of their abilities to elicit popular support. Modern revolutionary movements have been mass movements claiming the consent of the governed as the sole legitimate base of authority. The people's democracies of the east and the constitutional democracies of the west, each claimed that they and they alone are genuinely democratic. Thus we notice that the relationships between ideology and democracy is obvious.

Modern ideologies are the first attempt of modern man to cope with the novel environment. As distinguished from the political thought of earlier times, they are theories designed to face the unprecedented problems and opportunities posed by an age of growing mass participation in politics. This accounts for their common emphasis on democratic principles of legitimacy. Ever since the industrial revolution, men have no sooner caught up with one set of problems than they have been over-run by new ones. Under such circumstances, decisive and effective leadership could only come from men of bold and sanguine temper.

Modern ideologies have three characteristic features. In the first place, the goals to which they address are typically utopian and high and steady morale is needed to bear the strain of inconclusive battle. Modern ideologies normally tend to define these goals in optimistic terms. The liberal concepts of the free markets or the Marxist's concept of classless society are typical utopian trends.

In the second place, modern ideologies take things in oversimplified terms. This line of reasoning encourages the ideologistic shades of opinion to look on political differences as a matter of black and white. They and their associates are the forces of light, fighting for the interest of all mankind. Free men versus tyrants, proletarians versus capitalists, patriots versus imperialists, such clear cut alternatives are typical of the ideological way of seeing political realities.

The third characteristic of the modern ideologies is also worth keeping in mind. To the end of the 19th century, successful ideological movements have regularly derived much of their strength from the extreme optimism regarding the human progress. One of the significant features of the industrial revolution was that it has generally seemed to encourage the prospect of radical innovations. In an age of rapidly increasing technological progress, it was easy to conclude that the progressive improvement of human welfare was an inevitable function of time itself, and was bound to continue in the future. Since the supporters of modern ideologies, regularly believe that they alone are on the side of the Engels, the result has been to give them confidence in the ultimate victory as well as in the justice of their cause.[11]

Very broadly, ideologies have been classified into three different categories. In the first category, we can keep the ideologies of status quo. If a state pursues policies designed to reserve the status quo, it is regarded as the adherent of status quo ideology. This ideology has tremendous faith in peace and international law. They abhor all types of imperialism. They also hold faith in system of collective security and mutual assistance to ensure that the world peace is not disturbed. In the second category, we have the ideologies of imperialism. It is opposed to the ideology of status quo. This ideology does not have any faith in international law and seeks to disturb the status quo to promote their own interests. Hitler of Germany adhered to this ideology. The third category, refers to ideologies whose premises are not clear and are used by various states for their respective purposes. One of the best examples of this ideology is offered by 'principles of national self-determination' advocated by President Wilson during the First World War.

Generally speaking there have been a number of ideologies dealing with the multifarious problems of mankind all of which could not be relevant with the theme under discussion. However, a brief reference be made to a few of them to highlight the role each played at a given time of history. To start with idealism which has been discussed from the days of the Greek thinkers followed by Hegel, each of whom provided some valuable pillars to mansion of political idealism. Idealism: Greek thinkers, followed by Rousseau, Hegel, Kant, Green etc. provided valuable pillars to the mansion of political idealism. The early Greek thinkers, Plato and Aristotle looked upon the state as a moral entity. The state to them was the greatest moral institute whose sole purpose was ethical development of man. Aristotle defined the state as 'union of families and villages having for an end a perfect self-sufficient life'. The state embraced within it the whole complex of social cravings and needs of man. The state was regarded as representing and containing within itself all the individual's social aspirations and at the same time fulfilling all his social needs. Whatever claims the state may make upon the individual were held to be based upon an absolute authority.

Liberalism: Liberalism seeks to promote the welfare of men regardless of their social, economic, racial or national status. It does not permit sovereignty to stay in the way of protection and promotion of human rights and other democratic status. It favours the international institution where men shall have the right to take part in important decisions affecting them and find peaceful solutions. It also supports peaceful changes in accordance with the will of the majority.

It is not easy to define liberalism because it does not represent any coherent body of doctrine. It is rather a historical tendency embracing diverse and even contradictory currents of thoughts that manifested in certain countries at a given epoch. Liberalism in this wide sense should not be confused with the programme or creed of a particular political party which adopts the liberal designation but may or may not represent the essential philosophy of liberalism.[12] It is somewhat difficult to state what exactly constitutes the essential principles of liberalism. In the first place, the representative political thinkers of the liberal school themselves do not agree about it. Secondly, the circumstances in which the liberal states emerged in different countries have been so various that they have necessitated a corresponding change in the liberal outlook in those countries. Lastly, the liberal state has been susceptible to changing economic patterns in the same country requiring a restatement of the liberal ideology.[13]

The history of past 400 years of the western liberal democratic bourgeois countries and almost all the socio-economic and political developments and movements of the modern western world, are closely associated with liberalism. During the modern period liberalism has been interpreted by different thinkers and philosophers, and it has been enriched by different thinkers and political movements of the western world. Liberalism emerged as a revolutionary and progressive philosophy in the modern period and in the beginning its guns were directed against the medieval reactionary order represented by feudalist monarchy and papacy. It emerged as a philosophy of the emerging capitalist class and middle classes and with the changes in the socio-economic and political requirements of this class, liberalism also underwent changes.

Liberalism has inspired many socio-economic and political movements and has been central to the development of modern western philosophy. It has been an extremely flexible and dynamic ideology and in spite of various challenges and crises, it has not been in its essential form.

The word liberalism was coined only in the beginning of 19th century. It has been derived from Spanish word 'liberales' and in 1812 this name was used by the supporters of Spanish constitution for themselves. Very simple, liberalism is the theory and practice of individual liberty, juridical defence and the constitutional state.[14] Liberalism represents a system of ideas that aims at the realisation of the pluralist society, favouring diversity in politics, economics, religion and other cultural life. It is opposed to uniformity, it is opposed to conformity. It seeks in the simplest sense to advance the freedom on man. It is essentially anti-authoritarian. It seeks to increase individuality of man by increasing his area of choice and decision. It is essentially humanitarian in its appeal. Finally, it is flexible in the methods of its realisation.[15] Liberalism has been concerned with liberty—religious, political, social, economic, moral and cultural of an individual, and it maintains that social, economic and political systems should be so structured that they serve the ends of individual freedom.

If liberalism is the socio-economic and political philosophy which was directed against the medieval reactionary order represented by feudalism, monarchy and papacy, Marxism as its successor is the scientific outlook of the working class. The development of capitalism and industry based on the capitalist mode of production, gave birth to a new class—the working class. The working class was the essential product of the capitalistic development. After the industrial revolution, the condition of working class in the European world, especially in England, was extremely miserable. During this period, the slogans, ideals and ethical values of French enlightenment were no more in sight and there emerged a society based on brutal exploitation of the vast majority. Marxism upheld the ideals of the French Revolution and challenged the liberal systems based on private property, market model of society, unbridled individualism and capitalist mode of production.

Marxism was influenced by the French enlightenment, English economists, Hegelian dialectics, Feuerbach's materialism and utopian socialism. Twenty five systematic expositions are found in the writings of Karl Marx and Friedrich Engels. Marx did not appeal to the conscience of the capitalists to improve the conditions of the working class: he did not appear to the reason of the capitalist class; he did not also entrust the state with welfare functions to improve the conditions of the capitalist class; he did not also entrust the state with welfare functions to improve the conditions of the working class, but on the contrary he gave a revolutionary message for changing the society: "workers of the world unite, you have nothing to loose but your chains and you have a world to win." It is a scientific philosophy of socio-economic and political change. It is scientific, because it not only interprets the material world, but also suggests the ways of transforming the world into a new one.

Utilitarianism: Utilitarianism is primarily an ethical theory based upon the psychological doctrine known as Hedonism. According to the teachings of Hedonism, every man, as a matter of fact, seeks pleasure and avoids pain. Other motives may enter the calculation, but the ultimate motive is that of pleasure versus pain. The Hedonistic teachings are by no means new. It goes back to the Greek times, especially to the teaching of Austippus, the founder of the Cyrenaic school and in a modified form, to the teaching of Epicureans. While modern Hedonism differs widely from the ancient, both forms regard pleasure as the guiding principle. Earlier Hedonism was egoistic in character, while the modern is altruistic. Utilitarianism bases itself on the latter form. Hence it is sometimes called altruistic or universalistic Hedonism. Its goal is the greatest happiness of the greatest number.

Among the utilitarian thinkers Jeremy Bentham (1748-1832) was the most prominent. He laid the foundation of the Utilitarian School of thinking. He played a conspicuous part in curing injustice and in bringing about lasting reforms. The keynote of his philosophy is:'Nature has placed man under the governance of two sovereign masters, pain and pleasure'. They govern us in all we do, in all we say, in all we think: every effort we make to throw off our subject will serve but to demonstrate and confirm it! The principle of utility, he says, recognizes this subjection, because it approves or disapproves of every action whatsoever, according to the tendency to promote or oppose happiness. This principle he later describes as 'the greatest-happiness principle'. In the apportionment of lots of happiness, the principle to be applied he says, is 'each to count for one and no one for more than one'. The primary concern of Bentham was the good or welfare of the community. He believed that his principle of utility could be applied with advantage to all social questions and particularly to constitutional, legislative and law reforms.

Another great Utilitarian was John Stuart Mill (1806-73). J.S.Mill was the son of James Mill. James Mill was an ardent believer in utilitarianism. J.S. Mill was over educated and over drilled in utilitarianism. But at the same time when he reached maturity and began to reflect on things for himself he clearly saw the serious defects of utilitarianism. Besides, he was a man with a Catholic outlook willing to see the merit in others point of view. In this process of self-liberalisation Mill was helped by his wide reading of contemporary works such as those of St. Augustine, Comte, Thomas Carlyle, S.T. Coleridge, etc. The influence of Mrs. Taylor who many years later, on the death of her first husband became his wife was also important.

Mill, unlike Bentham, stressed that pleasures differ not only in quantity but also in quality. He realised that individual happiness and general happiness are closely interwined, and that, therefore, it was not necessary to force oneself to pursue the pleasures of others. Mill was of the opinion that every man possessed 'a feeling, for the happiness of mankind' and that consequently he should desire and promote general happiness.

Utilitarianism is often unjustly criticised as the utility theory or expediency philosophy. Utility means serving a purpose or end to achieve some good individual. The utilitarians conceive man not only as an individual, but as an individual who is by nature social. Utilitarianism has sometimes been regarded as synonymous with materialism of the worst type.

Fascism: Fascism emerged in the present century as the most heinous, anti-democratic, oppressive, anti-humanitarian, reactionary, and counter-revolutionary form of dictatorship. It was a curious amalgam of deception, orthodoxy, hero-worship, power-worship, aggressive irrationalism and spiritualism. Fascism based itself on attractive social democratic slogans and emphasized law, order discipline and unity. Fascism is a dictatorship which emerged in some developed capitalist states of European world after the first world war, and initially it had mass following. Fascist dictators, unlike military dictators or terrorists or oligarchs came to power through mass actions. Though the first world war was fought for the defence of democracy, various fascist dictatorships emerged in the European world. They rejected the ideas of parliamentary democracy, opposed the organised working class and the philosophy of socialism. They were violently nationalistic. They preached submission to authority, discipline and an irrational sense of community. Fascism had been a blood-stained ideology and was hated and feared by people throughout the world so much so that the term "Fascism" was used in day-to-day language more as a term of abuse.

Fascism was derived from an Italian word, "Fascio" meaning 'a bundle of wood'; it expressed unity, discipline and strength. Generally speaking, as the term fascism referred to the regimes of Mussolini and Hitler which were established in 1922 and 1933 in Italy and Germany respectively.

Fabianism: Fabianism was another ideology which developed subsequently after the formation of the fabian society in 1884 by some young progressive intellectuals who envisaged the emergence of a socialist society in Great Britain as a result of democratic, gradual, peaceful and constitutional means. Among the prominent members were Sidney Webb, G.B. Shaw, Graham Wallace, Sidney Olives, Annie Beasant, W. Clarke, E.R. Paes, H.G. Wells, G.D.H. Cole, Herman Finer and Harold J. Laski. Fabians were influenced by Henry George, J.S.Mill, Marx, Ricardo, Carlyle, Ruskin, Robert Owen, Proudhon and Lasalle.

Fabianism maintained that society must be reconstituted in such a manner as to secure general welfare and happiness. It rejected Marxian theory of socialist revolution and expressed firm faith in achieving a socialist society through gradual reforms along ordinary parliamentary lines. Instead of the Marxian idea that history is the history of class struggle Fabians maintained that history demonstrates the irresistible progress of democracy and almost continuous progress of socialism.[16] They rejected labour-value doctrines of both classical/economists and Marx and maintained that value has always been in the creation of society rather than of labour.[17] According to Fabians, the object of socialism is to obtain for all members of society the value which society creates, and this object could be achieved by gradually transferring lands and industrial capital to the community, while making the state more fully representative of the community. Thus, its object is to transfer ownership not to the workers but to the society for general benefit.

Through democratic processes the socio-economic, political, cultural and intellectual system of the society will gradually change and in this way, socialism will go on developing. Socialism will be and should be brought gradually and not through abrupt revolutionary change. Fabianism rejected the policy of forcing socialism on the society, from above and maintained that socialism must emerge from the bottom and go upward rather than to come from top to bottom. The Fabians were critical of free enterprise capitalism and criticised its oppressive nature.

Syndicalism: Syndicalism is the vision of a new stateless, classless society with the trade union at its base and fierce class struggle as the technique of social change. Syndicalism emerged in France in the closing years of 19th century and in the opening years of 20th century. The exponents of this version of socialism were both the active leaders of the Trade Union movement and a galaxy of brilliant intellectuals, Pelloutier, Pouget and others helped to formulate the main tenets of syndicalism. George Sorel, Hubert, Lagardelle and Edouard Berth gave intellectual justification to its philosophical foundation. The, main tenet of syndicalism was that the trade unions or the syndicate were the foundation of the emerging socialist society. General strike,

Sabotage and other kinds of direct action were the revolutionary instruments of social change.

Of all the social groupings, the trade union, the syndicalists argued, were the strongest and the most fundamental "because men in society were interested above everything else in the satisfaction of their economic needs."[18] Hence, the trade unions were the most effective in evoking in man's spontaneous and instinctive loyalty.

The syndicate or the Trade Union would form the base of syndicalist's society. It would consists of workers engaged in one trade and they would use social wealth for social benefit with the consent of the society. In the society of syndicalists vision, there was no place for the state with which the people were familiar. The place of the state would be occupied by the local and the national organisations in the new society.

Guild Socialism: Guild socialism arose as an eloquent protest against prevalent capitalism and emerging state socialism. The guild socialists recognised the limited role of the state in the society. They advocated withdrawal of state control from economic sphere, for they discovered in state socialism the role of bureaucracy. Penty, Orage and Hobson were the main exponents of this brand of socialism. G.D.H. Cole was the brightest star in the constellation of guild socialists. The guild socialists protested against the capitalist method of exploitation in which the surplus values of labour produced was pocketed by the capitalists. The guild socialists also protested against the painful debasement of man's inner spirit by machine civilization in which man is reduced to an 'automation' and hence fails to discover any creative joy or the thrill of creation in his work. The guild socialists plan was infused with this awareness and they envisioned instead a new institutional framework which would restore the man's pride and spontaneous joy in his work.

Anarchism: Anarchism believed in hostility to all forms of political authority. It also invoked disparagement of institutionalised religion and of the system of private property. Anarchism was a vision of a new society characterized by the absence of every form of authority. It was based on an axiom that man had a natural impulse to co-operation. The process of spontaneous cooperation was thwarted by the establishment of artificial authorities. Anarchist's society would emerge after the liquidation of the present state structure; it would be a web of free associations which an individual would have full liberty to join or to leave. This arrangement would be a proper and desirable substitute for the coercive political state. The autonomous associations would cater to the various needs of the community and thus render the state organisation unnecessary.

Emergence of Socialism: The close of the 19th century witnessed the doom of individualism. Dicey was quick to discover the collectivist trend in legislation in about 1870 in England. The present century opened its innings with little promise for traditional individualism. With passage of time, individualism began to lose its territory to the emerging doctrine of socialism. In the 20's and 30's socialism made an open revolt in politics. Under the challenge of socialist ideas, individualism, with its principle of non-intervention, staged a retreat in most of the countries of the west. Traditional individualism was found to be a clog in the wheel of progress and came to be increasingly rejected by the people either through the verdict of the ballot box or through the challenge of the open rebellion. Socialism in some form or other seized the temple of politics. The philosophers of laissezfaire equated industrial capitalism with an unending era of prosperity.

The 19th century world, for the most part was full of optimism. But soon it was found that the complex economic problem created by industrial capitalism could not be effectively tackled by traditional individualism. It was an inadequate response to the challenge of new problems. Adam Smith's favourite child-free competition-passed away before it would grow to full maturity. The growth of monopoly in the economy called for increasing state intervention. With its grip over the key and strategic points in the economy, monopoly was found to be a menace to both the consumers and small producers. The abundant control over supply enabled the monopolists to inflate the prices of the consumer goods and swell their coffer of profit at the expense of the consumers' interests. The small producers could not compete with the vast resources of the monopolist and consequently failed to stand competition. To curb the powers of the monopolists, the governments in different countries passed anti-monopoly legislations.

Thus unbridled capitalism produced socially disasterous consequences. The optimum allocation of resources, from the standpoint of social welfare, came to be increasingly disturbed. Men with heavier purse were able to tempt the resources into their lines of production where maximization of profit was the sole consideration. The wider objective of social welfare was missing in the scheme of economic development. Informed public opinion in the West demanded re-allocation of resources along socially desirable lines, In addition, unplanned production, without any comprehensive centralised mechanism linking up the communities' targets of production with carefully estimated total demand of the market, created frequent fluctuations in the level of income and employment.

The alternating waves of prosperity and depression were found to be deep-seated symptoms of the economic malice of capitalism. Mounting injustice, being an offshoot of the capitalist distribution of wealth and income, created tension in society. Fantastic inequality in income and wealth, rampant exploitation, collosal poverty and mass misery constituted a perrineal source of friction and a distinct threat to the solidarity and cohesion of identical societies. The distress and antipathy between the 'haves' and 'have nots' which often found expression in massive strikes by the workers suitably replied by arrogant lock-outs of factories by the employers, brought the society to the precipice of an open social disruption. Men with imagination joined hands with the socialist agitators to put pressure on the government to end the old individualist illusion. The governments in different countries under this pressure came out with welfare schemes for improving the living standards of the people and introducing distributive justice in the society.

All these forces were germinating in the matrix of developed socialist societies. They reached a climax in the thirties when the great depression embracing the whole of the globe, shook the capitalist system to its foundation. Individualism was totally discredited. The governments in different countries came to play a decisive role in the process of rehabilitation of the shattered economy. Planning, total or partial, came to occupy an important place in the programme of almost every government. The theory of socialism thus received a tribute from practical circumstances.

Socialism which "is based on a level sense of wrong crying for redress" is not a homogenous concept. Myriad social situations obtaining at different times and in different climes, and age old traditions have endowed the word 'Socialism' with varied meanings. Engels classified socialism into utopian and scientific. In his view socialism must live on two levels: one is utopianism and other is involvement in contemporary political convulsions. As David Riesman in his 'Faces in the Crowd' aptly remarks, "all over the world one can find the tragic casualties of a void effort to deny that there are two levels of policies—the detached utopian one and the effective commitment to current political turmoils. It is not only utopian politics but all life which appear to be lived at these two levels".

The year '1848' is considered to be the dividing line that marks off one phase of socialism from the other. Charles Fourier (1772-1837), Robert Owen (1771-1858) and others were the principal exponents of utopian socialism. They were not interested in political action for ushering in socialist society, nor did they try to appeal to the class fidelity of the multitude. These early socialists scored over the politicians through persuasion and example that they wanted to convert the people to the pressing need for a new social order. Owen, for example, through demonstration of humane and just relations in his own mills, sought to inspire the people in a socialist vision, believing that human character depended on environment, Owen wanted to replace the competitive system by a co-operative one where justice and harmony could prevail. Significantly enough, "that a pre-Marx socialist is not necessarily a Utopian in the sense of having an understanding of the organic growth of the society and of its associative core, is shown by St. Simon (1760-1825)". He was an eloquent champion of large-scale industrialisation and planning. In 1848 Marx and Engels through the publication of 'Communist Manifesto' imparted a new insight to socialist theory and sought to re-define socialism in tune with reality. Since then varied schools of socialism have developed in different countries local condition and influence and varying interpretations of Marxist teaching have led to the ramification of socialism into its different versions.

Leninism: Lenin (1870-1924) was the author of the 'Russian Revolution of 1917'. He was both a theorist and a man of action. He joined revolutionary movement as early as 1890 and spent many years abroad studying Marx and Engels. By a happy coincidence of circumstances he was brought back to his motherland by the Germans during World War I and he utilised this opportunity to overthrow the Czarist regime. He was the acknowledged leader of the Soviet party since November 1917. He applied Marxism with masterly brilliance to Russian conditions.

Lenin reinterpreted Marxism to suit Russian conditions. He found Marxism inadequate in some respects. Thus he sought to modify Marxism in the light of the experience culled from his intimate association with the socialist movement. Unlike Marx, Lenin believed that the maturation of the capitalist economy, the evolution of the relations of production, will only inculcate in the proletariat a trade union consciousness, an awareness of the workers trade union rights. Through some automatic movement of the capitalist economy there cannot be spontaneous emergence of the revolutionary consciousness of the socialist ideology. In Lenin's view, some outside force is necessary to inspire the proletarian class with a burning socialist awareness. In other words there must be a middle class intellectual leadership for endowing the workers with revolutionary socialist consciousness.

Lenin's principal contribution to communist thought—structure is his spelling of the imperialist stage of capitalism and of communist theory in that stage. In the advanced stage of capitalism characterised by the growth of giant monopolies covering world-wide market, there ensures, in the search for extended markets and adequate new materials, an international scramble for control of industrially backward areas. Thus the imperialist phase of capitalism ultimately leads to war between imperialist states for the control of underdeveloped regions.

Karl Marx did not formulate in detail the organisation of the dictatorship of the proletariat. He just provided the idea, Lenin spelt its organisational aspect. The dictatorship of the proletariat is a uniparity state which is guided by a band of class conscious leaders of the working class. The party of the working class people is the spear head of this revolutionary social order. It is a transient state whose task is to hold down the counter-revolutionary attempt of the old exploiting class and to pave the way for the final withering away of the state. It is a transitional stage in which the state is languishing. The stateless society, which is the final stage of mass's journey towards full freedom, will come through stages and carefully planned education. The first stage in Lenin's view is equal distribution of consumption goods. The final stage is the ideal stage in which the principle of 'from each according to his ability and to each according to his needs,' is the governing principle. In his formulation of this final stage, Lenin admitted that this ideal may not be realised as it depends upon a revolution in human nature and technique of production leading to the total abolition of distinctions between workers inter se. Thus "Lenin like Marx retained the moral propulsion of a utopian ideal but he did not confuse the ideal with the attainable."

Stalinism: Stalin who was the master of political strategy, was the advocate of "socialism in a Single country". In his view socialism could be built up in a country through accelerated industrial growth and collectivisation of agriculture. Stalin discovered "the possibility of building up socialism by the efforts of one country". In this struggle for power, Stalin came out victorious and the 14th congress of the Communist Party in April 1925, accepted Stalin's theory as the official creed of the party. The failure of a series of a revolutionary upsurge which came over different parts of Europe in the wake of Russian Revolution of 1917 dealt a blow to Trotsky's thesis embodying Europe's 'ripeness' for socialist revolution and finally led to the triumph of Stalin. Subsequently, the world of Trotsky became a 'planet without visa'.

The acceptance of Stalin's thesis of socialism in a single country led to a profound modification of the Marxist theory. For Marx, Engels and Lenin internationalism was the basic core of communism. But Stalin's mission was a powerful, triumphant Russia as a spear-head of world revolution. Communism thus, lost its genuine international consciousness and it found in

Stalin's ideas a close alliance with rationalism. Internationalism in Stalin's ideological scheme was just a backdrop. The author of the idea of "socialism in a single country" could not be anything but a staunch nationalist keeping aloft the interests of his own country. Further, the theory of "socialism in a single country" led to some modification of Marxist doctrine of the dictatorship of the proletariat. Stalin fully accepted the pivotal role of the party in the new revolutionary order.

Stalin gradually tightened the control of the party, and power became, during his regime, increasingly centralised and total. Stalin found it necessary because the speedy growth of Soviet Russia in a predominantly hostile capitalist world demanded increase in tightening, and not relaxation of authority. Thus in his view, till the menace of hostile capitalist encirclement was completely eliminated, the state authority in Soviet Russia could not decline in depth or in width. The state will wither away if the capitalist environment has been removed, and its place has been taken by a socialist environment. Stalin's influence in Soviet politics was short-lived and soon after him, a merciless debunking started, the latest being detombing of this builder of Russia.

Maoisim: Mao Tse-tung, the builder of new China, is the advocate of the people's democratic dictatorship or the new Democracy. In this type of democracy, Mao argues, freedom belongs to the people alone. The working class, the peasantry the petty bourgeoisie and the national bourgeoisie constitute the people. As Mao observed, "the combination of these two aspects, democracy for the people and the dictatorship over the reactionaries, means the people's democratic dictatorship."[19] The brief period of intellectual freedom allowed under Mao's slogan of 'let hundred flowers blossom' released a wave of intellectual ferment and protest against some of the postulates of the Chinese communist society. It proved irksome and uncomfortable for the men at the helm of affairs who soon re-established and further tightened the system of control. The 'cultural revolutions' showed clearly the stresses and conflicts within the Chinese society, and a drift towards merciless totalitarian rule. On the external plane, Mao's China maintains the bellicose temper of communism, and has not grown alive to its danger in a nuclear age of ours.[20] In China's view peace could only be preserved through militant struggle. The Chinese view of the international situation is that the balance of power has tilted in favour of the communist camp and that the west knows that it will be destroyed in a nuclear war and that the west will only use the nuclear threat for blackmail, but will avoid a nuclear showdown. China, however, accused the former Soviet Russia of following a policy of revisionism. However, the policy of China seems to have changed lately China's relation with USA have improved.

Conservatism: The term conservative was first used in its distinctively modern sense in this context—i.e. to indicate a political position opposed to ideological, politics—when Chateaubriand (1768-1848) gave the name 'Le Conservateur' to a journal he issued in order to resist the spread of the new politics, and especially the democratic ideas which were its main manifestation. The name was soon taken up by many other groups that opposed the progress of democracy, in its more radical forms at least. In the United States, for example, the American national republicans were calling themselves conservatives by 1830 and this term was used to describe the British Tory Party in 1832.

The conservative critique of the new ideological style of politics inspired by the French Revolution centred on the optimistic belief underlying it, according to which human reason and will are sufficiently powerful for us to be able to shape history in accordance with whatever ideals we may feel inspired to adopt. During the 19th century the most influential vehicle for this revolutionary optimism was liberalism, and conservative doctrine was consequently shaped primarily by the need to meet the challenge posed by liberal defenders of the democratic ideal. During the 20th century, however, socialism replaced liberalism as the principal vehicle for radicalism, and it is in opposition to this new enemy that conservative doctrine has therefore mainly been defined in our own age.

Although the enemy of conservatism is easy to identify, it must immediately be noticed that the conservative doctrine opposed to it has never been homogeneous. On the contrary, ever since the French Revolution it has always included very different, and ultimately conflicting, stands of thought.

Nevertheless, it is possible to detect a unifying conservative intellectual aspiration, even though it is worked out from entirely different philosophical standpoints, and is subject to entirely different practical interpretations. This intellectual aspiration consists of a quest for a theory of political order which views people and society in a way that is wholly untinged by utopian ideas and aspirations. Conservatism seeks, more precisely, to develop a theory of limits which will not only enable it to cut through the various ideological systems that characterize the modern world but will also provide a principled defence of political realism.

Realism in politics all too easily becomes the cynical doctrine that might is right or the Machiavellian proposition that end justifies means. In the more thoughtful form of conservatism however, realism is not a doctrine of mere power, but a doctrine of limits. As such, what it means is that any viable concept of order must begin from a clear recognition of the main feature of the human condition, which is the existence of objective limits that subject the core of life to inescapable tension. This tension arises because we are creatures inevitably divided between a multiplicity of complex dualities: dualities such as those between spirit and matter; between man and nature; between the individual and society, between governors and governed; between free enterprise and state regulation; between different groups within society, and between different states. These dualities or oppositions may indeed be partially harmonised, but never wholly eliminated. For conservatism, to dream of eliminating them from human existence is the hallmark of all utopian conceptions of order. The unifying theme of conservatism, then, is the quest for a realistic concept of order which acknowledges the ineliminable tension at the heart of human condition. It is a principled nature of conservative realism which provides the answer to cynics who discuss the doctrine as nothing more than a commitment to pure pragmatism, power, and success.

Nationalism: Nationalism has an aura of antiquity about it. After all, the existence of distinct cultures can be traced back into the mists of time, as the archaeological remains from Aztec, Hittite and countless other archaic civilizations which adorn 'our' museums still testify. Then there are the many ancient texts which refer to nations in conflict, such as Herodotus' writings on the wars between Greeks and Prussians, Caesar's descriptions of his militancy campaign in Gaull, or a passage in the Gospel of Saint Matthew prophecising that in the last days 'nations shall rise up against nations'. It would be tempting to conclude that nations and nationalism are natural phenomenon and as such are as old as human civilization itself. Yet Ernest Gellner speaks for most scholars who have reflected on this issue when he asserts nationalism tends to treat itself as a manifest and self-evident principle, accessible as such to all men and violated only through some perverse blindness, when in fact it owes its plausibility and compelling nature only to a very special set of circumstances, which do indeed obtain now, but which were alien to most of humanity and history. It will be a central theme to what follows that nationalism in its various permutations and nation-states based on them are indeed essentially modern, even in the many instances when they are associated with ethnic distinctiveness or with political states which may be as old as recorded history.

The recentness of nationalism is born out by its etymology. Nation is derived via the French from the Latin 'Nation' whose root occurs in 'nasci' to be born, and which in classical usage tended to be a pejorative term for a race, tribe or 'breed' of people considered uncouth by Roman standards. In the various Romance languages of the Victorian era which inherited the word 'nation' as 'part of' identified with the legacy of occupation, or the non-Latin languages which eventually adopted it under the influence of the Renaissance, 'nation' was to go through a number of semantic shifts before it was used expressly to denote the alleged cultural unity and political sovereignty vested in an entire people. Significantly, among the earliest documents of this usage are a pamphlet by the Abbe' Sieyes and the Declaration of Rights of Man and Citizen, both composed in the heat of the French Revolution in 1789. It was only after this that the term 'nationalism' first started gaining currency in European languages to refer to the animating energy of the new 'peoples power' which events in France had revealed to be capable of overthrowing not just a monarch, but monarchy itself, and not just in a seceding colony (as in the American

Revolution), but in one of Europe's oldest established absolutist states.

Philology also highlights the fact that, far from being a universal elatum of human experience, the concept of 'nationalism' with its revolutionary populist implications has a highly nuanced history as we move from society to society. Even in languages which have borrowed it, such as German and Polish, it acquires specific connotations, while those cultures which have in the last two hundred years generated home grown equivalents from native linguistic roots, such as Arabic or Chinese, have done so largely under the impact of contacts with the West and of modernization. In the process of coining the concept they have inevitably imbued it with untranslatable, culture-specific shades of meaning. Fascinating case studies in this are the Arabic term 'Ulatan', or the Japanese 'Kokumin', both of which only partially overlap semantically with the English term 'nation'.[21]

Nationalism is an ideology whose affective deriving force expresses itself in the sense of belonging to and serving a perceived national community. The carriers of this ideology attribute to their nation a distinctive cultural identity which sets it apart from other nations and gives it a special place in the historical process. This community is identified with a unique set of characteristics allegedly deriving from constitutional, historical, geographical, religious, linguistic, ethnic and/or genetic realities. The sentiments aroused by the sense of being a member of this community may be confined to a keen sense of pride in national culture and traditions without being associated with political demands (cultural nationalism). On the other hand when such sentiments play a major role in the dynamics of a 'political' movement, the thrust of nationalism is generally for the national community to be assumed to form 'naturally' a state (whether autonomous or part of a federation or confederation of states) in which the sovereignty held to reside in the people is exercised by its elected or self-appointed representatives within territorial boundaries recognized by the international political community. As long as the resulting 'nation state' upholds the principle of civil society on the basis of which all permanent residents fully enjoy the human rights conferred by citizenship, irrespective of ethnic criteria, then nationalism which can not be dissociated from political liberalism and gives rise to 'liberal nationalism'. Indeed a subjective 'secondary' national identity in the sense of 'love of one's country' (or patriotism), which may well not be conterminous with a primary sense of ethnic identity, is arguably vital to the social cohesion and political stability of all liberal democracies.

Feminism: A common starting point for all feminist ideas is the belief that women are disadvantaged in comparison to men, and that this advantage is not a natural and inevitable result of biological difference but something that can and should be challenged and changed. Unlike traditional political theories and ideologies, feminism provides a way of looking at the world that sees women's situation and the inequalities between men and women as central political issues; as such, it provides a fundamental challenge to dominant assumptions about the scope and nature of politics. Beyond this, there is enormous disagreement as to the nature, causes and cure for women's inequality, subordination or oppression, for feminism is certainly not a unified ideology but contains many competing strands. These have frequently been identified as 'liberal', 'Marxist', 'radical' and 'socialist' feminisms; 'black feminism' and, increasingly, 'post-modern feminism' also represent distinct and important approaches. Liberal feminism can be understood as 'equal rights' feminism. It asserts that women are rational beings like men, and that they should therefore have the same legal and political rights, and the opportunity to compete equally with men in politics and paid employment.

Marxist feminists argue against this that full equality will only be achieved when capitalism is replaced by genuine socialism. Both these approaches use existing theories and apply them to the situation of women; radical feminists, however, claim to provide a new perspective based on women's own experiences, and they argue that the patriachal domination of women by men is both the most basic form of power in society and one that has its source in such apparently private areas of life as the family and sexual relationships. This analysis involves a redefinition of power and politics, and an attack on the allegedly artificial distinction between public and private life. Modern socialist feminism seeks to combine this radical perspective with Marxist class analysis by exploring the inter-relationship between capitalism and patriarchy. Feminism has frequently been seen as the preserve of white middle-class women; some feminists now argue that the experiences of black women must not only be included in feminist analysis, but taken as its starting-point. Finally, a number of feminists have recently endorsed postmodernist critiques of western philosophy, and are attempting to use these as a basis for exploring new women centred forms of knowledge and understanding.

The term 'feminist' first came into use in English during the 1890s, the origin of modern feminism can be traced back at least to the late seventeenth century, when early capitalist development involved a marked change for the worse in the legal and economic situation of many women, and liberal challenges to establish political authority were extended by some writers to question the arbitrary power of men.[22] It is, however, Mary Wollstonecraft's "Vindication of the Rights of Woman" written in 1792 during the early years of the French Revolution, that provides the first full expression of early liberal feminism. At this time women not only lacked the vote, but were deemed unfit for education, were debarred from many occupations and had no more legal standing then children; a married woman had no legal property of her own, anything she might earn was legally the possession of her husband, and even if he abused her she had no real right to a divorce. Forcefully rejecting contemporary belief in female inferiority, Wollstonecraft (1759-97) argued that women are, like men, rational individuals and that, as such, they should have equal rights; and she established the principles underlying later campaigns for women's right to education, employment, property and vote. Half a century later, these principles found concrete expression at the first ever Women's Rights Convention held at Seneca Falls in America in 1848, and the latter part of the nineteenth century saw the growth of equal rights feminism throughout the industrializing world.[23] In Britain the eminent philosopher John Stuart Mill (1806-73) introduced the question of women's suffrage to the House of Commons in 1867, and his 'The Subjection of Women', first published in 1869, provided a full-scale analysis of women's situation and the advantages to society of giving them full legal and political equality with men. Although many rights have now been won his arguments still have a striking relevance today.

Some early feminist demands met with considerable success. By the end of the nineteenth century, women in Britain and America had won a considerable degree of legal independence and increased access to education and employment, and they were no longer completely excluded from public life and political debate. They were, however, still denied the franchise, and the frustrated demand for 'Votes for Women' was to produce an unprecedented wave of feminist activity by the turn of the century. Feminism was not similarly central to the revolutionary socialist ideas developed by Karl Marx (1818-83) later in the century. Nevertheless, his theory claims to provide a comprehensive analysis of human history and society, and later writers have applied it to feminist issues. It implied that family and sexual relationship are, like other forms of social organisation, the product of a particular stage of economic development; as such, they cannot be altered at will, but only as a result of socio-economic change expressed through class conflict and revolution. This understanding was developed by Fredrick Engels in 'The origin of the family, Private Property and the State', first published in 1884. In this Engels (1820-95) argued that Women's Oppression has not always existed, but that it began with the first private property and class society, for it was only then that men's desire to pass property to known heirs motivated them to control women. This motive would, Engels argued, disappear with the overthrow of capitalism. When women would no longer be economically dependent on men and the socialisation of housework and childcare would liberate them from domestic chores.

Women have made important gains during the 20th century and many of the principles for which they have fought are now part of the 'Commonsense' assumptions of our society. Thus, few today would challenge the right of women to education, employment or the vote, or advocate a return to the gross legal inequalities of the 19th century. Nevertheless, even in the most advanced countries, women remained disadvantaged in comparison with men. Positions of public power remain mainly in male hands. Women as a group continue to work much longer hours than men (particularly at home) and receive far less financial reward, while fear of sexual violence restricts their lives and they are denied full control over their reproduction. Feminism may seem less fashionable than a few years ago, but its assumptions have entered the consciousness of too many people to be easily cast aside. There is an increasing general acceptance of the radical feminist claim that the 'personal is political', and the power relations are not confined to the public words of law, the state and economics but they pervade all areas of life. This means that some issues of child care and domestic violence are re-defined as political, and can be the focus of collective feminist action; it means too that politics is not simply something that is out there, but a part of every-day experience. Feminism's redefinition of politics means that it represents a proposed challenge to other political ideologies which, it argues, are all too often based on the experiences, interests and perceptions of only half of the human race.

Ecologism: The roots of ecologism are to be found wherever and whenever people either thought or acted in ways similar to those advocated by the modern green movement. The bands of hunter-gatherers that roamed on the earth until about 10,000 years ago co-existed in a non-exploitive way with their environment and only took from it what was necessary to satisfy their vital needs. They may also have been animated by the view that nature has value in itself as much as it is useful for human beings. On both these scores, Paleolithic humans are close to modern green sentiments and are therefore sometimes cast as early political ecologists.[24]

Much more recently, eighteenth and nineteenth century romantics throughout Europe reacted to what they saw as the plight of nature as a result of rapid industrialisation by demanding the reestablishment of links between society and the natural world. Romantic poets wrote of the natural world as a source of moral and aesthetic value, and stressed upon the supposed unity between humanity and nature which industrialisation had broken down. Such back to nature views are clearly a part of contemporary green ideology.[25] Similarly, craft oriented thinkers such as William Morris (1834-96) with an aesthetic regard for the non-human natural world advocated closeness to nature as an antidote to what he regarded as the philistinism and ugliness of indentical life, and pressed the value of the countryside against urban life. Again these views are reflected in some aspects of contemporary ecologism.[26]

In the United States of America one important present-day debate was prefigured in the 19th century when John Muir (1838-1914) and others argued strenuously for the preservation of wilderness for its own sake, which Grifford Pinchot (1865-1946) took a more practical line in arguing for the conservation of natural resources because of their utility value.[27] This battle between camps that came to be known as the 'preservationists' (like Muir) and 'conservationists' (like Pinchot) has been handed down to us today. The history of ecologism can be shown to have deep roots and analyses of this sort serve usefully to remind us that while ecologism is a modern political ideology, it has old resources.

The second view of ecologism's history begins with those scientists in the nineteenth century who began to build on Thomas Malthus' (1766-1834) famous argument that population would increase geometrically and food production only arithmetically, thus causing wide spread famine. Studies in the biological and earth sciences in France, Britain, the USA, Russia and Germany led to an awareness of the possibility of resource and energy scarcity. Some geographers began to view the earth as an organism, and the Oxford English Dictionary credits the German Zoologist Ernst Maeckel with the first use of the world 'ecology' in 1873. Contemporary scientists' views (on scarcity in particular) have played a big part in today's green sense to see their nineteenth century counterparts as contributing to the history of ecologism.[28]

Ecologism faces the problem of putting its ideas into practice. Green political parties and pressure groups have certainly made an impact, as have exhortations to change lifestyles either at home or in sustainable communities, yet industrialism remains the practice across most planet, and the aspiration of the rest of it. In deciding the future of ecologism we need, as at the outlet, to distinguish it from environmentalism. The latter has a clear role to play in public policy-making from now on. Its profile will vary with the perceived state of the environment and it will certainly not always command centre stage, but governments at least pay it lip-service. To the extent that this has been brought about by the green movement's insistence on the environment as a political issue, ecologism has already won a significant battle. But it would be wrong to think that ecologism's future is already behind it, because the more radical demands for the dismantling of industrialism, the examination of the assumptions of anthropocentrism, and the move towards a decentralized, low-impact society are as far as ever from being met. In this respect it will continue to attract and repel in equal measure according to the constituencies to which it speaks: the only solution to industrialism's failure for some, and a doom-laden irrelevance for others. In actual future probably lies somewhere between these extremes, acting as a pure and good conscience for the paler green environmentalism which seems to have taken hold of governments around the world. Barring a sudden deterioration in the state of the environment, ecologism in the 1990s and beyond will play the role of all such movements; a source of inspiration to activists, and a position against which to 'check' less principled and radical forms of environmental politics.[29]

II

In the light of the preceding discussion about the role the various ideologies played in determining the basic conditions in which human society could be established on a stable basis, it would not be out of place to offer a brief critique in this context here. Ideology is understood more as a right or wrong reflection of reality on the human mind as it is associated with human psychology. Ideologies do not tell about ideals, theories and values only, but also guide the social activities of man. The importance of ideologies can be understood when they are understood with reference to the social activities. Without ideology, all social and political activities remain purposeless and ideology is itself meaningless if it cannot act as a guide of social activities of men. Political activity without ideological guidance becomes aimless and in turn ideology is unthinkable without social application.[30]

Ideology provides justification and a rationale to the policy of a country by providing goals for political actions and concealing all manifestations of a struggle for power. Ideology plays both cooperative and oppositional role. While common ideology unites the states, the opposite ideology divides them sharply. The ideology of nationalism has divided the mankind into small groups opposing each other. Ideology also provides a rigid framework for foreign policy makers. Ideologies are essentially irrational; they have a considerable emotional content, they can be used to obscure the real facts of a situation; they can be appealed to extremists and they can also make reasonable approach and compromises difficult or even impossible, they frustrate efforts to find areas of agreement.

Thus, ideology has immensely contributed in theorising politics. Even the end of ideology theory, which is itself an ideology has also added another dimension to this study. As some scholars view there has been a decline of ideology in recent years. For example Daniel Bell holds that the ideological fires in the western world have cooled down and ideology which was once the road to action has become a dead end. The impact of ideology in theorising politics would be incomplete if we do not discuss the end of ideology theory.

For several years the end of ideology theory has been the most fashionable sociological doctrine. It proclaims that we are living in a twilight of ideology when acute ideological conflicts are at the end. The theory of end of ideology is itself an ideology. It suggests that ideological commitments have been fast evaporating with more and more economic prosperity. It emphasized that the aim of both capitalism and socialism is to establish an industrial society and both are two different ways to achieve this aim. There is no difference between the economic structures of the capitalist and socialist societies.[31]

From 12th to 17th September 1955, about one hundred and fifty writers, politicians, journalists, university teachers met at Museo Nazionale Della Tecnica and Della Scienza in Milan, Italy. They gathered there to express their themes and ideas about "The future of Freedom"[32] It is also known by the name of Milan Congress of 1955. The most prominent participants of this Congress were F.A. Hayek, S. Hook, S.M.Lipset, Daniel Bell,

Raymond Aron, Edward Shils, R. Crossman, H. Gaitskell, A. Schlesinger, and B. Jouvenal. These prominent personalities met to forward the process of breaking the encrustation of liberal and socialist thought and to discover the common grounds in their thinking and push forward with the task of formulating more realistic and more inclusive ideas on the conditions of the free society. It was a conversation among a group of lively, well-informed, and disciplined scholars.

The papers presented by some eminent scholars were those prepared by M. Bertrand de Jouvenal on "Some Fundamental Similarities between the Soviet and Capitalistic Economic System", by John Plamentaz on "Threat to a Free Society", by Ely Devon, on "Changing Economic Ideologies in the United Kingdom", by M. Kamal Jumblat on "Reflections on Nationalism and Free Society", by Crossman on "Democratic Control of Foreign Policy", and by Arendt on "The Rise and Development of Totalitarianism and Authoritarian forms of government in 20th Century.

Some of the scholars differed on several but all of them converged on the critique of doctrinarism of fanatacism and of authoritarianism. They endorsed the view that there should not be any ideological conflicts in the free society and end of ideology was the requirement of the free society. In a society there should be an ideological accord and ideological conflicts should be replaced by consensus on ideological matters. Some more informal discussions among western ideologues took place at which this theory was thoroughly discussed. Many other sociological and economic concepts arose like single industrial society, convergence theory, post capitalist society, stages of economic growth, value-free social sciences etc. All these theories were associated with the theory of end of ideology.

The capitalist groups of scholars maintained that the nature of capitalism had changed and the contemporary western societies were post-capitalist societies. The socio-economic and political problems of industrial societies were the same and technological and scientific developments had virtually wiped off the differences between these societies.[33] The working class had socio-economic and political rights and there was no exploitation of the working class in these societies. The capitalists and the workers were equal partners in all the affairs, including profits in the industries. Class conflict was over and class harmony was a well established fact in the western societies. The state belonged to the whole community and not to any one section.

The end of ideology theory further maintained that instead of unplanned, free enterprise economy there was now a regulated and planned mixed economy by the state. This was a well accepted economic principle. The problems of both western and socialist industrial societies were not economic or ideological but purely and simply technological scientific and administrative. In such an industrial society the approach should be technical rather than ideological.[34] The end of ideology also firmly believes that the main issue in industrial society was not that of social revolution but of social engineering.

Referring to the underdeveloped regions of Asia, Indian delegate to the Milan Conference Piloo Mody was optimistic about the economic future of India. He was supported by Professor Arthur Lewis who maintained that it was more essential to have political liberty and representative institutions to ensure economic development in newly sovereign states of Asia and Africa. Jouvenel tried to show that there was no short cut for the economically under developed countries. They would have to go through an individual revolution which would not be less painful than the industrial revolution of the west.

Gaitskell talked on the need for economic and political independence in the under developed areas. Stress was also laid on the problems of freedom and welfare in those countries of Africa and Asia which had only recently acquired sovereignty. Speakers from Africa, Asia, Middle East urged for aid from more advanced countries of the world for the economic development of their region. They also stressed how precarious was the situation of liberty among them and expressed their belief that without an impressive rate of economic progress, liberty might collapse. In asking for economic assistance from the developed world the Afro-Asian leaders had only one aim in view—namely to strengthen the roots of democracy in the newly liberated world.

In a brilliant paper on "The Resilience of Liberty" Manes Sperber accepted with only a little regret the unideological character of the ordinary man's outlook even though he was fully aware that indifference towards public events reduced the effectiveness of democratic institutions and provided no bulwark against the emergence of tyranny, although once a tyranny exists it promises a limit to the expressive powers of the tyrannical authority.

Raymond Aron said that liberalism and socialism continued to inspire convictions and provoke controversies but it was becoming more and more difficult reasonably to transform such preferences into doctrines. Western capitalist society today comprised of a multitude of socialist institution. One can no longer count on collective ownership of planning to bring about a lot of dramatic improvement in a man. Technological progress lived upto man's expectations and has gone increasing by leaps and bounds. Perhaps some years or some decades hence it will have overcome the limitations of material resources. But its price and its limits are now generally realised. Mechanised societies are not pacific, they deliver man from the servitude of poverty and weakness, but they subject millions of workers to the logic of mass production, and they risk turning human beings into machines.

Aron believed that the theory of class struggle was falsified by a spurious analogy. The rivalry between bourgeoisie and proletariat differs in essence from the rivalry between aristocracy and bourgeoisie. The ideologists of the proletariat are bourgeois intellectuals. The proletariat never had a conception of the world opposed to that of the bourgeoisie. The so-called proletarian part in the countries where it has seized power had peasants rather than factory workers as its troops. The so called proletarian regimes that is regime governed by communist parties owed practically nothing to authentic working class culture.

Neither Russia nor the United States ever fully experienced the struggle between the aristocracy and the bourgeoisie whether liberal, socialist, conservative or Marxist. Our ideologies were the legacy of a century in which Europe was aware of the plurality of civilisation but doubted the universality of its message. Aron said that today factories, parliaments and schools were springing up in every latitude. The masses were in fervent and the intellectuals were taking power. Politics were differentiated not only by the economic and demographic ages of different countries but also by the traditions peculiar to each nation and each sphere of culture.

An intellectual's religion in the communist state has nothing to do with the religious profession of the intellectuals of the non-communist world. Communism recruits disciples from the intellectuals of Asia and Africa whereas the liberal democracy of the west derives its strength from the support of common men. Though it often wins elections democracy in the west finds scarcely any supporters ready to sacrifice all for the triumph of the democratic cause. They lacked the commitment to the concept where as the communists display a sort of religions fervour for their ideology. Communism sought to retain its ambition to improve the lot of the people but it sacrificed what was and what must have remained the heart and soul of the unending human venture involving freedom of inquiry, freedom of controversy, freedom of criticism. Communist vision succeeded according to Raymond Aron, because of intellectual weakness. No true theory would suppress the uncertainties of the present. It would maintain and encourage controversy. It offered no hope for speedy progress. Communist faith differed scarcely at all, from the contents of the other ideologies to which left wing intellectuals everywhere adhered. Communism was the first essentially European belief to have succeeded in converting millions of Asians. It gave a coherent expression to the political hopes of the west. Simple people were susceptible to these hopes.

Daniel Bell in his book "The End of Ideology" said that for two decades between 1930 and 1950, world-wide economic depression and sharp class struggles existed. During this period there was rise of fascism and racial imperialism. All this meant an end of hope to all apocalyptic thinking and to ideology as a concept. For ideology which was once a road to action had come to a dead end. Feuerbach, the most radical of all left Hegelians called himself Luther II. In his view man would be free if we could demytholise religion. God had been transformed from a parochial deity to a universal abstraction. Religion was capable only of creating false consciousness. Philosophy would reveal true consciousness by placing man, rather than God at the centre of consciousness. Thus Feuerbach sought to bring the infinite into the finite.

According to Bell, Marx said that men differed because of their class positions. All truths were masks but the real truth was the revolutionary truth. For Marx the only real action was in politics. Revolutionary action was not social change. It was, in its own way, the resumption of all the old, millerarian. It was in its new vision, a new ideology.

The key social division in society arose out of the distribution of property. Yet in a politico-technological world property had increasingly lost its force as a dominant element of power and sometimes even of wealth. In almost all modern societies technical skill becomes more important than inheritance as a determinant of occupation and political power takes precedence over economic factors.[35]

S.M. Lipset felt that the differences between the left and the right in the western democracies are no longer profound. The change in the western political life reflected the fact that the fundamental political problem of the industrial revolution had been solved. The workers had achieved industrial and political citizenship. The conservatives had accepted the welfare state and the democratic left had recognized that an increase in overall state power carried with it more danger to freedom than solutions for economic problems. This triumph of the democratic social revolution in the west ended domestic policies for those intellectuals who took resort to ideologies to envisage plans to political action.

The United States has been the wealthiest country in the world, and its working class lived on a scale to which most of middle classes in the rest of the world aspired. But according to Lipset the democratic class struggle would continue, though it would be a fight without ideologies, without red flags and without May Day parades. Those who viewed the gradual decline of ideology which was often all conducive to human freedom feared the inherent conformist aspect of bureaucratic organisation, an endemic aspect of modern industrial society, whether capitalist or socialist is reducing the scope of individual freedom because "organisation men" must continue to succeed. This point is sometimes linked to the decline in the intensity of political conflict, because politics is seen as changing into administration as the managers and experts take over in government as well as in business.

Politics of various underdeveloped countries was much more complex than it was in the western countries. In these states there was still a need for intense political controversy and ideology. The problems of industrialisation, religion and the character of political institutions were still unsettled and the arguments about them had become intertwined with international struggle. The post-political relations between former colonial countries and the West and between coloured and White people made the task even more difficult.[36]

According to Aron, Marxism was the last great ideology prior to the end of the ideological age. What people increasingly agreed upon was the need for a system that increased the volume of collective resources and reduced the disparity of status between groups with the minimum of delay and friction. Concensus instead of conflict was the goal of modern advanced societies. By comparison with the bitter ideological struggles of the 20's and 30's the disputes of the 50's were more like fencing matches.

Bernard Henri Levy in his best seller "Barbarism with a Human Face" takes a dismal view of socialism. Having concluded that Marxism was the opium of the masses, he was compelled to say that though socialism was on march in Europe, it was in crisis all over the world. In Italy young people were rebelling against communist party and so in Bologna which was then the most totalitarian state anywhere. The same was true in Naples, in Angola, in Eastern Europe, in Sweden and in Portugal. He said that between the barbarity of capitalism and the barbarity of socialism, he would choose the former.

Carter was inspired more by old fashioned religion than by new fangled political ideology. In his opinion God lived while Marx died. Largely because of Christian convictions Carter was optimistic about the west's chances of survival against what used to be called Godless communism. Referring to America Jimmy Carter said that ideology was out of fashion in his country. The word evoked the spectre of the cold war centred around monolithic communism. It connoted complacency about capitalist democracy and paranoia about Marxist dictatorship. An overdose of ideology in the American system contributed to the trauma of MaCarthyism which stood for a sort of witch hunting of those who even dared to talk about the welfare concept of the state. To McCarthy rank reactionary and conservative state should be order of the day as in his view the least interference by the state in administrative matters would create conditions in which human beings would flourish in peace and prosperity.

Those who believed that ideology was largely relevant to modern statesmanship based their view on the comprehensive nature of state functions that was the hallmark of the modern society. Kissinger was one of them who believed that the USA should deal with the Soviet Union not primarily as a competing system of ideas but as a rival superpower. He went a long way towards de-emphasising ideology in US foreign policy. The secretary of state in the Carter administration Cyrus Vance felt that Euro communism may pose an even greater threat to Soviet hegemony in Eastern Europe than it did to western interests.

The then US Ambassador in UN Andrew Young who was not hesitant to talk about communism in equally derogatory terms observed that Americans should stop worrying so much about communist infiltration in the third world but worry more about indigenous problems there. Anthony Lake the then Director of Policy Planning in the State Department, said that the spread of communism was not so dangerous to peace as the spread of nuclear reactors and conventional weapons. He further suggested some more issues which needed serious attention of the American people. Among these were over population, poverty, monopoly of resources and terrorism that cut across ideological lines.

The end of ideology theory was criticised by Marxists on the ground that it was a counter move to check an emergency philosophy which was meant for the welfare of mankind in general. According to Marxists, in a class divided society the social realities were different for different classes and because of this their ideologies were also different. Ideologies did not tell only about ideals, theories and values but also guided the social activities of men. The importance of ideologies could be understood only with reference to the social activities. Ideologies did not remain a psychological problem but also became a material force. Without ideology all social and political activities remained purposeless and ideology itself was meaningless if it could not act as a guide to the social activities of men. Political activity without ideological guidance became aimless and in turn ideology was unthinkable without social application.

The Marxists maintained that in a class-divided society, the economically dominant class—which had interest in the maintenance of status quo, which opposed change and was afraid of revolution was likely to support the end of ideology theory. But the economically weaker and the exploited working class which wanted to demolish the exploitative system, wanted a revolutionary change which would ensure freedom from exploitation, ultimately leading to the achievement of the ideal of classless society. Without a philosophy and ideology of its own, the working class could not pursue its socio-economic, political and revolutionary struggle. For working class end of ideology would mean end of the theory of communism. Such an aimless practice should not become the basis of any meaningful social change. Thus for the working class end of ideology would mean end of revolution, end of the way to liberation and it would mean an everlasting bondage to the capitalistic industrial society.[37]

The new philosophers were reflecting a state of mind that had been evident, if not common place in the rest of the west for some years. Arthur Koestler in 1950 in his essay "The God that Failed" wrote that how he had joined the communist party with great zeal in 1931, only to quit it seven years later in total bitterness. The significance of the new generation of philosophers was that they were criticising Marxism when the Marxian time bomb was politically alive and ticking. They denounced Marxism when the socialist-communist alliance in France had the best chance of winning and taking control of parliament. They branded communists as incipient dictators.

Daniel Bell argued that the rise of welfare state had exhausted all the 19th century ideologies. The ideologies as much as communism and socialism in France and Italy did have political weight or a driving momentum but still they had lost their power to persuade. In their view only through social engineering a new utopia of social harmony could be achieved and not through radical transformations.

REFERENCES

1. Henrey D. Aiken, *The Age of Ideology*, pp. 16-17.
2. Derek Heater, *Political Realities, Contemporary Political Ideas*, Longman, p. 26.
3. Louis Althusier, *Lenin Philosophy and Other Essays*, Ben Brewster, London, 1970, p. 123.
4. Partho Chatterjee, *Thinking About Ideology in Search of an Analytical Framework*. A Chapter in the book Contemporary Political Theory, Ed. Bains and Jain, Radiand Publishers (1980), p. 94.
5. Amal Ray and Mohit Bhattacharya, *Political Theory, Ideas and Institutions*, The World Press Pvt. Ltd., 1988, p. 602.
6. *Ibid.*, p. 603.
7. Deeck Heater, *Political Realities—Contemporary Political Ideas*, Longman, p. 26.
8. Allan R. Ball, *Modern Politics and Govt.*, Macmillan, 1973, p. 260.
9. F.M.Watkins, *The Age of Ideology—Political Thought, 1750 to Present*, Prentice Hall of India Pvt. Ltd., New Delhi, 1968, Preface.
10. *Ibid.*, p. 384.
11. Amal Ray and Mohit Bhattacharya, *Political Theory, Ideas and Institution:* The World Press Pvt. Ltd., 1988, p. 603.
12. Laski, *The Social and Political Ideas of Some Representative Thinkers of the Victorial Age*, Chapter V, p. 100.
13. Tocqueville, *Recollections*, P-99, *quoted by Hosky in his essay on Tocqueville*.
14. G.Sartori, *Democratic Theory*, Calcutta, 1965, p.364.
15. A.P.Grimes, *The Pragmatic Corrse of Liberalism*, in Wesrtern Political Quarterly, Vol. IX, No. 3, (Sept. 1956) p. 6-64.
16. Sidney Webb, *The Historical Basis of Socialism*, in Fabian Essays.
17. G.B.Shaw, *Economic Basis of Socialism*, in Fabian Essays.

18. Sabine, *Syndicalism in France*, pp. 124.
19. E.Gellner, *Nations and Nationalism*, Blackwell, Oxford, 198, p.125.
20. A.Smith, *The Ethnic Origin of Nations*, Basil Blackwell, Oxford, 1986.
21. See R. Scruton, *'In Defence of the Nation'*, in J.C.D. Clark (ed.), *Ideas and Politics in Modern Britain*, Macmillan, London, 1990, pp. 58-9; and C. Gluck, *Japan's Modern Myths*, Princeton University Press, Princeton, 1985.
22. See Moira Ferguson (ed.), *First Feminists:* British Women Writers 1578-1799, Indian University Press, Bloomington, 1985.
23. See Richard Evans, *The Feminists: Women's Emancipation Movements in Europe, America and Australasia 1840-1920*, Croom Helm, London, 1977, and Olive Banks, *Faces of Feminism*, Basil Blackwell, Oxford, 1986.
24. See Max Oelschlaeger, *The Idea of Utilderness: From Prehistory to the Age of Ecology*, Yale University Press, New Haven and London, 1991, Ch.1.
25. See Anna Bramwell, *Ecology in the 20th Century*, Yale University, New Haven and London, 1989.
26. See Peter C. Gould, *Early Green Politics: Back to Nature, Back to the Land and Socialism in Britain 1880-1900*, Harvester and St. Martin's Press, Brighton and New York, 1988.
27. See Douglas H. Strong, *Dreamers and Defenders: American Conservationists*, University of Nebraska Press, Lincoln and London, 1988, Chapters 3 and 4.
28. James Lovelock's Gara, Oxford University Press, Oxford, 1979, *Argues Similarly, and has had an Important Influence on Contemporary Ecologism.*
29. Roger Eatwell and Anthony Wright (ed.) *Contemporary Political Ideologies*, Printer Publishers, London, 1993, p. 50-54, 147-149, 192-196, 216-218. Author of Articles in this book: *Conservatism:* Noel O'Suillivan, *Nationalism:* Roger Griffin, *Feminism:* Valerie Bryson, *Ecologism:* Andrew Dobson.
30. L.N.Moskvichov, *The End of Ideology Theory, Illusion and Reality*, Moscow, 1964, p.115.
31. *Ibid.*, p. 10.
32. Edward Shils, *The End of Ideology, Encounter*, Nov. 1956, Vol. 5.
33. P.A.Sorokin, *Motval Convergence of the United States and the USSR to the Mixed Socio-cultural Type*, Mexico, 1961.

34. Daniel Bell, R.E. Hane, *Schlesinger have supported the idea of technological approach rather than ideological approach to the problem of industrial societies.*

35. Daniel Bell, *The End of Ideology,* The Free Press, 1960.

36. S.M.Lipset, *Political Man,* Double days and Compay Inc.

37. J.K.Galbrith, *The New Industiral State,* London, 1967.

3

THE SOVIET IDEOLOGY: ORIGIN EVOLUTION AND FORMULATIONS

Historical Background

It is said that political power is based on force, yet force alone is an inadequate basis for a political system. This paradox is frequently resolved by explaining that the monopoly entails only the legitimate exercise of force. But what is legitimate depends on the attitudes of the population of the territory or at least on the attitudes of a dominant element among the population. Attitudes reflect widely held expectations concerning proper political behaviour, customs and beliefs which constitute the political culture of a society. The effort to determine the political culture involves direct surveys of the attitudes of the population. But in a closed system like the Soviet, this approach was forbidden.

To understand Soviet system, we must understand that it is the creation of a consciously articulated body of ideas—the ideology. Political culture like most popular customs was extremely persistent. What preceeded the Bolshevik revolution of 1917, was more of a shameful memory of the past rather than a proud heritage. The Czarist regime prevailed in the same territory for centuries prior to the establishment of the USSR. Czarism was essentially a Russian phenomenon.

One of the most striking parallels between Czarism and Bolshevism is the existence of an unusual measure of centralised, unrestricted power in both systems. Czarist rule was synonymous with autocracy. Just before the Bolshevik revolution some modifications were introduced in the autocratic system. For instance the institution of an elected legislative assembly did enable public opinion to exercise some pressure upon the Czar. If one goes back to the history of the East Slavs—from whom the Russians along with other nationalities descended—one finds evidence of embryonic democratic institutions. However, Russia has probably less experience with limited governments or representative institutions than any other European country.

The factors which contributed prominently to the absolutistic nature of Russian government and to the relations betwen the church and the state. The orthodox faith, to which traditionally an overwhelming majority of Russians have adhered to have been an extremely important element in the country's history. In the Byzantine Empire, from which the Russians obtained their Christian faith in the late tenth century, orthodoxy had developed the peculiar institution of "Caesaro-papism". In this system, the emperor was both autocratic ruler of the state and supreme head of the church. The separation of ecclesiastical and temporal power—whether between the Pope and the Holy Roman Emperor, or between the secular state and the church—did not exist.

The Mongol invasion of the thirteenth century was also a major cause in the development of absolutism. Living in the broadest portion of the great Eurasian plain, almost unprotected by natural barriers, the East Slavs were easily subjected by the Mongol cavalry. The Mongol invasion gave rise to new distribution of power in Eastern Europe. The principal Russian beneficiaries of Mongol rule were the princes of Moscow, who became the vassals and lieutenants of the Mongol Khans. It is not at all clear from where the Mongol Khans found their patterns of rule. They required a degree of self-abasement from their subjects commonly associated with oriental despotism. The Muscovite princes adopted many of the despotic attitudes and practices of the Mongol rulers.[1]

The high water-mark of Czarist autocracy came under Catherine II (the Great) in the eighteenth century. Catherine was German by birth and most of the intellectual underpinning in her rule was provided by West Europeans. The era was the culmination of the divine right theory of monarchy in the west, a justification for absolute rule that had been developed from the above noted influences on Russia. In perfecting autocracy in the Russian Empire, Catherine and her immediate predecessors were following the almost predominant model of European statecraft.

For centuries, most men took social inequality for granted. Unequal distribution of wealth, rank and even legal privilege were widespread. One of the most significant developments of the 19th century was the concern for such social stratification. The phenomenon was described as a class structure though social thinkers presented and continued to present widely varying definition of class. The superficial impression is that of a glittering aristocracy, an intense but morbid intellectual milieu and a down trodden though enduring peasantry.

In western Europe the nobility considered itself to be true aristocracy. Though usually of the same race and nationality as the rest of its country's population, the nobility had for centuries enjoyed the status of hereditary privileged class. As a result, the nobles regarded themselves as wholly distinct and superior, entitled to rule and to enjoy the fruits of rule. The Russians were in close contact with these West European nobles. Since the early part of the 18th century, the Russian Empire had included the Baltic provinces, where a small ruling class of German origin dominated a Latvian and Estonian peasantry. Such a concept of class differentiation influenced the Slavophiles' view of the West European nobility's mentality. In the Russian lands of the Empire, the position of the upper stratum was different. The nobles were distinct from the remainder of the population and they enjoyed many privileges. Unlike the typical Western noble, the Russian noble was essentially a servant of the autocracy. No traditions of family honour of class autonomy shielded him from the full force of absolute rule.

The three quarters of vast population was of peasants. Until 1861, most of the peasants in the Russian Empire were serfs, the property of noble landlords or of the crown. Under Catherine the Great, the peasants had been little better than a chattel slave, subject to removal from his ancestral farm, to almost unrestricted sale as property and to arbitrary and brutal chastisement. The government kept close watch over his activities through the "land captains". Primary control of the peasant's movement was left to the village community who was responsible for the tax and redemption payments for the land allotted to the peasants. This practice also encouraged autocracy. The professionals constituted a part of the social group that had no precise western counter-part. The scholar, the artist, the professional tended to constitute the intelligent power. They were disgusted with the situation in the Russian Empire, embarrassed at the backwardness of its economic and political development and ashamed of the oppression and neglect of the peasantry. Instead of a stabling element, the intelligentsia tended to be two spearheads of the forces working for the profound description of the Czarist order.

The importance of the intellegentsia's dissatisfaction as an element in the climate of opinion favourable to revolution was obvious. The collectivist aspects of the village community hampered individual economic development. The demand for unanimity in the village took the form of pervasive censorship of expression. The censorship was more effective during the last years of the 19th century. The rapid growth of scientific thought in Russia, marked the emergence of figures of world importance such as the Chemist Demitry. I.Mendeleyev, the psychologist Ivan P. Pavlov and the mathematician Nikolai Lobachevsky, indicates the acceptance of a kind of rationality that inevitably would have induced more systematic approaches to general problems of knowledge. The very considerable progress in general education, which promised to reduce illiteracy to modern levels within a generation following the reforms of 1905, provided a solid foundation for liberal institution and social progress.[2]

By the end of the 19th century, the Russian Empire embraced over 166 million inhabitants in an area of 8 million square miles. Over half of the population was non-Russian. Many of the remainders were East Slavs, closely related to the Russians and most of the others were Europeans living in the border areas. The greatest expansion of the empire had taken place in Asia. There were Czarist proconsuls who believed that they were entitled to impose the benefits of Russian culture and material progress.

Russians on the whole did not share the rigid attitudes of racial superiority and segregation that characterised many west European colonizers. Unlike the West European colonial empires, separted by thousand of miles of ocean from their home countries and inhabited by people whose physical characteristics differentiated them from the Europeans, the Russian Empire stretched in an unbroken mass across Eurasia. The physical characteristics of the empire's population represented a series of gradual changes from the blond, semi-Nordic types of the Baltic coast to the darker, flatter Mongol features of the Altai. The Russian contact with the non-Europeans had lasted for more than a millennium, involving relationships of subjection as well as ascendancy. This aspect of Russian heritage, the combination of strong national pride to the point of messianic complex, and a relatively tolerant attitude towards racial differences—has exerted an important influence on more recent Soviet contacts with the non-European world.

The first revolution of 1917, in March was quite unplanned. Under the terrible strain of World War I, the rigid and inefficient structure of the Czarist regime broke down. For a few months, liberals and moderates imbued with Western concepts of governmental and social order maintained a precarious grip on the cultural authority. In November, they were swept away, almost without bloodshed, by the Bolshevik Revolution. A few thousand determined revolutionaries guided by the ideological and organisational theories inherited the place of the Czarist bureaucracy. Among the main reasons for their success was their willingness to promise immediate distribution of land to the peasants. Within a few months, the Bolsheviks were engaged in a desperate struggle against a variety of domestic counter-revolutionary movements which were sporadically and ineffectively supported by the central powers and the western allies. By 1920 the Bolsheviks had triumphed fully.

After the charismatic leader Lenin, leadership came in the hands of Stalin. He launched the programme of industrialisation and the Five-Year Plans. He also carried out the collectivisation of agriculture. During the period 1934 to 1938, Stalin consolidated his absolute dictatorship. For seven and a half years after the end of World War II, Stalin retained his undisputed dictatorial powers. While the USSR was busy in rebuilding devastated economy. Stalin rigidly maintained barriers to intercourse between the Soviet population and the outside world.[3]

In all societies, political culture is an amalgam of traditional, often subconscious, influences and deliberate indoctrination by dominant institutions. In 'the American Dilemma' Gunnar Myrdal was able to identify an "American Creed" which included those democratic principles inculcated by the schools, the churches, the mass media and other institutions, as well as those traditions transmitted from generation to generation. Similar political-cultural amalgam have been detected in most other modern societies. The traditional element is strong in the USSR, too. The Soviet regime claimed to exercise its monopoly in favour of a single body of ideas as the Communist ideology. The ideology claims to be systematic and scientific doctrine capable of guiding the process of human transformation. An examination of this supposed scientific approach to social problems is the prerequisite of understanding the Soviet system.

Officially, the body of communist ideology is called Marxism-Leninism. The ideology is not an indigenous Russian growth, for Karl Marx and his collaborator, Friedrich Engels, were German by birth. Their works and Lenin's constitute the Soviet ideology. Lenin built upon the basic Marxist structure and he modified it in many respects. His successors have introduced additional modifications but Leninism and Marxism remains the foundation of Soviet ideological thinking.

Materialism—the most fundamental premise of the doctrine, has also remained unchanged since Marx. Accoding to Marxism-Leninism, all being is determined by the nature of the material base. The situation of mankind is said to depend upon the relationships of production. In each epoch of human history different types of tools are available and human labour utilises them in a certain way. The nature of this relationship of man and his tools requires a special form of social organistion—"the relationship of production". All other aspects of human society—family relations, religion, government, law, art, philosophy, literature—are included in the "superstructure". Materialism had tremendous psychological implication on the Soviet ideology. Marxism, Leninism has always been rigorously atheistic, not merely agnostic. The world in both its physical and human aspects is explained scientifically. As a result, the discoveries of the natural sciences received enormous emphasis in the USSR. Except when it seems to conflict with Leninist-principles or with the personal interests of a leader of the regime, scientific investigation receives great support.[4]

According to Marx, dialectical materialism is an indivisible whole. Its fundamental aspect is the simultaneous presence of contradictory elements—thesis and antithesis. The interaction of the contradictory elements leads to change—the formation of a new state—synthesis. Stalin was moving in the direction of rejecting much of dialectic theory. He declared that certain elements of human activity e.g., languages and apparently the natural sciences stood outside the framework of dialectical development in history. After Stalin's death, the return of Leninism had cast doubt upon those alterations which tended to bring Soviet thought—somewhat close to western ideas.

Historical materialism, that is application of the dialectics to history, offers the only valid explanation of social development. Marx's original stress upon dialectic development did have the virtue of focusing attention on those elements of change and inter-relations of social phenomenon that many of his contemporaries and immediate predecessors had neglected. Marx contended that every stage of history has been marked by divisions of human society corrersponding to man's relationship to tools. As the tools change, the relationship changes. Hence the existing social order becomes unstable as the contradictory elements within it emerge. A new dominant class rises to replace the old. Thus, the feudal nobility replaced the slave owners of antiquity and capitalist entrepreneurs replaced the nobility.

Russia was ripe for a revolution but not yet inevitably drawn to proletarian revolution. Both Marx and Lenin maintained that theory and action are inseparable, but Lenin's emphasis on organising a revolution, was much stronger than Marx's. To carry out the proletarian revolution, according to Lenin, a highly organised party was necessary. Without the leadership of this vanguard of the proletariat, the working class lacked consciousness of its own true interests. This party should embrace all the conscious elements of the proletariat and persons of other classes who adhered to the proletarian cause. All members must actively participate in the party's work.

The guiding organisational principle of the party was democratic centralism. This concept meant choosing leaders from the rank and file, followed by building decisions from above. Between elections, the party leaders were supreme and any effort to agitate or go against their decisions was treason to the party. In the pre-revolutionary times, debates and elections could not take place with any regularity in the underground party.[5]

For decades, Lenin's dictum on the necessity of violent revolution was never questioned by Soviet leaders. Both Marx and Lenin had thought that the stage in which compulsion is still necessary would be brief. To Marx, the great economic machine run by capitalism, once in the hands of the workers, would be almost able to furnish the abundance of the goods required by the formula of true communism, from each according to his ability, to each according to his needs. Lenin realised that such abundance would not be achieved for many years through the backward Russian economy, but he believed that the revolution, once started would as a chain reaction spread to more industrialised countries. Lenin concentrated in strengthening the proletarian dictatorship achieved in Russia. This was the beginning of the practice of socialism in one country which Stalin elevated to the level of theory.

The role of the state is very intimately related to the transition to full communism, the ultimate goal of all Marxists. While stressing this goal, Marx himself was wise enough to avoid setting up of a precise schedule for its attainment or in defining its characteristics. In this both Lenin and Stalin were equally cautious. In 1961, however, when Khrushchev was at the height of his power, the Soviet communist party adopted a new programme declaring that the USSR was making transition towards full communism.

The two basic prerequisites were to come close to being attained namely the provision of goods "to each according to his needs" and the establishment of single system of public ownership of the means of production. These were in contrast to the division between socialist and co-operative property. "To each according to his needs" could not entail the satisfaction of unlimited desires. Material production would be fully adequate, Soviet spokesman said, to supply real necessities. Gradually, more needs like medical services and education which was already free would be satisfied by free distribution, in place of present money exchange system. Among the goods to be distributed free of charge were listed noon lunches, local transportation, and housing. Money wages would gradually be levelled, although wage differentials would remain for sometimes.[6]

The elimination of money incentives is regarded as an essential aspect of the achievement of full communism, for each must work according to his ability without any regard to material reward. The regime's ideologues recognised that attainment of this goal, really needed, a radical transformation of human psychology. The new Communist man must be created. The observance of the rules of Communist conduct must become an organic need and habit. A major change must be the elimination of the difference between manual and intellectual labour. Soviet society officially contained two classes of toilers—the industrial workers and the peasants and a stratum of intellectuals and white collar workers. Full Communism, on the other hand, must be classless. Ultimately, even national distinctions, especially language, must be effaced, but the party programme recognised that this process would take much longer than the elimination of the classes. As less and less time is spent on material production, the individual will have more time and freedom to develop his talents. His leisure will be beneficially employed for his own cultural, intellectual, and physical development, for sports and artistic endeavour and for public service.

The transition to communism described in the 1961 party programme was still a part of the official ideology. The resolution of 1966, Party congress referred to the ultimate attainment of communism, but the matter was not discussed in detail nor set any date for the realisation of this goal. After 1961, in the former Soviet Union, several policy developments seemed to point that there had been little emphasis on wage leveling. Soviet citizens had been encouraged to use their earnings to acquire personal property. One such instance was the provision of housing for all. The system encouraged individuals to provide for their own housing needs. When Khrushchev was in power, individual home construction was discouraged but afterwards both individual and co-operative construction was considered essential. The scheme provided for one-third of all urban housing which was highly praised. Private gardening by farmers, which was once discouraged, was then treated as a laudable initiative.

The retreat from the drive towards full communism was related to a change in the regime's perception of world conditions. It was said that until a developed communist society is achieved and the final settlement of the contradictions between capitalism and communism in the world arena in favour of communism takes place, the soviet state cannot wither away. Khrushchev had optimistically acclaimed the shining image of a communist party that is marching forward victoriously through—out the whole world. But, since 1961, the Soviet leadership had come to realise that the final settlement with capitalism was a distant dream. The determination exhibited by the United States and its allies during the 1962 Cuban missile confrontation and in subsequent crises, plus the recovery of the US economic growth rate to levels equal to those of the USSR, had demonstrated that capitalism was far from collapse.

The 1961 programme had also insisted that while the USSR was opening the new road to communism, it would have to facilitate the advance of other states of the socialist camp, in order that they could all achieve full communism, more or less simultaneously in the same historical epoch. But, even under the most favourable conditions, it would be enormously difficult to provide hundreds of millions of impoverished Chinese with the material abundance the Soviet regime considered a prerequisite for communism. The inept policies of the Peking Communist regime have restricted China's limited potential for economic advance. The bitter controversies between the Soviet and Chinese regimes had made it impossible for the USSR to play an effective role in preparing China for Communism and had, perhaps, caused the Soviet leaders to wonder whether it was really desirable for the Chinese Communists to achieve a powerful economy. The Soviet citizens who suffered terribly for decades and more recently, endured considerable deprivation in order to move towards Communism will be disheartened if the regime reneges on the definite promise of the 1961 programme—the Party solemnly proclaimed: the present generation of Soviet people shall live under Communism.[7]

But, eliminating the time-table for attaining communism would not merely cost the regime's popularity. Communist ideology has always insisted that Communism is not just a highly desirable goal that one should strive to attain but a historical development that can be also scientifically predicted. According to the ideology, Marxism-Leninism is just as scientific in its analysis of social development as are the natural sciences. Marx predicted the increasing impoverishment of the proletariat in the industrialised countries; the opposite took place. Lenin adapted the original theory by adding the new concept of imperialism. Lenin himself, regarding imperialism as the last stage of capitalism, predicted imminent world revolution. When instead, dictatorships like Nazism arose, Communist ideologues declared that these fascist regimes represented capitalism's final attempt to stave off revolution. Obviously, any theory can be "preserved" if it is altered whenever factual developments contradict it. But such a theory has neither predictive utility nor scientific value.

Marxism-Leninsm provies not only a sure guide to social development but an absolute assurance of eventual human perfection. The attainment of Communism, however, is by far the most important development the ideology envisages. Therefore, once a prediction of the time for attaining communism has been publicly incorporated into the body of the ideology, indefinitely postponing the time is tantamount to renouncing the predictive power of the ideology. The problem, then, goes beyond mere disappointment of the citizenry; Soviet citizens could actually lose faith in Communist ideology. But because of the rigid mechanism of party system they could not have the slightest chance to raise their little finger in protest.

The regime appeared to be temporizing, tacitly dropping the emphasis on attaining communism, but avoiding a public revision of the time table. Earlier faulty predictions could be explained away, since either they were made by theoreticians like Marx and Lenin, who had not yet attained power or they were not so intimately related to the sacrifices and aspirations of the Soviet people. Nevertheless, Marxism-Leninism had shown itself to be a remarkably persistent and flexible doctrine. Its skilled ideologues may yet find a way to restore its credibility. However, there was another side to the unavowed flexibility of Marxist-Leninist doctrine. Because the basic tenets were actually subject to revision, there was no dogma in true sense of the word.

The dominant element in the Communist Party determine what was orthodox and those who clung to another interpretation, even one undisputed in earlier years, became heretics and no ecclesiastical appeal to the clergy could save them. Obviously, this aspect of the ideology strengthened the absolutist claims of the then leadership. By opening up a broad area of ideological uncertainty, it also promoted a high degree of dynamism in the system. The Soviet Communists knew that they could not justify themselves by ideological orthodoxy. Consequently they try to assure their position by maximum practical service to the regime and by anticipation of its shifting theoretical requirements. For the hard core of the former Soviet regime's supporters, faith in the ideology as a consistent belief system was not the only basis of loyalty.[8]

The Party

The Communist party was the core institution of the Soviet political system. In a pluralist system there were almost always two or more parties. The leaders of each party assumed the continued existence of at least one opposing party, though they devoutly hoped to keep their opponents out of power, in the role of "loyal opposition". Each party acted as a legitimate institution for articulating the political demands of a number of groups in the society. In a multiparty system, the range of demands articulated by each such party was comparatively narrow, for every set of interests tended to be represented by a different party. In a two-party system each party not only articulated a wide range of interests but also served to "aggregate" these interests—that is, to combine and compromise them in a way that usually promoted the smooth functioning of the pluralist political system as a whole.

In its conception, the Soviet Communist Party was an entirely different phenomenon. Lenin regarded party as the indispensable instrument by which the Marxist vision of a perfect society was to be attained. From the outset, the Party was a conspirational instrument for overthrowing the existing Czarist political system rather than a legitimate instrument for articulating demands within the system. The compromises that inevitably attached to legitimacy were rejected by Lenin, who saw them as tantamount to "reformism". Following the Revolution, the Party was the essence of the "dictatorship of the proletariat," a role it held for many decades. In this capacity, the party was explicitly given the monopoly of political articulation and all other parties were suppressed.

Lenin and his followers rejected the concept of the single party as an overarching institution of interest aggregation, for they regarded the party as a force to transform, rather than to mediate, the interests and political culture of the existing society. The Communist Party became the institutional guardian and interpreter of the ideology and was charged with indoctrinating the population with the ideas and values that would make them psychologically capable of living under full communism. Stalin, as an absolute dictator, distrusted any institutional locus of power. He limited the sway of the Party, devolving many functions in the execution of his will upon state organs, particularly the police. It took, however, all the power of an absolute ruler to reduce the scope of the Party. Even then, Stalin never tried to reduce the theoretical significance of the Party. Every Communist was taught that the party was the only infallible guide to the course of history and that its command was beyond question. For most of the Party transmitted the teachings of Marx, Engles and Lenin, even though they were partially distorted by Stalin's reinterpretations. Therefore, the Communists were taught to accept the Party as the essential institution of the Soviet system.[9]

The Party regained complete ascendancy soon after Stalin's death. This re-emergence of the party as the dominant institutional force in the former USSR was very closely associated with the rise of Nikita Khrushchev. Even in Stalin's lifetime, Khrushchev had insisted on the paramount position of the party. The party is responsible for everything. Whether it is army work, police work, economic work or Soviet work; all is subordinate to the Party leadership, and if anyone thinks otherwise, that means he is not a Bolshevik. After Stalin's death, Malenkov, who appeared as successor, resigned as a member of the party secretariat while retaining the position of the head of the Soviet Government. Khrushchev became the highest party boss. It is clear that the prestige and the power levers concentrated in the party were major factors in enabling Khrushchev to win in the struggle for supreme authority in the former USSR. Regardless of their rank in government agencies, other Soviet leaders were also party members formally bound to obey orders issued in the name of the Party. Within each branch of the Soviet bureaucracy, many officials were tied to power alignments that led them to follow the Party leadership rather than their nominal superiors. So we can say that the Party was very important in the former USSR but Party's institutional pre-eminence depended mainly on the existence of personal rule.

In sheer size, the Soviet Communist Party resembled the mass membership parties of pluralist societies. Soviet writers have always explicitly rejected the term mass organisation for the party. Instead they followed Lenin's prescription that selection of members be made with great care, so that the Party may act as a lever within the whole social structure rather than become submerged in it. In sharp contrast to pluralist parties, the communist party does not solicit volunteer adherents, but chooses its members. The mere fact of the enrolment of merely all eminent Soviet citizens provided a propaganda advantage. The regime constantly boasted that the outstanding citizens were communists and used this assertion as a proof that the party embodied the best of Soviet society. Consequently, the prize winning physicist, the record breaking milkmaid, the popular novelist, the renowned Arctic explorer, were all prime targets for recruitment into the Party. In crisis situations, such as war, extraordinary effort to the point of complete neglect of the ideological background or intellectual capacity of the candidates was devoted to bring all "heroic" figures into the Party to serve as examples to their fellows. Ordinarily, prospective members were carefully screened. Each must be recommended by three persons who had already been party members for at least five years. The prime duty of each communist was to safeguard the Party against the infiltration of persons unworthy of the lofty title of communist; sponsors were held responsible for a new member's derelictions.[10]

The Party's Ideological Life

Eversince CPSU was established, it had a full ideological life, a life exceptionally rich in content and diverse in form. It reflected in a concentrated form all the processes that took place in science, culture, education and upbringing i.e. in all spheres of Soviet society's cultural life. The party was the ideological and theoretical centre of the Soviet people. It critically processed the sum total of human knowledge and all the achievements not only of Soviets but world science and culture, absorbed all their values and made them serve the interests of the working people and the interests of communist construction.

The CPSU was inseperably linked with the entire cultural life of the Soviet people. The party's ideological life exerted a comprehensive and decisive influence on the cultural life of the Soviet society. The party responded vigorously to all the questions of cultural construction and society's spiritual development posed by reality. It interpreted them thoroughly to answer them from a truly Marxist-Leninist point of view.

Marxism-Leninism was the CPSU's ideological weapon, well tested in revolutionary struggle and constructive labour. The party was founded on the firm foundations of Marxism-Leninism, the teaching that constituted its basis, the core of its entire ideological life. CPSU always gave utmost attention to thorough study of the communist philosophy by the communists. The party always resolutely and uncompromisingly opposed those who underestimated revolutionary theory. Lenin wrote, "There can be no strong socialist party without a revolutionary theory which unites all socialists, from which they draw all their connections, and which they apply in their methods of struggle and means of action."[11]

Lenin stressed that in that period the significance of revolutionary theory for the party becomes stronger because the party was only just forming and developing. For the party to become a truly revolutionary vanguard of the proletariat and to be able to overcome the resistance of opportunists and vested interests. It had to rely firmly and consistently upon the basic principles of Marxism. In addition the party had to analyse the entire international experience of the working-class movement of that time, preserved its best elements while dicarding all the eroneous ones. This could be done only by means of revolutionary theory. This demanded that the party be highly trained ideologically and politically on the basis of revolutionary theory.

The party with Lenin at the head rose to the occasion. It showed not in words but in deeds an example of a careful, thoughtful and creative attitude towards revolutionary theory. This helped the party successfully to fulfil its mission as a leading and guiding force in the struggle of the working masses for the overthrow of czarism and capitalism.

When the CPSU became the ruling party, it, armed with Marxist-Leninist theory, boldly and resolutely led the masses in the building of a new society. In these conditions revolutionary theory, in the direct meaning of the word, became not only a means for explaining the world, but for changing and transforming it. Revolutionary theory represented an inexhaustible source, wherefrom the Party derived confidence in its strength, its courage and optimism and its will power to achieve the victory of communism. The 23rd congress of CPSU emphasised: "No society has ever stood in such great need of scientific theory as the socialist society. This is why theory must continue to blaze the way for practice and ensure a strictly scientific approach to the management of the Soviet people's economic and cultural life.[12]

The revolutionary theory provided the key to understand and resolve all the cardinal problems of social development. It allowed one to find his bearings in a specific situation, to see the historical perspective, and to assess developments correctly, from class positions. It also helped to determine the directions of socio-economic and political development for many years to come. That is why no matter what tasks the CPSU undertook, it referred again and again to the very rich ideological legacy of Lenin, its founder. The CPSU invariably and consistently followed Lenin's instructions that "we must not remove theoretical questions from our agenda, but raise all the practical work of our Party to the level of theoretical clarification of the tasks of a workers' party."[13]

The CPSU always proceeded and continued to proceed from the fact that theory must really belong to the whole Party, to each communist. That is why it wanted all communists to completely master and consciously grasp Marxism-Leninism to take active part in the Party's and country's ideological life and to realise their ideological connection in practical participation in building communism. The Leninist tradition of the CPSU that communists should thoroughly master revolutionary theory.

In guiding communist construction, the CPSU understood that this formidable task could not be successfully achieved without the comprehensive development of man himself and that without a high level of consciousness, culture, education, and ideological and spiritual maturity communism would be unfeasible as it would be also unthinkable without an appropriate material and technological base. In other words, the party proceeded from the fact that the moulding of the new man was not only a primary objective, but an indispensable prerequisite of communist construction.

The Party was intermittently concerned with raising the level of political consciousness of the many million strong masses of the working people and cultivating in them the readiness, willpower and skills needed to build communism. The Soviet man, convinced of the righteousness of communism's ideals, matured, hardened and grew in the course of revolutionary struggle and revolutionary construction. The high political and moral qualities the Soviet people were moulded by the socialist system, not merely by the Soviet way of life, but primarily by the Party's purposeful and persistent ideological and educational work. The party tried to secure the fusion of ideological labour and moral education.

The Party wanted that Marxism-Leninism be spread by all communists. The main objective of Party propaganda was to make Party policies fuse with the practical activities of the masses and to make Party education a means to teach people, as Lenin put it, "to act in the way communism really demands."[14] The objective was to achieve in reality unity of all aspects of communist ideology, the theoretical institutional as well as organisational.

The party attached exceptionally great significance to bring people to an understanding of the laws, course and prospects of social development, politics and events taking place on the domestic and international scene. The party strove to connect ideological work with work to fulfil the key economic and socio-political tasks. Party organisations set up groups of lecturers, political information officers, and propaganda teams. They carried to the masses the party's ideas and thoughts. The party constantly directed ideological cadres to conduct all ideological, educational and mass political work in a lively interesting and understandable manner so as not to bypass important topics.

A major task which was undertaken by the party in the sphere of ideology was to foster in Soviet people a new communist attitude towards labour. Lenin said, "It will take many decades to create a new labour discipline, new forms of social ties between people, and new forms and methods of drawing people into labour. It is the most gratifying and noble work."[15]

Literature and act played a major role in moulding a comprehensively developed personality, and the world outlook, moral convictions and spiritual culture of Soviet people. The great proletarian writer Gorky called writers the engineers of human souls. It is quite understandable, therefore, that the party gave the most serious attention to raising the ideological and artistic levels of literature and art in order that they served in the best possible way the cause of communist construction. The Party believed that the primary duty of men of letters and art was to depict in a talented and vivid manner the labour achievements of the Soviet people. Thus by taking care to create the necessary conditions for the comprehensive development of man, the party through ideological activity actively affected the moulding of the new man, and constantly directed this process.[16]

The CPSU was a party of scientific communism. By introducing and establishing in the minds of the masses a truly scientific, Marxist-Leninist ideology, the party waged a resolute and uncompromising struggle against bourgeois ideology. This approach was caused by the very essence of the party's ideology, by life itself, by the objective logic of class struggle. The CPSU represented a system of political, legal, moral, philosophical, religious and artistic views and ideas. Socialist, Marxist-Leninist ideology, being the world outlook of the working class, expressed its interests, its communist objectives and ideals to the fullest extent. Its very essence opposed bourgeois ideology, which in reflecting and defending bourgeois, exploiter interests, sought in every possible way to indicate and perpetuate the capitalist system. These two ideologies were not only conflicting, but diametrically opposed and irreconcilable to the same degree. That is why, ideological struggle was a basic form of class struggle of the two ideologies. The only choice was—either bourgeois or socialist ideology. There was no middle course. Hence to belittle the socialist ideology in any way, to turn aside from it in the slightest degree meant to strengthen bourgeois ideology."[17]

The CPSU was invariably guided by the Leninist tenet. The party educated the masses politically, instilled in them a scientific world view and educated the working people in the spirit of communist ideals. The party also waged a struggle against the bourgeois, petty-bourgeois, reformist and revisionist ideologies. The party spared nothing in order to arm the working people with the ideas of scientific communism with an understanding of the laws of social development and class struggle. This helped awaken the class consciousness of the working people and played a large part in bringing about the victory of the Great October Socialist Revolution. The party would have failed to lead the Soviet people to the full triumph of socialism if it had not waged a merciless, consistent struggle, both before and after the establishment of Soviet Power against bourgeois and petty, bourgeois ideology, against revisionism, Trotskyism right wing and left wing opportunism and against all the opponents of the revolution.

As a result of the fundamental socio-economic transformation achieved in the USSR and the party's purposeful theoretical, ideological and educational activities, following the complete victory of socialism, the communist ideology, the ideology of the evolving class had become dominant in Soviet society and got firmly established in the minds of millions of people. Lenin pointed out: "By educating the party workers, Marxism educates the vanguard of the proletariat capable of assuming power and leading the whole people to socialism, of directing and organising the new system, of being the teacher, the guide, the leader of all the working and exploited people in organising their social life without the bourgeoisie and against the bourgeoisie."[18] Foreseeing how difficult and complex the struggle to build socialism and communism would be, Lenin taught; "Without a party of iron that has been tempered in the struggle, a party enjoying the confidence of all honest people, a party capable of watching and influencing the mood of the masses, such a struggle cannot be waged successfully."[19]

The Apparatus: The Soviet political system had been rocked by severe conflicts. These conflicts involved prominent leaders and those lower officials who had been their adherents, but in all cases, the divergent groups were centred around segments of the Soviet structure of formal large scale institutions. What communist ideology, as an element of political culture, accomplished was to keep the resolutions of these conflicts largely within the institutional framework of the communist party. Because of Lenin's extreme aversion to factionalism, no bureaucratic group openly constituted and aligned with the party though its purpose was to promote the general welfare of the system.

Lenin envisaged the necessity for one man rule but in practice he did not make most of the basic decisions of the Soviet regime during his time. Stalin ruled as an absolute despot. He made all important decisions himself. He clothed his rule in secrecy, often avoiding the discussion of pending matters even with his own hand picked circle of high officials. Stalin was slavishly acclaimed as the greatest geniuses of mankind, omniscent and infallible. At the same time, he undermined any force, institutional or personal, that could possibly compete with him for power. He humiliated his associates in numerous ways, and in hundreds of cases had them executed without even publishing accusations against them.[20]

None of Stalin's Lieutenants was able to assume full control of the Soviet system. Between March 1953 and January 1955, a real collective leadership based on the Politburo made many basic decisions. This was in some respects, a return of the pre-1937 situation. However, in the post-Stalin period Politburo members found it harder and harder to exert influence. In every modern political system there is probably a tendency to have one man whether he be an American President or a British Prime Minister which symbolizes authority. In the Soviet system, this tendency was vastly enhanced by the absence of legitimate institutional mechanisms for articulating and resolving differences. Khrushchev acquired a dominant position in the party apparatus—the body of full time officials that not only carried on the day-to-day execution of decisions but also manipulated elections and discussions in party meetings. Because the apparatus performed these key functions, any group that opposed the apparatus was likely to be outmaneuvered. Its adherents were not elected to formal decision-making assemblies like the Congress, and efforts to concert policies opposed to those of the apparatus were denounced as factionalism. Under the party rules, the Politburo had a legitimate place in the decision-making process. But the Politburo was not formally the supreme decision-making body.

In the long intervals between congress, supreme authority was formally delegated to the Central Committee. After Stalin's death the Central Committee was held as the repository of collective leadership. Most of the important officials of the then USSR were among its several hundred members. They were drawn from all major segments of the bureaucratic state, economic, military, police but the party apparatus predominated. In the years between 1953-1957, there was a considerable turn over in membership of the Central Committee. Khrushchev, as chief of the apparatus, was able to take advantage of this turn over to install his followers. Khrushchev's rivals had been more closely associated with the most repugnant features of Stalin's rule, specially his destruction of 70 per cent of the Central Committee elected in 1934. During spring of the year 1937, Khrushchev took two decisive steps against his rivals. He secured Central Committee approval of a sweeping scheme for reorganising the bureaucracy that supervised industry. Instead of primary reliance on centralised ministeries in Moscow, a "sovnarkhoz" (Council of People's economy) in each province was assigned primary responsibility for maintaining economic stability of the State. The cumbersome ministries were long due for reorganisation.

What the reform accomplished was to break up central government apparatus associated with Moscow. Khrushchev moved directly against his rivals by threatening to expose their complicity in Stalin's brutal annhilation of earlier party leaders. In desperation, Khrushchev's opponents used their Politburo majority to demand his resignation. A special Central Committee plenum, hastily assembled with the aid of military command in June 1957, overwhelmingly endorsed Khrushchev. His opponents were expelled from all major posts. A new Politburo, composed mainly of Khrushchev's close associates, was elected.[21]

Khrushchev was identified with a number of dramatic policy decisions, including major changes in agriculture and in an aggressive assertion of communist interests abroad. As long as these policies appeared promising, Khrushchev was almost indispensable as a symbol of Soviet authority. When poor harvests and foreign policy reverses (like the Cuban missile crisis) occurred, his value as a prestige symbol diminished and he became more of a liability than an asset. Khrushchev sponsored a division of the apparatus between the Russian and non-Russian republics. In 1962 he introduced a further division between the agricultural and industrial centres of control. This complicated rearrangement was confusing and burdensome for established party officials, and of dubious value from an efficiency standpoint. Khrushchev's bifurcation of the apparatus may have appeared to many officials as a scheme to "divide and conquer". Bifurcation, infact, drastically reduced the scope of the authority of most established party officials.

Since 1964, real collective leadership appeared to have prevailed. The principal party and the government posts were separated, and the Politburo apparently discussed the most important questions. The party leaders still appealed to the Central Committee against a Politburo majority. But the Central Committee functioned only in times of crisis. Its regular plenums took place only two or three times a year and usually lasted only a few days. The plenums were characterized by set speeches rather than by free discussions. While all the bureaucratic interest groups were represented in the Central Committee, its members were drawn from all segments of the Soviet bureaucracy, but they did not serve as the delegates of these segments. In these circumstances the Central Committee was hardly the locus of ordinary decision-making or the recognised aggregating institutions of the Soviet system. What the Central Committee could do—was to act as a legitimizing institution for leadership change.[22]

Instruments of Coercion: Though political power requires the monopoly of force, force alone is an inadequate basis for a political system. The Soviet system was not based on force alone. Political culture, the result of a blend of traditional attitude and totalitarian communist ideology, was of critical importance. The institutional framework of the Communist Party enabled a self-chosen and self-perpetuating elite to maintain a monopoly over decision-making. Indoctrination stressed the unique legitimacy of the party's decisions, inculcation of belief in the inevitability of a perfect communist social order, almost exclusive control over career advancement, pervasive control of communication channels, were among the powerful factors that maintained this monopoly. Lenin and all his successors chose to employ force. The communists had a strong base of sympathisers in the strategically located urban sectors. The regime never neglected persuasion and indoctrination. There is no doubt, however, that without an extensive employment of force, the Soviet regime could not have been stabilised.

Until the late 1940's however, the Soviet system was subject to more sporadic outbreaks of armed opposition than were usual in advanced societies. Some of these rebellions were encouraged by powerful enemies abroad. Under these circumstances, the Soviet regime relied in part on military instruments for maintaining a monopoly of force. The most important military element had been the ground forces, known until 1946 as the

Red Army and after that, as the Soviet army. The navy had always been distinctly secondary and so was the airforce. The army played a major role in defending the USSR in its encounters with great powers—during the Civil War of 1918-20, in the limited wars with Japan in 1938-39, and during World War II. The army had also been the principal means by which the Soviet regime imposed communist governments on peripheral areas of Europe and Asia.[23]

The Problem of Nationalities

Lenin sharply criticized parliamentary government, leaders. In his view legislative bodies in the parliamentary form of government were "bourgeois talk shops". Lenin needed a new form of legislative body and he found it in the "Soviets" ("Soviet" means simply "Council" in Russian). The original Soviets were merely adhoc bodies formed by worker groups to direct the general strike at the start of the unsuccessful 1905 Revolution. Lenin's Bolsheviks neither originated nor dominated these Soviets but he welcomed them as a proletarian creation that, unlike parliaments, combined execution with deliberation. When the Soviets were revived during the 1917 Revolution, the Bolsheviks eventually did succeed in dominating the Soviets, which were then adopted as the symbol of Bolshevik regime.

The main foundations of the construction of the former USSR were the principles of socialism. The leaders of the October 1917 Revolution in Russia where orthodox followers of the socialist doctrine as propounded by Marx and Engels. The first two constitutions of the post-revolution Russia, those of 1918 and 1924, were framed with the specific purpose of rooting out the exploiting classes of the former regime. The bourgeoisie, the landlords and the Kulaks were rooted for laying down firmly the foundations of a socialist society wherein all power would be in the hands of the working masses. The constitutions completly overhauled the economic and political structure of the country by abolishing landlordism and giving the land to the tiller, by abolishing capitalism and establishing in its place, a socialist system of economy and also by abolishing the parliamentry democratic governmental system and giving all power to the Soviet's.[24]

By 1936, the Soviet leaders began to make the claim that the foundations of socialism had been laid in the USSR. Stalin even claimed that all exploiting classes had been eliminated and that there remained the working class, the peasant class and the intelligentsia, all of them with complete socialist orientation. Socialist principles underlying the country's constitutional system left no place for the 'idle' rich in the USSR. Work was declared to be a duty and a matter of pride. For every able bodied citizen an edict was laid down in accordance with the principle: 'He who does not work, neither shall he eat'. The constitution confered a number of very important rights to Soviet citizens. The Soviet constitution guaranteed to every citizen the right to work. The rights of Soviet citizens provided a unique system of social security which not merely provided for maintenance in old age but also in case of sickness or loss of capacity to work. It also included the right to rest and leisure. Soviet constitution conformed to the principles of socialism by conferring upon women complete equality with men in all spheres of economic, political, cultural and social life. It recognised the principle of equal pay for equal work.

Socialism and Communism

Marxists make a distinction between socialism and communism, looking upon the former as the first stage of the latter. The Stalin constitution was based on the principle: "From each according to is ability, to each according to his work". Under communism, a stage which was never achieved in the USSR, the guiding principle was to be: "From each according to his ability, to each according to his needs". It was said that this higher stage would be attained when production had increased to such an extent that it could no longer be necessary to apportion reward in accordance with work and when such necessities as food would be available to everyone without payment. The USSR was a federation of Soviet Socialist Republics. It was claimed that the Soviets to which all power belonged, made the USSR a new type of state. The Soviet was a peculiar type of representative institution. Its unique feature was that it was a purely proletarian institution. Unlike other elected assemblies, a Soviet contained no representative of the exploiting classes, viz., capitalists, landlords, employers of labour and idlers. The Soviets were, thus, said to represent a new type of democracy. "In contrast with bourgeois democracy which conceals the class character of the state, Soviet theory openly acknowledged the inevitable class character of every sort of state until the complete disappearance of the division of society into classes and therewith of all state authority of every sort".[25]

In the light of this belief, the Soviet writers declared that 'democracy' in bourgeoisie states is only formal'. About democracy, Lenin said that at each step in the most democratic bourgeois state, the oppressed masses encounter a lamentable contradiction between the formal equality proclaimed by capitalist 'democracy', and the thousands of factual limitations and complications making hired slaves of the proletariat. In other words, democracy in capitalist countries was a sham. Behind the facade of universal franchise, 'free' sham elections and fundamental rights, it ensured the dominance of the bourgeois class. While sovereignty belonged nominally to the people, power was really exercised by the exploiting minority. According to Lenin, parliaments in the capitalist countries are "merely show windows to delude the masses". Consequently it is maintained, a parliamentary type of democracy suits the interests of a capitalist state. In a worker's state, such as the USSR claimed to be, the proletariat needed its own representative institutions, but these must be fundamentally different from the parliaments of bourgeoisie states.

In the second Congress of the Third International, it was declared that the only form of proletarian dictatorship was a "Republic of Soviets". The Soviets were superior to parliaments in the respect that they excluded the exploiting classes from authority and associated the entire mass of workers with the exercise of political powers. Their aim was to draw the whole of the poor into the practical work of administration. Lenin claimed that the Soviet system "is immensely superior to bourgeoisie parliamentary for drawing in the freest, broadest and most energetic manner all the masses in the work of government. It is a power that is open to all, that does everything in the sight of the masses". A Soviet is thus, "the direct organ of the masses and of their will." According to Vyshinsky, the fundamental difference between the Soviet form of State power and the parliamentary form is that "in the Soviet form it is realised by the universal participation of the working people, one and all, in the management of the state".[26]

The Soviet system differed from the parliamentary form in another respect. In the latter, the principle of separation of powers was employed to separate the power which made laws from the power that executed them. Parliaments were empowered to legislate but the laws framed by them were applied by the executive branch and the bureaucracy. The bureaucracy, however, was not always amenable to the control of the masses to whom sovereignty formally belonged. The result was that parliament became 'talking shops' absolved of the responsibility of working the laws they made while the bureaucracy acquired power without responsibility. The proletariat, according to Marx, had no need for parliaments which merely talked, it needed "not a parliament but a working corporation, legislature and executive at one and the same time." Lenin had declared that if the people are to rule, they must have direct control on executive as well as on legislative power. Accordingly, the Soviets in the USSR were empowered to exercise all functions of government. This, however, was so only in theory. The Supreme Soviet of the USSR was controlled by the executive and the party. The Judiciary was not independent; it was under the control of the Presidium of the Supreme Soviet, the Ministry of Interior and Procurator General (nominally elected by the Supreme Soviet). The power to "interpret" laws and decrees was exercised not by the courts but by the Presidium, which therefore, wielded legislative, executive as well as judicial powers.

Soviet System

The entire governmental system of the USSR was a hierarchy of Soviets. There was a Soviet in every village, in every factory, in towns and the regiments of the Red Army. These were 'primary' Soviets. They formed the base of the Soviet Pyramid. Above them were in an ascending order, the Soviets of districts (raions), provinces (Oblasti) constituent (union) republics and, finally, the Supreme Soviet of the USSR. The Soviets first appeared as an organisations of industrial workers during the revolutionary disturbances in 1905. These Soviets or Councils had arisen spontaneously in several Russian cities and provided leadership for the revolutionary movements. The important thing about these Soviets was that they were organisations of workers themselves and consisted of representatives chosen by workers alone. The revolutionary Soviets were quickly suppressed, but they reappeared during the February-March 1917 Revolution. This time, they spread rapidly from large cities to smaller provincial towns and villages and to the army. They were composed of the elected delegates of workmen in factories, shops and mines in the towns, of peasants in the villages and of soldiers in the regiments. These Soviets had arisen almost spontaneously.

After the revolution, the Soviets naturally became the basis of the new constitutional system. The reason why the Bolsheviks chose the Soviets as instruments of the new political system was partly ideological and partly tactical. The Bolsheviks could hardly hope to control a popularly elected parliament chosen by all sections of the people; but they could confidently expect to dominate the Soviets composed predominantly of urban workers. Since 1918, the Soviets had been the basic organs of government in every administrative area of the USSR, village, town, district, province, union republic and the Union. Prior to 1936, only the primary Soviets viz., the Soviets of villages and towns were elected indirectly. Thus, village and town Soviets elected delegates to the district Soviets which, in turn, elected representatives to the provincial Soviets (or Congress). The provincial Soviets sent delegates to All-Republic Congress of Soviets and the All-Union Congress of Soviets. The electoral system then in operation, discriminated against the rural areas by giving the towns the right to send additional delegates directly to the provincial, All-Republic and All-Union Congress of Soviets. Besides, the Soviets were elected on a restricted franchise. The right to vote was denied to certain types of persons, e.g., those who employed hired labour for profit, traders, monks and clergymen, persons who had served in the old Czarist police and members of the ruling dynasty. The constitution of 1936 removed all these restrictions and conferred franchise on all citizens, male or female, at the age of eighteen.

Elections to all Soviets had been made direct and by secret ballot. The Soviets, at all levels carry on government functions either directly or through committees or agencies appointed by them. When it was said that all power in the USSR was exercised through the Soviets, it must be added that alongside the hierarchy of Soviets was the pyramid of party organisations and that the latter controlled the working of the former directly or indirectly.

"The principle of nationality," writes Towster, "is one of the basic pillars of the Soviet structure of political power".[27] One of the most generally acknowledged achievements of the Soviet constitutional system had been the welding of a large number of nationalities into a strong and united state. It is well-known that the USSR was a multi-national state, containing nearly 185 national groups. According to Turin, the main nationalities with their percentages in the total population of the USSR were as follows: Great Russians (53), Ukrainians (21), White Russians (3), Finns (3), Tartars (3), Jews (2), Georgians (1). Armenians and Greeks (1) Germans(1), Pales, Lithuanians and Latvians (1), Uzbeks, Yakuts and Bashkires(3). Some of the ethnic minorities in the USSR were counted in tens of millions, some in hundreds of thousands while the rest consisted of a few thousand persons each. These nationalities and national minorities were characterized by wide diversities of race, language, religion, culture and level of civilization. Even those observers who were, in general, highly critical of the Soviet political system, agreed that the Soviet federal system, based as it was on the nationality principle, had succeeded in creating a single politico-economic system out of the conglomerate Russian community.

During the pre-revolutionary period, Czarist Russia—'an outstanding example of the racially conglomerate state'—followed the policy of ruthlessly suppressing the non-Russian nationalities. Unity was imposed on the heterogeneous people of the Empire by methods of brutal repression and complete disregard of the rights of nationalities. Non-Russian minorities, constituting nearly a half of the population, were subjected to a deliberate policy of 'Russification', a policy calculated to destroy their own cultures and to impose on them the Russian language and culture. They lived under varying degrees of political, social, and economic disabilities. The ruling Russian nationality had forced a distinctly inferior status on them. No wonder, Czarist Russia had been described by Soviet writers as 'the prison of peoples'. As was natural, the oppressed nationalities frequently revolted against the Czarist policy, but all revolts were crushed with savage ruthlessness. In putting down the Polish insurrection of 1863, the Czarist authorities killed 33,000 Poles in battle and executed another 10,500. As late as 1916, several thousand people were slaughtered in order to put down a revolt in Central Asia.

In sharp contrast to the Czarist policy in respect of the nationality problem in Russia, the Soviet authorities had, from the outset, followed the policy of achieving political unity by giving the fullest recognition to distinct national groups. The Constitution of 1918 proclaimed: "the equality to the citizens regardless of race or nationality", and declared it "contrary to the fundamental law of the Republic to repress national minorities or to limit their rights in any way." Eversince, the nationality policy of the USSR had rested on the following principles; (1) equality and sovereign rights of the people of Russia, (2) the rights of the people to determine freely how they were to be governed, (3) revocation of all national privileges and restrictions, and (4) free development of national minorities and ethnographic groups inhabiting the Russian territory.

These principles were said to form the basis of the federal structure of the Soviet Union. On the basis of national groupings, the territories of the USSR were divided into Union Republics, Autonomous Republics, Autonomous Regions and National Areas. Each Union Republic was inhabited mainly by a major nationality. But smaller national groups within its boundaries were also given an autonomous status by organising compact areas. Thus, the Russian Soviet, Federative Socialist Republic (RSFSR) contained within its territories 13 autonomous republics, 45 autonomous regions and 10 autonomous national areas. The same was true, in varying degrees, of most other Union Republics. Union Republics enjoy the largest measure of autonomy including the right of secession i.e., of withdrawing from the USSR. For obvious geographical reasons, the right was not given to smaller territorial divisions. But in each division the dominant national group was allowed to use its own language in the legislature, in the courts and as medium of instruction in educational institutions. They were encouraged to develop their own industries and employ their own people as officials and teachers. It desires to be noted that some of the nationalities which were as backward as not to have any written language of their own had been encouraged to develop their dialects into full-fledged languages which now possesses rich literature.

The religious and social customs of national minorities were allowed to flourish in complete freedom. It was of special interest to Indian students to know that there were a number of Muslim Union Republics in the USSR, (e.g., Azerbaijan, Uzbek, Kirghiz and Tadjik). They enjoyed full autonomy in matters of religion, language and culture. That explained why despite their legal right to go out of the 'Godless Soviet Union', they had shown no desire to make use of the right. Of course, it was largely true that in actual practice, the exercise of the right of secession was nearly impossible. But the Soviet Union could rightly claim credit for having integrated the various nationalities inhabiting the country into a federal system which combined a large measure of autonomy for the nationalities in cultural matters with a high degree of centralisation in economic and political matters. The political personality of the nationalities had been recognised by making the areas inhabited by their units of the Soviet federation. Besides, the interests of the nationalities were safeguarded by laying down a uniform scale of representation for the territorial units of the federation in the Soviet of Nationalities, there being an equal number of seats for territories of the same category. The economic interests of the nationalities had been promoted by the policy of modernising the economies of previously backward and under privileged nationalities so as to bring about the economic equalisation of the different peoples of the Soviet Union.

Constitutional Set-up

The legislative power of the USSR was vested in the federal legislature called the Supreme Soviet of USSR. The legislature was bi-cameral and was organised on the federal principle. The Supreme Soviet of the USSR was formally declared to be the highest organ of power in the USSR and was supposed to exercise the legislative power of the Soviet Union exclusively. Its actual functions could be more appropriately described as approving and acclaiming the policies and decisions adopted by Presidium and the Council of Ministers, rather than as passing laws in the ordinary sense of the phrase. The Council of Ministers of the USSR constituted the executive branch of the Soviet Central Government. The ministers were elected by the two houses of the Supreme Soviet in a joint session. When the Supreme Soviet was not in session the ministers could be appointed by the Presidium but were subjected to ratification by the Supreme Soviet. The judicial authority of the Soviet Union was vested in the Supreme Court of the USSR which was the highest court in the country and stood at the top of its judicial hierarchy. It was the only federal judicial organ, there being no lower federal courts in the USSR. The Supreme Court was not the final interpreter of the Soviet constitution as there was no provision for judicial review in the constitution. No account of the judiciary of the Soviet Union could be complete without a reference to the office of the Procurator General. All organs of the federal government—and this applied equally to organs of the government of all national and territorial divisions of the Soviet Union—worked in close cooperation with and under the ultimate control of the Communist Party.

The Constitution of the Soviet Union recognised the Supreme position of the federal legislature of the USSR. The Supreme Soviet of the USSR was described in Article 108 of the constitution as "the highest body of State authority of USSR. The Supreme Soviet of the USSR was a bi-cameral legislature, its two chambers being known as the Soviet of the Union and the Soviet of Nationalities. The Soviet of the Union represented the common interests of the citizens of the USSR. The other chamber the Soviet of Nationalities, stood for the federal principle and represented the interests of the nationalities and national minorities of the USSR organised as the constituent units of the Soviet Union.

Under the new (1977) constitution the two Houses of the Supreme Soviet of the USSR had equal number of members, the total for both being, 1500. The deputies of the Supreme Soviet of the USSR indicate a broader representation of the many types of people who made up the population of the Soviet Union. A deputy of the Supreme Soviet of the USSR enjoyed certain rights and privileges but at the same time, performed a number of duties. The Constitution of USSR laid down a Five-Year-Term for both chambers of the Supreme Soviet. In the event of an irreconcilable disagreement between the two chambers, the Presidium dissolved the Supreme Soviet even before the expiration of its full term. On the expiration of its regular term, or, in the event of earlier dissolution, the Presidium was required to schedule the election of a new Supreme Soviet not later than three months after its dissolution. An important feature of the Supreme Soviet of the USSR was that its two chambers had co-equal and co-ordinate powers.

Unlike legislatures of democratic countries of the Western type, there was no opposition in Supreme Soviet. The Supreme Soviet controlled defence, foreign affairs, foreign trade, taxation and revenues, economic planning for the Union, admission of new republics in the Union, transport, monetary and credit system, state insurance, public debts, banking, industrial, agricultural and trading establishments of all-Union importance, civil and criminal law, citizenship etc.

Presidium was a standing committee of the Supreme Court of the USSR but its powers were incomparably greater than those of a standing committee of any other legislature in the world. Members of the Presidium of the Supreme Soviet of the USSR were elected in a joint session of the Supreme Soviet. The tenure of the Presidium was concurrent with that of the Supreme Soviet which elected it and ended a little after its dissolution. The powers and prerogatives of the Presidium were enumerated in Article 49 of the Constitution according to which the Presidium *(a)* convened the sessions of the Supreme Soviet of the USSR, *(b)* interpreted the laws of the Soviet Union, *(c)* issued decrees, *(d)* dissolved the Supreme Soviet in case of irreconcilable disagreement between the two houses and ordered a fresh election, *(e)* conducted a referendum on its own initiative or on the demand of one of the Union Republics, *(f)* appointed and removed Ministers of the USSR on the recommendations of the Chairman of the Council of Ministers (Prime Minister) and was subjected to subsequent confirmation by the Supreme Soviet. The

Supreme Soviet met for very brief sessions after long intervals. The Presidium was virtually in constant session and had been correctly described as a 'daily working organ of the government.'

According to the Soviet Constitution, the highest executive and administrative body of the state authority of the USSR was the Council of Ministers which, until 1946, was known as the Council of People's Commisars. The Council of Ministers was elected by the two houses of the Supreme Soviet of USSR in a joint session. An unusual feature of the Soviet Council of Ministers was that there were two different types of Ministries represented in it. They were *(a)* All-Union Ministries; and *(b)* Union Republic Ministries.

Marx and Engels believed that, like the state, law was a class institution. Hence, in a capitalist society, law was nothing but the will of the bourgeoisie made into law for all whose essential character and direction were determined by the economic interests of the ruling class. They declared that the much advertised principle of equality before the law was really a cloak for actual inequality. This was so because the poor could not afford to pay the cost of legal proceedings or the fees of the best lawyers and, even more so, because judges were themselves the members of the exploiting classes and were therefore, naturally predisposed towards the interest, of property and finally, because the laws which these judges interpreted and applied were so framed as to safeguard the privileges and the interests of the propertied class. The two communist philosophers Marx and Engels regarded crime as the product of environment and particularly of unjust economic conditions. They thought that under communism no coercive law would be needed and the power of public opinion would be enough to impel all individual, in socially desirable ways.

Under the Constitution of the USSR, law and justice fell in the jurisdiction in the All-Union government. In the Soviet Union, therefore, there was one simple integrated judicial system for the entire country. The Soviet Union had a single hierarchical system of courts. The Soviet judiciary was organised in a pyramidal form. At the base of the pyramid stood two types of local courts viz. Comradely Courts and People's Courts. Above these stood the superior courts of regions and territories. Next above were, in order the Supreme Courts of Autonomous Republics and Union Republics respectively. At the summit of the pyramid stood the Special Courts and the Supreme Courts of the USSR. The Supreme Court of USSR was the highest judicial body of the Soviet Union and was elected by the Supreme Soviet of the USSR for a five-year term. It was composed of a Chairman, Deputy Chairman, Judges and people's assessors. The number of judges and people's assessors varied from time to time. The Supreme Court of the USSR functioned in five division or 'collegia'—i.e., the civil, the criminal, the military, the rail-road, the transport and the water transport collegia. When the collegium sat as a court of original jurisdiction, it was composed of one judge and two people's assessors. When, however, a collegium sat as an appellate court, it consisted of three judges. A significant feature in which the Supreme Court of the USSR differed from the Supreme Court of most other feueral states such as the USA and India was that the Soviet Supreme Court did not possess the power of judicial review over legislation.[28]

Procedural Justice

In matters of administering justice the record of the communist state in Russia was very dismal. It was mostly characterised by the barbaric practice which was prevalent in the medieval ages. The police terror which was the order of the day consisted of secret arrest and arbitrary condemnation after a closed hearing. Arrests were usually made late at night. Families and friends of the arrested person frequently were not informed of his where-abouts for months. During this time, "confessions"—often prepared by the police investigtors—were extorted from the accused, both to condemn him and to provide "evidence" against others whom the police wished to incriminate. Interrogations took place in the small hours of the morning, when the prisoner was most susceptible to trickery, psychological pressure and plain torture. After the confession was secured, the prisoner was brought before a police "special board" empowered to set sentences of up to five years in concentration camps. Apparently, the special boards sometimes even exceeded this legal limit, though death, sentences were usually set by secret sessions of military tribunals attached to the regular court system. The special boards operated in complete secrecy. The accused was not informed of the charges until he appeared before the board and was not permitted counsel.[29]

Arbitrary and inhuman as the Soviet security police was in its heyday, it rarely resorted to public beating and lynchings that marked Nazi and Fascist police measures. These circumstances did not help the victims, but they did enable the regime to avoid the appearance of barbarity. Moreover, even under Stalin, the vast majority of ordinary crimes fell under the jurisdiction of a regular judicial system. The former USSR and the Czarist government before it had always adhered to the continental European inquestorial legal system. This system had many advantages for a person accused of an ordinary crime, but it was especially susceptible to abuse when an arbitrary regime considered its interests were at stake. A large part of the administration of justice was in the hands of Procurator who was supposed to carry out completely impartial investigation of crimes, report to the court all circumstances favouring or inculcating the accused, and even appeal cases in which the defendant's rights were violated. The Procurator General and his subordinates were officers of a central agency, formally independent of all local judicial, police and party authorities. In theory, the procurator acted as a safeguard of the rights of the accused as well as a vigorous defender of the interest of society.

All judges were supposed to give priority to the interests of the state and the law always regarded crimes affecting the state as more serious than offences affecting individuals alone. Nevertheless, the courts constituted a distinct part of the governmental mechanism. Most cases were tried in the "people's court". Fairly small judicial districts were established for a people's court, but a court may have several judges, with the work being divided on territorial basis or by types of cases. Judges were nominally chosen by popular election, as elsewhere in the Soviet electoral system. In practice there used to be only one nominee who, in effect, was chosen by the Communist party.[30]

Under Stalin, every worker was legally bound to his job. Changes could take place only with the permission of management. Absence or even tardiness was a criminal offense, although the penalties were eased in the last years of Stalin's life. Probably no single aspect of the Soviet system was more bitterly resented by the common man. The labour discipline laws were, therefore, abolished in 1956. But many restrictions on freedom of movement remained. Unauthorized job change could cost a worker his social-security benefits. Every Soviet citizen must carry domestic passport and report every change of residence to the police. Transportation to another locality was often hard to obtain unless one had an official requisiton. The police were authorized to expel "loafers" from many of the most important (and attractive) cities. Graduates of universities and other higher educational institutions were legally bound to work at assigned jobs for several years. Party members must accept job assignments on penalty of expulsion. But all of these restrictions, it seems, had not been able to ensure the complete devotion to work demanded by the feverish tempo of Soviet economic development. Even with considerable increase in the availability of consumer's goods, incentive pay was inadequate to induce all workers to devote their full capacities to production. Attempts to gain money by using state property or by speculating (buying and selling for a profit) had been criminal for decades. At that time those who resorted to large-scale thefts of state property or currency speculation had been condemned to death—a far harsher punishment than was meted out for property crimes in capitalist societies.[31]

Summing Up

To sum up, the Marxist-Lenin type of political culture pervaded in the former Soviet Union for over 70 years during which period it created many complex problems in its attempt to solve some of the long standing issues which faced the people of old Russia. If one accepts the declarations of the regime, in the past, at their face value, the ideology was the core of the system. Some of the elements of the ideology had been altered and re-altered by Lenin's successors who failed to negotiate with the old assumptions. Marxism-Leninism has always stressed the need for continual interaction of theory and practice. But with the passage of time, we saw some ideological drift, with the result that psychological force of the doctrine had correspondingly altered. The Bolshevik revolutionary, dedicated to destroying the old order so as to be able to proceed to rapid construction of a perfect society, has long since been replaced by the Party bureaucrats. Because of the historical inevitability, the spread of Communism through-out the world was a fundamental Leninist tenet, but these reversals implied an indefinite postponement of this concept. Several transitional measures took place. Many of the prescriptions such as limitations on farmers' garden plots, opposition to personally owned housing and automobiles and the use of collective bodies of enforcing discipline had been abandoned.

The regime insisted on the necessity of eventually eliminating private property, material incentives and state coercive agencies, but this was never accomplished. The regime held firmly to one basic element of the materialist aspect of communist ideology—atheism. Belief in science as a force that, under Communist everything fits in neatly with the concept of Marxism-Leninism as the supreme science of society and with the Communist officials' self-image as an engineer of society. Just as obviously, this creed of materialism rules out transcendental belief; there is no clear evidence that attacks on religion in the USSR have abated. The place of the Party also seemed secure into minds of those who accepted the ideology.[32] The role of the Party as a legitimizing institution was indispensable. However, it was speculated that the advanced stage would compel the present elite to cede power to a new generation and the latter may move from orthodox conservatism to reliance on a more pragmatic ideology or the younger elite may seek to restore the dynamic aspects of communism. But it is not yet clear as to which way the ideological trends would take their course. History also has not provided a reliable response to risk query. Future alone may reveal what it holds in store for mankind.[33]

REFERENCES

1. Charques, R.D., *A Short History of Russia*, New York: E.P. Dutton and Company; Everyman Paperback, 1956.

2. Ellison, Herbert.J. *History of Russia*. New York: Holt, Rinehart and Winston, 1964.

3. Lenin, Viladimir I. *Imperialism and State and Revolution*. New York: The Vanguard Press, 1929.

4. Hunt, Robert N.C. *The Theory and Practice of Communism*. New York: The Macmillan Company, 1954.

5. Monnerot, Jules. *Sociology and Psychology of Communism*, Boston: Beacon Press, 1953.

6. Wetter, Gustav A. *Dialectical Materialism*. New York: Frederick A. Praeger, 1959.

7. Stalin, Joseph V. *The History of the Communist Party of the Soviet Union (Bolsheviks)*. New York: International Publishers, 1939.

8. Marcuse, Herbert. *Soviet Marxism*. New York: Columbia University Press, 1958.

9. Meyer, Alfred G. *The Soviet Political System: An Interpretation*. New York: Random House, 1965.

10. Reshetar, John S.A. *Concise History of the Communist Party of the Soviet Union*, New York: Frederick A. Praeger, 1960.

11. V.I.Lenin, *"Our Programme"*, Collected Works, Vol. 4, p. 211.

12. *23rd Congress of the CPSU*, Novosti Press Agency Publishing House, Moscow, 1966, p. 144.

13. V.I.Lenin, *"The Fifth Congress of Russian Social-Democratic Labour Party*, April 30-May 19, 1907". Speech, Collected Works, Vol. 12, 1972, p. 441.

14. V.I.Lenin, *"The Tasks of the Youth Leagues"*, Collected Works, Vol. 31, p. 285.

15. V.I.Lenin, *"From the Destruction of the Old Social System to the Creation of the New*, Collected Works, Vol. 30, p. 518.

16. Igor Shvets and Ivan Yudin, *"The CPSU: Ideological, Political and Organisational Principles,"* Progress Publishers, Moscow, 1985, pp. 220-242.

17. V.I.Lenin, *"What is to be done?"*, Collected Works, Vol. 5, p. 384.

18. V.I. Lenin, *"The State and Revolution"*, Collected Works, Vol. 25, 1977, p. 409.

19. V.I.Lenin, *"Left Wing' Communism—an Infantile. Disorder"* Collected Works, Vol. 31, pp. 44-45.

20. Fyodorov, Aleksei. *The Underground R.C. Carries On Moscow:* Foreign Languages Publishing House, 1952.

21. Pistrak, Lazar. *The Grand Tactician*, New York: Frederick A. Praeger, 1961.

22. Rush, Myron: *Political Succession in the USSR*, New York: Columbia University Press, 1965.

23. Hazard, John N. *Law and Social Change in the USSR.*, London: Stevens and Sons, 1953.

24. Armstrong, John A. *Ukrainian Nationalism. New York,:* Columbia University Press, 1956.

25. A.V. Vyshinsky: *The Law of the Soviet State,* pp. 152.

26. Vyshinsky: *The Law of the Soviet State,* p. 84.

27. Julian Towster: *Political Power in the USSR,* p.50

28. K.R.Bombwall, *"Major Contemporary Constitutional Systems"* Modern Publications, Ambala Cantt., 1986, p. 324-386.

29. Conquest, Robert. *Russia After Khrushchev,* New York: Frederick A. Praeger, 1965.

30. Baykov, Alexander. *The Development of the Soviet Economic System.* New York: The Macmillan Company, 1947.

31. Nove, Alec. Rev. ed. *The Soviet Economy: An Introduction.* New York: Frederick A. Praeger, 1966.

32. Armstrong, John A., *"Ideology, Politics, and Government in the Soviet Union: An Introduction"*, Frederick A. Praeger, Publishers New York, 1967.

33 . Stephen White, *Political Culture and Soviet Politics,* The Macmillan Press, London, 1979, p.64.

4

IDEOLOGICAL SOCIALIST BLOC: EMERGENCE ROLE AND CONFIGURATION

The first bourgeois-democratic revolution in Russia took place in 1905-07, but for a variety of reasons it ended in defeat of the revolutionary forces. The dramatic deterioration in the standard of living of Russia's working masses after the revolutionary explosion of 1905-07 caused a new upsurge of the revolutionary movement among the popular masses of Russia as early as the second decade of the 20th century. The First World War (1914-1918) in which Czarist Russia fought on the side of the entente caused a brief interruption in the revolutionary upsurge of 1910-14. The period witnessed the rising tide of the revolutionary movement, bringing the crisis to a head which culminated in the overthrow of Czarism in February 1917.

The February bourgeois-democratic revolution did not bring the working masses of Russia either liberation from the domination of their exploiters, or Russia's withdrawal from the imperialist war. The masses needed an efficient and energetic leadership and they found it in their vanguard, the Bolshevik Party led by Lenin.

The political situation in the country at that time was extremely complex. After the overthrow of the Czarist monarchy workers, soldiers and peasants throughout the country had begun to set up the Soviets, their own revolutionary bodies in power. The Petrograd Soviet, which became the city's body of workers and soldiers power was the first to be set up. Elections to the Soviets were held on a democratic basis. The Soviets were highly representative organisations of working people and they were closely connected with the masses and as such they best reflected their moods and aspirations.

But the Soviets were not the only body of power in the country. After the overthrow of the Czarism, dual power emerged in the country. Formal power was vested in the provisional government, while real power was in the hands of the Soviets. The situation was further complicated by the fact that the majority of the Soviet leadership had been seized by representatives of the petty bourgeois parties, the Mansheviks and the Socialist Revolutionaries who were prepared to come to terms with the provisional government.

It was Lenin who worked out a programme of action for a genuinely revolutionary Marxist party, the Bolsheviks, in this extremely complicated and fluid situation. Lenin set out his brilliant plan for further struggle for a transition from a bourgeois—democratic revolution to a socialist one. After analysing the situation in the country Lenin concluded that the specific feature of the situation in Russia was that the country, was passing from the first stage of the revolution which owing to the insufficient class-consciousness and organisation of the proletariat-placed power in the hands of the bourgeoisie and in the second stage it must place power in the hands of the proletariat and the poorest sections of the peasants. In the context of the struggle for the development of the revolution, Lenin assigned the central place to the Soviets. Lenin put forward the slogans "All Power to the Soviets". Lenin never advocated for the immediate overthrow of the provisional government since the government at that stage had the Soviet support. But soon after Lenin consolidated his position. He demanded the withdrawal of Soviet support to the bourgeois government exposing the falsehood of all its promises and propagating the need for transferring all power to the Soviets. Their petty-bourgeois illusions disappeared and the working people of Russia had to purge the Soviets of all conciliators to make them the only plenipotentiary bodies of government. That was the scientifically sound plan for the peaceful development of the revolution.

As Lenin saw it, the peaceful way of the revolution had nothing in common with the reformist interpretations. Lenin pointed out that the peaceful way by no means implied that the bourgeoisie and the land owners would give up power voluntarily. Counter revolutionaries would undoubtedly offer resistance, but this resistance would not necessarily take the form of civil war since the bourgeoisie and the land owners in that particular situation lacked adequate forces. The Bolshevik Party made energetic efforts to implement their plan. The party was educating the working people politically amidst fierce clashes with the counter-revolutionaries and conciliators. Under the leadership of the Bolsheviks millions upon millions of the working people were mastering the ABC of revolution in the crucible of revolutionary battles.

The war in which Russian Czarism took such an active part, continued even after the downfall of Czarism. Just as before millions of working men in soldiers' uniforms continued to shed their blood for interests that were alien to them. The counter-revolutionary Provisional Government was to blame for this, as were the conciliatory parties which controlled the leadership of most Soviets at that time. Right from the very start of the imperialist war the Bolsheviks never ceased to expose its anti-popular essence. After the victory of the February Revolution the Communist Party redoubled its efforts against the war. In as much as the Socialist Revolutionary and Menshevik leadership of the Soviets were in favour of continuing the war, the Bolsheviks' struggle against it was at the same time a struggle to revolutionise the Soviets. The Bolsheviks stand on this issue met with understanding and support of the mass of the working people. The struggle over the issue of war graphically demonstrated the anti-popular essence of the Provisional Government and widened the gap between the Socialist Revolutionary and Menshevik leadership of most of the Soviets and the electorate.

Long before the February revolution the Russian bourgeoisie was in effect the country's economic ruler. The continuity of the economic policy of the government was formalised in a series of official documents. Russian industry was heading straight for a serious crisis. In March-April 1917 alone over 100 industrial enterprises were closed down and nearly 10,000 workers lost their jobs. The railway transport situation deteriorated to a point where the Provisional Government was compelled to recognise it as a national emergency. The food crisis was becoming more acute, and the country's finances were in shambles and was almost on the verge of bankruptcy. Needless to say the economic dislocation caused by the war hit the working class hardest.

The revolutionary movement of the masses was led by the workers who launched a determined struggle for an eight-hour working day and the payment of wages during the strikes. The workers pressed not only for an improvement in working conditions, they also showed concern for the maintenance of production. A mass movement emerged for removing reactionary managers to establish workers control. Factory committees were set up to exercise this control. During the fight the workers could see that only the Bolsheviks were consistent champions of their interest and that the Socialist Revolutionaries and Mensheviks were inclined to a compromise with the employers.

For a country like Russia most of whose population was peasants, the question of the land was of exceptional importance. The 30,000 land owners had as much land as the country's ten million peasants had. An estimated 65 per cent of the peasants lived below the poverty line. The peasants looked to the rural Soviets set up after the revolution to find a truly revolutionary solution to the land question. The Bolsheviks urged the Soviets to turn the land owners' land over to the people and recommended that the peasants should lose no time in starting to till it. But since the majority of the rural Soviets were dominated by the Socialist Revolutionaries and petty bourgeoisies elements who sympathised with them, every manner of pretext was put forth to cause delay deliberately in the solution to the land question while the Socialist Revolutionaries were looking for a way of coming to terms with the Provisional Government of capitalists and landowners. The Bolshevik Party was increasingly gaining the support among broad sections of the peasantry. The peasant movement was gaining momentum daily. The mass movement of oppressed peoples for their national emancipation was increasingly merging with the revolutionary struggle of the Russian proletariat and peasants.

The Bolshevik party's struggle to win over the masses was headed by Lenin who led and guided the party's central committee, the editorial board of the Party's newspaper, Pravda, and who maintained close contacts with the party organisations in the provinces. Within the short space of three months after his return to Russia, Lenin wrote some 200 brochures, articles, appeals and draft resolutions of party conferences and central committee meetings. Lenin's appearance on the platform invariably triggered off the acclamations and enthusiasm among the audience. The Bolshevik Party's influence steadily grew as it consistently defended the interests of the working people. As a result a mass movement to expell the Socialist Revolutionaries and Mensheviks from the Soviets began. Apart from resulting in an increased number of Bolshevik deputies, the re-elections for the Soviet city of Kronstadt changed the political situation in the city radically. In a mammoth rally on May 11, 1917 the sailors and soldiers of Kronstadt passed a decision to demand the transfer of all power in the country to the Soviets. The Soviet executive two days later declared the same. Similar situations took shape in May-June 1917 in Narva, Riga, Ivanono-Voznesensk, Podolsk, Krasnayarsk, and in some other cities. But a tense struggle to Bolshevise the rest of the Soviets, of which there were nearly 400 by the summer of 1917, lay ahead.

During the war the Soviet Government had banned many of the country's trade unions. The February Revolution of 1917 marked the start of a rapid revival of the trade unions as the biggest mass organisation of the working class. In many towns and cities worker militias were set up. In villages peasants' committees sprang up and in army units—soldiers committees. All these mass organisations of the working people contributed to the growing organisation and revolutionary activity of the masses. The deterioration of the country's economic and political situation, the rising tide of the revolutionary struggle of the masses combined to precipitate a series of acute political crises the first of which occurred in April. The Provincial Government was in a state of shock. The Petrograd Soviet could sweep it aside without much effort.[1] But the Socialist Revolutionary and Menshevik leaders of the Petrograd reached a compromise with the counter-revolutionaries and in this way helped the Provisional government get out of the crisis.

For the second, the Provisional Government found itself teetering over the edge of the precipice in June 1917 at the time of the First Congress of Soviets of Workers' and Soldiers' Deputies. Addressing the delegates on behalf of the Socialist Revolutionary and Menshevik bloc on the question of power, a minister of the Provisional Government declared: at the moment there is no political party in Russia which says "Give us all power, go away, we will take your place." This drew a response from the audience: "Yes, there is!" That came from Lenin speaking on behalf of the Bolshevik party. The working people demanded the Congress of Soviets take over full power in the country. In June 1917 this was quite possible. But the Socialist Revolutionary and Menshevik majority at the Congress failed to take advantage of this opportunity.

Both the dual power and the peaceful period of the revolution came to an end to be followed by a period of armed struggle. In these circumstances the Bolshevik party led by Lenin mapped out a new course which was formalised in the decisions of the Sixth Congress of the RSDLP(B). In August 1917, the counter revolutionaries attempted to destroy the revolutionary forces once and for all and establish military dictatorship in the country. They engineered a revolt led by General Kornilor. The Bolshevik Party launched an impassioned appeal to the nation to rise in defence of the revolution with the slogan: "The revolution is in peril to arms!" Factories began to form Red Guard detachments on a mass scale. An estimated 60,000 Red Guards, revolutionary sailors and soldiers blocked the road to the capital. General Kornilor was arrested and one of his closest associates shot himself dead.

On August 31, the majority of the Petrograd Soviet for the first line voted for a Bolshevik resolution on the question of power. Early in September the Bosheviks commanded the support of 250 Soviets and the number grew daily. Under the impact of the rising tide of revolution in Russia the revolutionary movements in Western Europe began to show signs of revival. Unrest in the German Navy in May 1917 had developed into full scale revolt by August. The frontline troops in France also showed signs of discontent. They were supported by workers who held political strikes. In September 1917 the slogan "All power to the Soviets!" had a totally different meaning. Now it was a call for an armed uprising against the counter-revolutionary dictatorship of the Provisional Government, and no longer for a peaceful revolution.

On October 12, the Petrograd Soviet formed a Revolutionary Military Committee (RMC) which swung into action to prepare the armed rising and set up a special Red Guard department. The Bolshevik party was preparing all the organisations of working people for a decisive battle against the counter-revolutionaries. Units of counter revolutionary officers seized the Bolshevik printing house, thereby starting the first armed clash between the forces of revolution and counter revolution. The last bastion of counter-revolution fell on the night of October 25-26, 1917. This marked the victory of the armed uprising of the working people in the capital of Russia, Petrogard, which ushered in a new era in human history. In the evening of October 25, 1917, the second All-Russia Congress of Soviets of Workers' and Soldiers' Deputies met in the Smolny Palace. The congress announced for the world to hear the triumph of the socialist revolution and the establishment of the proletariat in Russia. The congress transferred all powers in the centre and in the provinces to the Soviets.

The second all-Russia Congress of Soviets put the formal seal on the victory of the Great October Socialist Revolution. Once it had risen in Petrograd, the wave of socialist revolution swept across the whole of the country. The Central Committee of the Bolshevik Party and the Soviet Government went into action to set up new government institutions. The problem was complicated by the fact that percentage of workers who could read and write was extremely low. By special decree the Council of People's Commissars set up the All-Russia Extra-ordinary Commission to combat counter revolution and sabotage (Cheka), headed by Felix Dzerzhinsky, a prominent leader of the

Bolshevik Party. In January 1918, the Council of People's Comissars issued the decree on the formation of the Workers' and Peasants' Red Army and in February another decree on the formation of the Workers' and Peasants' Navy. The new army and navy personnel were recruited from among workers and working peasants. Exploiter elements were barred from military service. It was decreed that all propertied classes were to be completely disarmed.

The first session of the Council's Presidium was addressed by Lenin who outlined a detailed action programme for this new organ of the revolution. The council's job among other function was to guide and control the nationalisation of large scale industries, to organise and regulate transport services, to introduce universal labour conscription. Under the leadership of the economic bodies created by the revolution workers' control in industry began to be organised in a planned manner. In introducing this control, Soviet power did not strip employers of their property rights but created conditions in which their property would be used primarily in the interests of the people. Thus, workers' control was a transitional measure during the passage from capitalist ways of managing production to Socialist ones.

Under the dictatorship of the proletariat, the socialist transformation of the country had begun by freezing social relations of the vestiges of feudalism. With the abolition of the landed estates the deepest roots of the division of society into estates were destroyed and the estates ranks, noble titles like prince, count etc. were also abolished for all time. Each member of the new society was proclaimed a citizen of the Russian Soviet Republic. Within a week of the victories of the armed uprising in Petrograd the Soviet Government adopted the Declaration of Rights of the Peoples of Russia which proclaimed:

1. The equality and sovereignty of the peoples of Russia;
2. The right of all nations of Russia to self-determination including secession and the formation of independent states;
3. The elimination of all national religions, privileges and restrictions;

4. The free development of the national minorities and ethnic groups inhabiting Russia. This document played a crucial role in the formation of the Soviet national republics.

The establishment of complete equality of men and women in economic, political and family relations was of exceptional importance. Immediately after the victorious Great October Socialist Revolution the church was separated from the state and the school from the church. Soviet power proclaimed the right of every citizen to profess any religion or to practise atheism. In doing so, Soviet power carried the cause of the Paris Commune a stage further by stripping the church of all rights. Soviet power showed great concern for the education of the rising generation. The richest art collections were nationalised and put on view for the public; large sums were allocated to renovate the Moscow, Kremlin and other historical monuments. In showing solicitious concern for the development of science Soviet power made every effort to create the most favourable conditions to enable the country's scientists to work fruitfully. All the measures adopted by the Soviet Government to carry out socialist changes in the economic, political and cultural fields came up against the fierce resistance of the counter-revolutionaries.

The third Congress of Soviets put the formal seal on the new state machine and chartered the course of the future socialist construction in the country. The Seventh Congress of the RSDLP(B) met in Petrograd in March 1918. The Congress approved the conclusion of the peace treaty with Germany. On Lenin's initiative the Congress adopted a new name for the Party. The Russian Communist Party (Bolsheviks) the RCP(B). The Fifth Congress of Soviets (July 1918) which approved the world's first constitution of the state of workers and peasants, now known as the Russian Socialist Federative Soviet Republic (RSFSR), was a landmark in the life of the Land of Soviets. The fundamental law of the land of Soviets put the formal seal on state ownership of the land. It also formalised the status of the Soviets as the sole bodies of power at the centre and in the provinces. The Supreme and the local organs of power were integrated into a single system. All the Soviets were elective organs, which exercised full power within their terms of competence. A fine system of local government was established. The relationships between the local bodies of power were based on democratic centralism. The constitution consistently implemented the principle of the equality of nations. The working people were granted the most democratic rights and freedoms in the world. The freedom of conscience, the freedom of association, the freedom of assembly, the freedom of the press, the right to work, to education and to rest. The constitution guaranteed these rights.

The Great October Socialist Revolution marked the transition of mankind from capitalism to socialism, thereby ushering in a new era in human history, the era of the triumph of communism. For the first time in history of the revolution wrested power from the exploiter classes, transferring it to the working people who rallied round the Leninist Communist Party, the most revolutionary party in the world which guided their constructive endeavour. The October Revolution abolished private ownership of the land and of the basic means of production for all time, turning them into the property of the whole people. The revolution destroyed the economic basis of social injustice and with it started the process of liquidating the exploitation of man by man.[2] The revolution liberated all the peoples of Russia from age-old oppression, rallying workers and peasants of different nationalities under the banner of proletarian internationalism.

Achievements of the Revolution

The October Revolution triumphed so rapidly and painlessly in the former Soviet Union that it was resolutely and openly supported by the overwhelming majority of the population. The revolution took place in the name of the basic interests of the working people. It also had powerful, dangerous and implacable enemies. These were above all the landowners. They included also the owner of large factories which were nationalised. The greedy bureaucracy were also against it as they had been deprived of their privileges. All these enemies were defeated in the course of the revolution, but inspite of laying down their arms they decided to continue the struggle against workers and peasants powers.

The forces of counter-revolution were, despite the dangers they presented, comparatively weak. The Soviet state relying on the support of the overwhelming majority of the country's population, quite rapidly suppressed the 'opposition of the internal-counter revolutionary forces'. Soviet power triumphed throughout the unbounded expanses of Russia. On December 15, 1920, 'Pravda' published an announcement by the field headquarters of the Military Revolutionary Council that with the conclusion of military action on the fronts the release of daily summaries of battle operations would cease. This marked the beginning of the long-awaited peace. It did not indicate that all military activities had ended or that the entire country had been liberated from the interventionals and white guards. Peace had been won and the peaceful socialist construction had been placed on the agenda. Many industrial enterprises under went modernization during the restoration of the national economy. They produced up-to-date machinery and electrical equipment. However, Soviet Russia's economy still remained insufficiently developed. The country was still agrarian, with a low level of industrial development and low labour productivity.

The new Russia was faced with the task of overcoming, in the briefest of historical intervals, the gap between the advanced political system and the backward economy, which had borne before the revolution an overridingly agrarian character. It was necessary to create a modern, heavy industry, transform poverty-stricken and destitute Russia into an advanced power. The fate of the revolution hinged upon this task.

It was necessary to determine the basic directions to be pursued in the building of a new, socialist economy. History knew of no similar experience. The Soviet people, the Communist Party had to travel an uncharted path, to pave the road for themselves. It was imperative to find methods and forms of managing a socialist economy and of clarifying the basic links in the development of industry, the proper pace of an industrial construction. In December 1925, the best representatives of the party, gathered for the Fourteenth Party Congress which adopted historic resolutions establishing the course for the socialist industrialisation of the country. The congress resolutions underscored that socialist industrialisation indicated, above all, the development of heavy industry and, in first order, of the engineering industry. It meant the production of the means of production, which would provide for the re-equipping of the entire economy on the basis of the advanced machine technology. It would ensure the victory of the socialist forms of the economy and the technological and economic independence of the country. It would strengthen the country's defence capacity. In order to carry out the industrialisation of the country old plant facilities had to be modernised and new ones built. Entire branches of modern industry had to be created from scratch. The execution of such imposing tasks demanded immense resources and huge capital investment. The Soviets believed that the capitalist powers had created large scale heavy industry both on resources accumulated within the country through the exploitation of the working people, and on resources drawn from without through the plundering of colonies.

The Soviet Union could not take advantage of such sources of accumulation, since such action was incompatible with the nature of a socialist state. The Soviet Union could not avail itself of foreign loans either, for such a path would threaten it with the loss of economic independence. There remained one path to the resolution of the problem of accumulation-funds had to be generated by the country's own efforts and its internal resources. Such resources were found in the expropriation of the landowners and capitalists, and the transfer of land, factories, banks and railways to the domain of public property. The annulment of Czarist Russia's debts freed the country from the payment of thousands of millions of roubles to foreign capitalists. State socialist ownership of factories, transport, the land, and banks, a monopoly over foreign trade, concentration of the bulk of internal trade in the hands of state and co-operative organisations, the planned development of the national economy, the unremitting growth of labour productivity—all of these measures ensured the socialist state of dependable sources of accumulation.

The Fifteenth Congress of the Communist Party adopted a resolution to draw up the First Five Year Plan for the development of the national economy of the USSR. The Five-Year Plan envisioned a major effort to raise the cultural level of the masses. Universal education was to be stimulated. Professional and technical education was to be stimulated. Broad plans for the development of science, and the training of qualified specialists and scientific personnel were drawn up. The Five Year Plan envisioned a major effort to raise the cultural level of the masses.

Throughout the Soviet Union industrial construction went into full swing. Inspired by the party and filled with faith in the correctness of its policies and economic plans, Soviet people demonstrated marvels of labour heroism. The country was turned in to a huge construction site. Industrial complexes appeared in the country's outlying districts. People experienced the power of free and creative labour, the might of collective effort. Everything was suddenly possible: the reclamation of the wastelands, the draining of swamplands, the construction of mammoth projects, and the erection of new cities. Millions of people left their homes and familiar places to participate in the gigantic construction projects of socialism. Canvas tents and mud dugouts became the temporary homes of these enthusiasts. Despite all difficulties new factories, settlements and cities were built in record time.

The massive collective farm movement unfolded in the autumn of 1929. In the last three months of that year 2,400 thousand peasant households joined collective farms. The peasantry understood the overall need for and his personal economic interest in the liquidation of the petty-commodity economy and the creation of a new socio-economic order in the countryside. Upto mid-1929 primarily poor peasants and hired labourers joined the collective farms; in the latter half of the year there was an influx of middle peasants, the backbone of the agricultural population. Thus from this point the collective farm movement took on a mass character, creating the conditions for the successful enactment of full collectivisation not only of separate villages but of entire regions.

By the end of 1932 the first Five-Year Plan was fulfilled ahead of schedule. The Soviet Union had virtually trebled the industrial output compared to that of Czarist Russia. Fifteen hundred major industrial enterprises had been constructed throughout the country. A large scale and technologically modern industry had been created. Modern enterprises unknown in the pre-revolutionary Russia sprang up in the most important sectors of industrial production, for the aviation, tractor building, automobile, chemical and machine-tool industries. Tractors and automobiles, airplanes and machine-tools, agricultural machinery and mineral fertilizers—all were now produced by Soviet factories. The engineering industry progressed at a particularly rapid rate. During the First Five Year Plan its output rose fourfold. The production of a number of types of machines and equipment climbed astronomically: metal cutting tools by 10 times, lorries by 35 times, tractors by 39 times, etc. Major progress was achieved in the electrification of the country. The production capacity of heavy industry was augumented. Iron smelting, coal and oil extraction rose. Some 179 new mines and over 1200 oil wells were brought into operation. Major progress was also achieved in the development of all other branches of industry.

The rapid growth of socialist industry, fundamentally altered the country's economy. Thus the Soviet Union had been transformed from a backward agrarian to an advanced industrial power. The erection of new factories and plants, mines and pits went forth not only in the centre of the country but also in the non-Russian outlying districts. The profile of backward districts was radically altered. In the Transcaucasian republic the oil industry was successfully developed, and so was the non-ferrous metals industry in the Central Asian republics. Industrial construction on a large scale was undertaken in the Ukraine, Bylorussia and the autonomous republics and regions of the Russian Federation. Agriculture was radically changed in almost all grain producing regions.

As a result of the socialist transformation the Soviet Union was transformed from a country of small holding peasant households into one boasting of the largest scale agriculture in the world. The collective and state farms bringing together more than 60 per cent of the peasantry were outfitted with the most up-to-date techniques. The industrialisation of the country and collectivisation of agriculture did away with capitalist elements and ensured the successful establishment of the foundation for the socialist economy.

Having achieved major progress in the development of the economy, the Soviet Union entered a period in which the foremost task was the further consolidation of socialism. The rapid development of the Soviet social and state system, and advances in agricultural and industrial growth—contributed immensely to the improvements in the material and cultural well being of the people. The Five Year Plans were being fulf'lled ahead in time. By 1955 in terms of industrial production the USSR already exceeded by 220 per cent the prewar (1940) level and by 95 per cent the 1950 level. The number of new factories, mines and open pits increased throughout the country. The socialist economic system ensured a rapid growth rate in industrial output. The average annual growth rate for national income and industrial output in the USSR was roughly double that of the corresponding indicators for the United States of America.

In the particular period the all round progress made in the economic sphere in the country was indeed phenomenal. A striking feature of the economic development of the Soviet Union in the 1950's was the wide-scale application of the achievements of science and technology and the rapid growth of productive forces on this basis. Such economic sectors as electronics, radio-engineering and machine building developed at a rapid pace. Major progress was achieved in the technical modernisation of the leading sectors of the economy. In 1956-58 alone, Soviet industry began production of more than 4,500 types of new machines, instruments and apparatuses. Major technical advances were made in the field of power-generating machine building. Transport was placed on a fundamentally new technological basis. There were a significant upswing in agricultural production.[3] Developmental work was in full swing in the former USSR and at one time it looked like that the victory of socialism would engulf the whole world.

Emergence of Super Powers

War is one of the major factors that consolidates or alters the power position of the countries. After a war, sometimes major powers are reduced to secondary status, and secondary powers emerge as major powers in the politics of a given region. For instance in the beginning of the 20th century, Prussia, Japan and Russia were considered great powers. After the First World War, Britain, France, Austria-Hungary came to be reckoned as great powers, with the United States slowly catching up. Thus, the First World War brought about major changes in international politics in general and in the position of great powers in particular. While Austria-Hungary got disintegrated, Russia went through a Bolshevik revolution. Germany was exhausted, France was defeated and Britain's power status was disturbed. The United States and Japan emerged with improved status. Between the two world wars the Soviet Union consolidated the Bolshevik revolution and achieved tremendous industrial progress. Britain and France despite considerable economic progress remained weak in comparison with Germany—a fact proved during the second world war. The Second World War, like the previous one significantly altered the international scene. One of the most important changes caused by the World War II was the emergence of the Soviet Union and the United States as the two most powerful states. The Axis powers of the Western Europe were totally shattered after their defeat and the Allied powers, though not the losers, lost much in terms of men, money and material.[4] This weakening of the European states created a power vacuum that was speedily filled in by the US and the USSR. Though these two states incurred heavy losses during the war, they were able to retain a position of superiority, in terms of economic, military and industrial capacity vis-a-vis the Western Europe. This superiority enabled the US and USSR to dominate the politics of their respective regions to such an extent that international politics came to be described by many as "Bipolar" politics.

It was during the conduct of the Allied strategy against the Axis powers during the war that America and Soviet Union emerged as the new leaders within the world community. The eminence of these two powers was based not merely on their superiority in arms strategy and industry but also on their respective leadership—that of Roosevelt and Stalin—that decided the destinies of a number of smaller countries in East and West. From the very beginning of the birth of Communist Russia in 1917 had evoked either a directly hostile or a non-friendly response in the capitalist world. The Communist leadership was aware of this hostility. The presence of free economic enterprise in capitalist countries was in direct contrast to the state ownership of means of production in the Soviet Union. Nevertheless this ideological difference seemed to have been submerged during the Second World War due to the imminent danger of Nazi expansion. However, with the removal of the common threat of Nazism after the war, these differences surfaced again. The rise of the US and the USSR as two leaders was mainly due to the great change in the balance of power after World War II.

The Allied victory reversed completely the position of Germany, Italy and Japan. France was to begin reconstruction in every field after living through German invasion and occupation, and Britain's former power and prestige were greatly undermined. Despite the loss incurred during the war, the US and USSR retained their dominant positions. It was during these years that the ideological divergence between the two became much more evident than it was ever before. The enormous territorial extension of Soviet Union in Eastern Europe resulted in the creation of a Soviet sphere of influence consisting of smaller eastern European nations. American expansion was manifested through important programmes for economic and military reconstruction like the Marshall plan and the NATO. These programmes subsequently culminated in the creation of American spheres of influence. In the process, the world after the Second World War got divided into two major blocs, led by United States, believing in capitalism and the Soviet Union upholding the Communist ideology.[5] Over a period of time the US and the USSR moved further apart from each other due to both conflict of opinion and of interest.

The conflict between the two was both ideological and political. For instance in Greece, the Soviet support to the leftist forces was an extension of Soviet ideology, whereas the American stand over the same issue was an expression of American fear of a communist take over. On the other hand the physical expansion of Soviet Union in East Europe and the expansion of the American presence in areas physically remote from the US were the attempts of these two powers to extend their spheres of influences as far as possible. This division of the world into two camps was described by Arnold Toynbee as 'bipolar politics'. Emphasising the supremacy of the US and the USSR in world politics, Toynbee wrote, "All other states of the world are in some measure dependent, most of them on US and a few of them on Russia, but non-completely independent of one or the other of the two powers". Even the emergence of the non-aligned groups and People's Republic of China has not altered this super power hegemony. The presence of major powers within and out side the cluster of the two super powers does not dilute the concept of bipolarism. For instance, Britain still maintains strong commercial links in many parts of the world. France, over the years, had shown a remarkable capacity for asserting herself by withdrawing her military command from NATO. This assertion was mainly due to the acquisition of nuclear technology and power by France. East and West Germany, despite ravages of war have been able to make tremendous progress in economic field, and in industrial spheres. However, all these factors put together do not negate the 'super' status of the US and the USSR.

The term 'super powers' was first coined by William T. Fox. He defined a super power as "a great power whose armed force is so mobile that it can be deployed in any strategic theatre, as opposed to a single regional theatre. Thus the major difference between a super power and a major power is the possession of two military characteristics by the super power: one "the full range of strategic nuclear armoury, and to the capacity to deploy its forces, whether armed conventionally or with nuclear weapons, in any strategic theatre of the world". In other words the definition implies that a super power has the capacity to intervene, interfere and move in any part of the world without affecting its own powers, prestige and popularity in any substantial way. This definition though conceived in 1944, stands valid today as the nuclear armoury has become a cardinal fact underlying the world powers structure, and has added tremendously to the power of the US and the USSR. Apart from the other attributes of power, the possession of nuclear weapons, along with the expanded military forces at sea, land, and air has entitled the US and the USSR to their present super power status in global affairs.

Super Powers vis-a-vis the Major Powers

The usually accepted components of national power are natural resources, sufficient manpower to utilize these resources, sufficiently gifted national leadership, economic sufficiency, military superiority, technological advancement and more recently, the possession of nuclear technology and a highly competent armed force. A country would not be rated as a major power as her role in any regional dispute continues to be conditioned by her own and her neighbour's relations with the super powers. Iran for one, with all her military might and oil power, was not able to assert herself even within the region. A country may possess abundant natural resources, sufficient manpower and even a committed and capable leadership yet may still be dependent on others for technological cooperation and military aid. This has been the case with a number of new nations with colonial background. If any of these is pitted against a non-colonial military power, it is the latter which will be regarded as major in terms of national power. For example, when Britain and France supported Israel in her attack on Egypt, these were undoubtedly superior compared to Egypt. Thus a nation could be described as a major power as different from a super power, when she is able to assert or dictate her position beyond her region.

The relativity of power also becomes evident when there is a change in national leadership or when there is a shift in the regional balance of power. A country could be described as a major power when she possesses all the concomitants of power along with nuclear capability and also a capacity to maintain balance of power within a given region. However, nuclear capability need not convert a country into a major war.[6] It is the capacity to maintain or upset the balance of power in a region which is more important. For example, USSR did not have to use her nuclear weapons in South East Asia to extend her influence.[7]

Events Leading to Soviet and American Supremacy

The basic need for the Soviet Union, immediately after the Second World War was a further consolidation of the communist rule at home and physical extension of the Eastern European frontier. At the domestic level the communist consolidation of power was achieved through a combination of several forces. These were the revolutionary and authoritarian heritage of Leninism, the traditional nationalism of Czarism, the stabilising equilibrium of conservative social institutions, the dynamics of rapid industrialization and the mechanisms of a police state under Stalin. Soviet Union became a leading industrial and military power in the span of a few decades. Rapid industrialization was achieved through a combination of different factors. It began with a massive investment in the expansion of elementary and higher education. This was followed by great emphasis that was placed on training of the engineers, technicians and the scientists. The system of incentives to reward the skills essential to the production forces was re-organised and the industrial elite were accorded a prestigious place in Soviet Society. During the post-World War II Soviet state had two choices, one to adopt a passive attitude that would have implied a risk of the disintegration of the existing Soviet State, or the active physical extension; the Soviet leadership opted for the latter. Thus Soviet extension in Eastern Europe came to clash with the US desire to acquire her own spheres of influence. During the conferences that were held between the Allied powers after the defeat of Germany, there were a number of issues on which the two (US and USSR) disagreed. At the Potsdam conference the major areas of conflict were all in Eastern Europe, deep within the zone of Soviet military occupation. The real expansion of Soviet power took place in Poland, Hungary, Bulgaria, Rumania and Czecholsovakia and the eastern region of Germany and Austria.

By 1953, the Soviet Union had recovered from the ravages of World War II and was able to achieve parity with the US in the scientific and technological process. Having discovered in 1949 the technique of making a nuclear bomb, Khrushchev in 1954 asserted the capacity of the Soviet Union to develop a hydrogen bomb, and warned the west that a nuclear war would mean the end of capitalism. It was not an empty threat as was indicated from the fact that in 1956 the Soviet Union had as an experiment blasted the hydrogen bomb. The stunning speed with which the USSR caught up with American achievements in military, industrial and technological fields, enabled her to reach beyond the confines of Eurasia. The European frontiers were sustained by a belt of Communist ruled countries under Moscow's domination. This provided the USSR with a secure western flank, and also provided for a Soviet domination for eastern, central and southern Europe. This European expansion of Soviet Union narrowed the possibilities of Soviet influence in other regions that were speedily approached by US for military alliances. Some of the countries, that were outside Soviet orbit, accepted these military alliances, like NATO, SEATO and CENTO.[7]

In 1956 Khrushchev denounced Lenin's doctrine that war between capitalist states was inevitable. He abandoned the old image of capitalist encirclement of the Soviet Union, proclaimed the possibility of peaceful overthrow of a capitalist system and of different roads to socialism after revolution. These were summed up in the two basic principles of Soviet foreign policy viz., "to support the national liberation movements and to effect all round cooperation with young developing countries" and to "uphold the principle of peaceful co-existence of states with different social system", "to offer decisive resistance to the aggressive forces of imperialism and save mankind for a new world order". During Khrushchev's regime, the image of Soviet Union also underwent a change in the western world. From "Stalin's Russia", she began to be referred more often as Communist Russia. The rigidity and the repression associated with Stalin were replaced by a less rigid attitude and made it obvious at the 20th party Congress of the CPSU.[8] USSR sought to limit the dangers of a major war and utilized these dangers to urge upto the West the necessity and prudence of accepting the great power status of USSR and therefore her right to pursue her worldwide interests.

De-Stalinization abroad implied a rationalization of intra-bloc relationships of the many, the three most important objectives of Soviet foreign policy were to let her adversaries, particularly the US know about the Soviet acquisition of a nuclear parity with the West. Thus Khrushchev revealed in 1960 that the USSR possessed enough nuclear weapons and rockets to "wipe out any country that attacked USSR." The second objective of the Soviet foreign policy was to achieve a more positive communication with the West and this was attempted at during Khrushchev's visit to US in 1959. The third was an energetic and successful projection of USSR's image in the developing countries, which became evident in Khrushchev's visit to India in 1956, and Soviet military aid to the non-Communist Third World countries like Egypt. In 1956, Soviet Union also realized that a direct confrontation with the US would be disastrous for both the countries. This was evident in a series of messages exchanged with American President during the Cuban Missile Crisis of 1962. The post-Khrushchev leadership retained the doctrinaire continuity of Soviet foreign policy. State power in USSR has often been explained as co-terminus with the moral and intellectual influence of Marxism.

In 1956 the Soviet state used that power to enforce Hungary's conformity by directly intervening in that country. In 1968 it was illustrated by Soviet intervention in Czechoslovakia. Since 1945, the number of countries that had joined the Soviet camp had been quite impressive, for instance in 1946 Bulgaria, in 1947 Hungary and Poland, in 1948 Czechoslovakia and East Germany, in 1954 North Vietnam, in 1960 Cuba, in 1969 South Yeman, in 1975 Angola, Laos and Vietnam, in 1977 Ethiopia and Mozambique, in 1978 Afghanistan, and in 1979 Cambodia. Though Soviet intervention in many parts of the world conferred the super-power status on the Soviet Union creating a number of Soviet supported regimes, yet she utilized intervention only when it had been militarily feasible. For example when the anti Allende coup was staged by the US in Chile, the Soviet Union maintained a discreet non-involvement even though Allende was a Marxist. The whole of Latin America, with the exception of Cuba remained open for American influence. Even a pro-Moscow socialist Cuba, could not remove the American military presence. Similarly, the Soviets avoided a direct military confrontation with the US during their presence in Vietnam. Short of physical military presence the Soviets extended every kind of assistance to Vietnam in her fight against the US. It was also noticed that the US watched helplessly the Soviet presence in Cuba, Vietnam, East Europe and Afghanistan avoiding a direct confrontation. This studied silence over each other's expansionist activities speaks of the mutual acceptance of the prevailing partition of the globe into spheres of influence. American transformation from a major to a super power status was much smoother than that of the Soviet Union.[9]

The United States superiority within the Allied powers had already been established during the concluding years of the war. The World War II brought about major changes in the status of European colonial powers. Italy was made to sign peace treaties with the Allied powers, that not only deprived her of her Empire but also drastically reduced her power status. Though Britain and France remained colonial powers after the Second World War, yet as a result of decolonisation policy, a number of British and French colonies were granted self rule and independence subsequently forming the bulk of the Third World Countries. After the departure of Germans from Greece during last phase of the war the British forces occupied Greece. The Soviet Union acknowledged the British presence in Greece by signing a treaty with Britain. Meanwhile there began a clash between the royalists and the leftists inside Greece, with Britain supporting the former while the latter were supported by their communist neighbours. The British forced the communists into exile or to seek shelter in the mountains. In 1947, monarchy was restored in Greece, after a plebiscite, through the communist offensive governments of Bulgaria, Albania and Yugoslavia. The British found it impossible to suppress the terrorist activities and directly appealed to the US for help.

Alarmed at the prospects of communist presence in Greece and neighbouring Turkey, President Truman of the US appealed to the Congress for a sanction of 400 million dollars in order to help Greece and Turkey remain free from communist domination. Truman Doctrine put an end to American isolationism and brought the US to the threshold of involvement-political-economic and military in the affairs of those people all over the world who were either supposedly fighting communism or who had to be "rescued" from communist influence. Simultaneously a new posture was adopted by the US to contend with the expanding surge of communism under the leadership of the Soviet Union. Interpreting Soviet diplomacy as expansionist, George Kennan, the then Director of the Policy Planning Staff at the State Department recommended a policy of containment as the only effective measure to check the spread of Soviet influence. The subsequent expansion of American presence in relatively remote areas like Vietnam and Laos etc., could be explained only in the context of this idea of containment. It essentially implied a physical encirclement of the communist bloc by the American presence, thus containing communism from physically spilling over into other regions.[10]

Marshall Plan

Extension of political support to the war distressed area of Europe had to be backed by concrete economic steps. Subsequently in 1947 the US launched a European Recovery Programme in the form of Marshall plan. After the war the whole of Europe faced severe economic crisis and it was felt in the US that the economic crisis in France, Britain, Belgium, Italy and West Germany would facilitate the communist extension in an otherwise 'free' world. It was agreed that as long as economic depression and scarcity of food would remain in Western Europe, 'there will steadily develop social unease and political confusion on every side, and mankind security would be seriously threatened'. The Marshall plan thus originated in the fear that communist extension in an economically depressed Europe would endanger the US influence in that region which was one of the main stipulations of Marshall Plan and that the Programme of economic recovery was to be initiated by the countries themselves. Soviet Union and both the communist and non-communist countries were invited to accept it. Soviet Union rejected the offer on the ground that the plan aimed at giving economic aid to Europe as a whole instead of individual countries. Further, it was opposed to the basic principles of the UN and held the view that it was a ploy of the US to create an economic empire exploiting the economic conditions of Europe.

The implementation of the plan led to a remarkable economic recovery in these countries. In the field of industrial products and hydro-electrical power a radical improvement was attained. With industrial development, economic self-sufficiency, and military security, stability returned to the countries of Western Europe. In this whole transformation the US gained the loyalty and friendship of the European nations. Their strength and stability was thus considered to be an American achievement. Military alliances concerning Europe, Middle East, South East Asia and the Pacific region provided another dimension to ascendancy of these two super powers in international politics. The Warsaw pact sponsored by the Soviet Union provided a military umbrella to the Communist bloc countries, and was a response to NATO but the American expansion continued through a series of multi-lateral and bilateral agreements. Apart from these, both the US and the Soviet Union had steadily extended arms to a number of developing countries, enormously adding to the super power hegemony in international affairs. The American and Soviet Supremacy had conditioned the conduct of international affairs, and the concept of national sovereignty of a number of third world countries became meaningless reducing them to mere puppets when they were caught in the mutual rivalry of the US and the USSR.

Cold War

The term 'cold war' was coined by Walter Lippman to describe the tension and conflict in the bilateral relationship of the US and the USSR after World War II. As a concept in international relations, it referred to a state of constant conflict and strife, maintained and perpetuated without a direct armed conflict between the antagonists. Every expression of hostility and tension was used without direct use of arms, hence the term 'cold war'. It has also been defined as "a state of intensive competition, political, economic and ideological, which falls below the threshold of armed conflict between States." However, since its beginning in 1945, cold war had been increasingly used not only by the Soviet Union and America but also by other nations of the world. Unfriendly or hostile neighbours or traditional enemies often took recourse to cold war tactics to express their mutual hostility. For instance, the constant propaganda between two hostile neighbours against each other like India and Pakistan and Iran and Iraq may also be described as a cold war tactics because these nations (when not actually engaged in armed conflict) maintain or perpetuate their hostilities through cold war.

Origins of Cold War

Some writers have tried to trace the origin of cold war in the general pattern of international relations in the 20th century. The differences between Soviet Union and America were not merely projections of their super power status but were also symbolic of two contradicting ideologies of Communism and Capitalism. As such, most of the early disputes between these two also reflected an interaction of two different systems of thought which questioned their mutual validity. After the Second World War this ideological conflict became more manifested and reflected in every move of the Allied powers to share the spoils of the war. From concrete issues of acquisition and adjustments of territories to the more abstract issues of societal conflict and economic growth, the Soviet American relations became heavily tainted with ideology. While the structure of the empire developed by the older world powers rapidly dissolved, the US and the USSR emerged as major powers. Almost simultaneously the old style imperialism in Middle East, Asia and Africa disappeared. This led to the emergence of several young states who were exposed to the economic, political and ideological pressures of the two major powers.

The major factors which led to a cold war atmosphere between the two super powers became identifiable during the post war conferences. Mutual suspicion of each other's motives and an unwillingness or incapacity to perceive the problems confronting each other, caused the tensions and the disagreements which marked these conferences. However, this scepticism and scare had a background beginning with the communist revolution in 1917. One of the earliest invasions which the new Soviet state had to encounter was the Allied invasion on Communist Russia immediately after the First World War. The presence of western troops within Soviet Union, after the termination of the First World War, was used by the Western powers against the new Soviet state. This added to the strength, of the counter-revolutionaries within the new state, significantly affecting the peace and development of the communist revolution.

Given this kind of experience, the Soviet leaders were rightly suspicious of every move of the Allies in 1945. Faced with a hostile, unfriendly western world the Soviet Union turned to

Germany for friendship and co-operation during the twenties. In the thirties, the Soviet Union had embarked upon a course of rapid industrialisation and technological growth. To cope with the unfriendly atmosphere at the international level, she had to become strong. To catch up with the west and to leave them behind was the motto. In this drive for development and growth the Soviet state needed both technical and economic cooperation and this was provided to her, amply by Germany. The US recognition of the Soviet Union came only in 1933.

The Course of Nazi expansionism caused great concern for the Soviet leadership and when her efforts to involve the western powers in restricting the eastward expansion of Germany failed, the Soviet Union entered into a secret agreement with Germany in 1939. This was interpreted in the West as an unfriendly act of the Soviet Union. The western leadership remained suspicious of the Soviet action during the entire course of Allied strategy against the Axis, quoting this secret agreement between the Communists and the Nazis.

During the course of the war, the Soviets accused the western allies of delaying the opening of a second military front against the Germans in eastern Europe. Stalin interpreted this delay as a design of the western allies to weaken the Soviet Union. After 1945, no effort was made on the western circles to hide the fear, and hatred of the Soviet Union. The famous Iron curtain speech made by Churchill, the American opinion about the desirability of the Nazis and the communists destroying each other and also the speculation of using the atom bomb against the communists, made a permanent wedge between the West and the Soviet Union. For a Soviet Union which was yet to catch up with the US in nuclear technology, these statements represented the essence of western attitude towards USSR.[11] Given this background, it is not surprising that the wartime alliance was regarded by both the powers as an unnatural alliance based on temporary need to defend themselves against a common enemy.

The Major Issues

The cold war originated from the German issue and remained confined mostly to Europe for a long time. The surrender of Germany after the war created an extremely sensitive area between the western powers and Soviet Union. The German problem had two main aspects; that of German unity and that of the future of Berlin. It was decided at the Yalta and Potsdam conferences that there would be a joint control of the four powers i.e., U.K., France, the US and the USSR over Germany. The Nazi-Soviet pact of 1939 was a crucial factor hindering a unanimous allied approach to the German problem. The potentialities of Germany as a great power accentuated the divisions between the Soviet Union on the one hand, and France, UK and USA, on the other. Both the sides required Germany as an ally against the other. Since agreement had been reached effecting a joint control of Germany it was also decided to totally eliminate the Nazi influence to completely disarm, and to restore democracy in Germany.

However, these decisions were not implemented. Despite the agreement to retain a United Germany, she was partitioned into four occupied zones. Subsequently an Allied Control Council was created which united the British, the French and the American zones into one unit. This merger subsequently led to the emergence of a West German State, which became a leading member of the NATO, and a recipient of the American aid through Marshall plan. Simultaneously the Russian occupied zone emerged as the East German state and became a very significant member of the Soviet bloc. The failure of the Allied powers to retain a united Germany was mainly due to mutual suspicion, conflict of ideology and of interest and a mutual fear of each other's domination, by both the Soviet Union and the US. It was against this background that a fresh crisis emerged in the form of Berlin blockade. Though Berlin was practically inside the eastern, Soviet zone of Germany, it was also divided into Soviet and the western zones.

In 1948, as a part of the programme for economic reconstruction through Marshall plan, currency reforms were introduced in the Western sector. By February 1948, the Soviet Union claimed that Berlin was a part of the Soviet zone and that the western powers were abusing their position. The introduction of a new deflated currency in the western zone was designed to eliminate excess money supplies and to curb inflation. Despite a meeting with the Soviet Government to discuss the effects of that move on Berlin, no agreement was reached as the Soviet Union insisted that West Berlin currency should not differ from that of the Berlin currency. Russia declared her own currency reform immediately and applied the new eastern zone currency to the whole of Berlin. The Soviets closed all land access from the west to the former German capital. The US reacted with its famous "Berlin Airlift" after considering and abandoning the alternative of "shooting a way into Berlin."

The crisis mounted swiftly during 1948, reached a height of tension, and then stalemated. Moscow would not release the blockade and US would not abandon the airlift. In the course of the controversy both states assumed firm positions that were to provide a base for the subsequent 'Berlin question'. The Soviet Union insisted that the west should evacuate Berlin and the US announced its refusal to be pushed out of Berlin and its intention of remaining there until Germany was re-united. Conferences were held to settle the dispute by negotiations which however failed. A reference of the dispute to the UN displayed the helpless nature of the UN because of the existence of Veto in the Security Council. Though the compromise to the Berlin crisis was negotiated at the UN in substance the understanding that brought the conflict to a halt was bilateral.

A minimal agreement was reached, based upon minor adjustments sufficient to permit both sides to retreat from their profitless positions and the final solution to the problems of Berlin blockade was made at a meeting at Bonn. A federal constitution for the Western zone was drafted leading to the emergence of Federal Republic of West Germany with Dr. Adeneur as the first Chancellor. The Russian response was quick and a new state, German Democratic Republic was carved out of the eastern sector. Thus, German unification which had been accepted by both the sides as desirable could never be attained due to ideological differences. The West German membership of NATO further widened the rift between the two sides. Though there was a lull in cold war because of armistice agreement at Geneva.

The Korean War

The emergence of People's Republic of China as the second biggest communist state perfected the Capitalist Vs Communist dimension of the cold war crisis. In a conflict between the communist North Korea and the non-communist South Korea, the US extended help to South Korea as a part of its containment policy. The United Nations troops were assigned the task of repelling the aggression by North Korea. American troops constituted the bulk of the UN forces under the command of General Mac Arthur and the Korean war was fought more as American Vs. the communists than as the UN troops against the aggressors.

With a direct help from the communist China the North Korean troops drove the UN forces back across the 38th parallel. The US pursued its cold war purpose throughout the operation under the aegis of UN. The Security Council intervention into Korean crises was made possible only by the Soviet boycott of the Security Council.

Later when the problem was shifted to General Assembly through the Uniting for Peace resolution sponsored by the US, it was felt that through this shift, a Soviet Veto could be avoided over any issue concerning the settlement of the Korean problem. However, the Korean crisis established the importance of the neutral and non-aligned group in the General Assembly, which forced the US for the return of peace in that region. The Korean war was the first instance when the Super powers used a third party to continue their mutual conflict and to test each other's strength.

The Suez Crisis

One of the most fascinating aspects of cold war has been the exposure of internal schisms within two power blocs, uniting the traditional adversaries on a major issue and in the process exposing the schisms within. This aspect of cold war surfaced in the Suez crisis of 1956. The refusal of the US to finance the Aswan Dam to be built over river Nile led to the nationalisation of the Suez Canal by President Nasser in 1956. When negotiations between Egypt and the Anglo-French governments failed to persuade Nasser to modify his position, an Anglo-

French Israeli invasion of the Suez Canal zone was undertaken. This time a United States resolution for a ceasefire in the Canal zone was vetoed by Britain and France. This was not merely an instance of disagreement in the Western bloc but of rift among the leading powers within NATO. For the first time the US and the USSR voted identically against UK and France who were the NATO allies of US.

Israel's position in the Suez episode, although central to the Middle Eastern aspect of the problem was peripheral to the cold war. But in terms of strategic confrontation of the cold war, the crucial fact about the Suez Crisis was the willingness of the two key European allies of the US to defy American wishes in pursuit of their own interests. Neither European power profited from the Suez venture and the alliance structure of the West was seriously weakened. The US learned from Charles de Gaulle during the 1960s that the Atlantic alliance never recovered from the shock it received in 1956. In the mid-sixties French-American tensions within NATO have been traced to the Suez venture. It also scarred Anglo-American relations. The US proved itself willing to turn to a non-western power against the key western allies. This subsequently led to a complete dependence of Britain on US. However, the intensity of the cold war began to decline after 1956, only to attain a fresh pitch in the Berlin wall and Cuban crises.

The Berlin Wall Crisis

The Soviet Union never succeeded in bringing about any modification in the American position that the West was in the city by right of conquest. The original four-power agreement governing access to the city remained and the movement within it was still in force. In the meantime the freedom of movement from one section of Berlin to another resulted in the wholesale flight of refugees from East Germany to West Germany. The crisis developed initially over technical points regarding the right of the East German government to control access of Western military personnel into East Berlin, the United States insisting upon adhering to the full letter of the original occupation agreement that made no mention of the East Germans. In August a wall was constructed separating the Soviet from Western sectors of the Berlin city. Yet, the open confrontation of the two powers at the wall, far from being a prelude to disaster, was the high water mark of tension. Both the sides withdrew their tanks, the climate grew less ominous and finally an arrangement acceptable to both the powers was made.

In 1962, the Castro regime in Cuba and its growing dependence upon the Soviet Union for economic aid, and the latter's demand for the placement of Soviet missiles and troops on Cuban territory became the cause of serious tension between the two super powers. After verifying the information about the presence of Soviet missiles in Cuba, Kennedy imposed a naval quarantine on Cuba to last until the missiles were removed. Soviet ships heading for Cuba turned back, some missiles were removed and the US lifted the quarantine. The Kennedy-Khrushchev correspondence during the crisis published later reveals that both the sides were equally anxious to prevent the crisis escalating into a hot war. Throughout the Cuban crisis both Washington and Moscow dealt only with each other. There was no pretence of allied solidarity or joint action and in moments of real crisis and high danger, bipolarity was replaced by a classical atmosphere of a great power diplomacy.

Both Berlin and Cuba were examples of an evolving dynamics of Soviet-American conflict, where the necessity of maintaining control over events and restrictive ceiling of permissible tension was realised, something which could not have been possible in case of the third party involvement. The rivalry and the competition of the two superpowers continued. The cold war also got reflected in the supply of arms to the third world countries by US and USSR. The virtual dependence of the third world countries on the US, USSR for arms supply added one more dimension to the continuation of cold war in international relations. The indiscriminate provision of arms to hostile neighbours provided both a testing ground for their weapons apart from providing markets for their industry. It also reflected in the failure of all talks regarding conventional or nuclear disarmament and in the management of third world economies through international economic agencies like World Bank, IMF or IBRD. The institutionalisation of super national consensus in the form of UN provided an opportunity to carry the cold war to conference table.

The emergence of the ideological socialist bloc was due to the long and continuous struggle for supremacy in between the US and the USSR. The cold war between the Soviet Union and the United States somewhat subsided in the sixties and the seventies again hot up towards the close of the 1970's. The origin of the new cold war is generally traced back to December 1979 when Soviet Union intervened in Afghanistan. America followed a policy of detente towards Soviet Union because it desperately needed SALT (Strategic Arms Liberation Treaty) to offset the loss of face in Vietnam. Further, this could help in maintaining the status quo, which was in favour of USA, by acknowledging the Soviet parity in nuclear strategic capability so that it did not offset the global balance of power. In the mid-seventies the Americans saw a number of thaws in the position of Soviet Union i.e., the Sino-Soviet rift, moving of Egypt under the Sadat away from Soviet Union; the pressure of King of Saudi Arabia and Shah of Iran as important factors contributing to influence the USA in the area, elimination of Allande of Chile, technological superiority of US nuclear armoury, all this went well with the national interests of USA and encouraged them to maintain status quo in the international system.

However, the developments in the second-half of the seventies went against the American interests. In Africa the Americans suffered a set-back when the Cubans were invited to Angola so that in collaboration with other African nationals they could continue their conflict with the South African racist regime. In 1976-77 the Shah of Iran and Saudi Arabia tried to wean away Sardar Daud of Afghanistan from Soviet Union, which led to Saur revolution and subsequent Soviet intervention in Afghanistan. In Aden as a result of a coup Rubayya Ali was eliminated, and the Soviet influence increased. Similarly, the switch over of Soviet support from Somalia to Ethiopia in the Horn of Africa, helped the Soviet Union to increase its influence in Ethiopia. In view of all these developments the attitude of the USA towards Soviet Union underwent a change.

President Carter adopted more assertive policy to restore USA's international position. On the one hand he tried to project himself as the champion of human rights campaign and wrote a personal letter to Andrei Sakharov, the leading Soviet dissident, and received Vladimir Bokovsky, another Soviet dissidant. The Carter administration also criticised the leaders of South Africa, Latin American dictators and South Korea for denial of human rights, but by and large this criticism was directed against Soviet Union. In mid 1977 Carter took a decision to produce and deploy air-launched cruise missiles which contributed to the escalation of arms race. In 1978 USA's attitude towards Soviet Union began to get tougher. Brzezinski paid a visit to China and made a bid to involve her in various joint actions. This was seen by the Russian as an alliance aimed against them. The normalisation of USA's diplomatic relations with China was seen by Moscow as a calculated move directed against it. In 1979 Carter and Brezhnev signed SALT II treaty at Vienna but Carter began to have doubts about it before he reached Washington. At this juncture USA discovered the presence of a Soviet brigade in Cuba and demanded its withdrawal or face the possibility that SALT II was withdrawn by USA. It also boycotted Olympic Games in Moscow in 1980 and imposed a grain embargo on Soviet Union.

In the meanwhile the Shah of Iran was overthrown in 1979. This imparted new urgency to the American Plan for Rapid Deployment Force, which was already under consideration. America also made a bid to secure base facilities in Kenya, Somalia and Oman to protect the American interests in the Indian Ocean and Persian Gulf Region. This naturally raised suspicions in the minds of Russia that America was trying to establish its hegemony over Persian Gulf. Towards the close of 1979, NATO took a decision to deploy American made cruise missiles and the advanced medium-range Pershing II missile in Western Europe from 1983. The NATO powers claimed that they took this decision to counter the threat posed by the Soviet deployment of a powerful new medium range missile SS-20, targeted on Western Europe. On its part Russia argued that it was obliged to deploy SS-20 missile to counter the employment of British submarine-based Polaris missiles, French nuclear weapons, American F-111K aircrafts based in Britain etc. It is indeed difficult to say as to who was to blame for this East-West arms race, but it cannot be denied that as a result of these decisions the tension between the two Power Blocs greatly increased.

In the midst of these developments, the decision by Soviet Union to invade Afghanistan in December 1979 further aggravated the situation. Soviet Union probably intervened in Afghanistan hoping that the intervention would be short and soon it would be able to withdraw However, the things proved quite difficult. The Carter administration with the help of the Chinese and through CIA arranged secret supply of arms to Afghan rebels to pressurise Russia to negotiate. But as the Russians were not willing to withdraw from Afghanistan until the American assured that they would not interfere in Afghanistan, Reagan administration also extended greater help to the rebels. On the other hand in El Salvador (in Central America) where America intervened, the Soviets, Cubans, East Germans and Several others were accused of involvement in the clandestine supply of arms to insurgents and imparting them training in terrorist tactics, with a view to ultimately impose a Marxist-Leninist dictatorship.[12] US Administration under Reagan tried to project the El Salvador issue as an international confrontation between West and Russians and tried to rope in Europe and Japan on its side in this struggle, though it had not completely succeeded in this regard.

Arms race was another phenomenon which helped in the emergence of two ideological blocs. Acquisition of more and more sophisticated arms became the fashion for becoming more powerful for both the USA and the USSR. In modern times the arms race can be traced back to the late sixties of the nineteenth century when Bismarck, the iron Chancellor of Germany started the system of conscription and tried to make Germany a world power. The spirit of intense rivalry and competition among the French and the English also contributed largely to this race. This race assumed serious dimensions during the period between 1884 and 1914 because, as Professor Philip Noel-Baker has put it "armaments produce fear, and fear produces more armaments."

The situation was further aggravated in the first decade of the twentieth century when Japan, in the wake of her victory over Russia in 1904-5 also jumped into the fray. During this period not only arms were produced in large quantities but improvement was also effected in their quality. This process continued till the outbreak of the First World War in 1914. During this period more sophisticated weapons, warships, submarines, fighter planes, tanks, bombers, poisonous gas and arms of various other varieties were discovered and perfected. It may be noted that although all the powers claimed they were piling up the arms for their defence and preservation of peace, this created a sense of fear, suspicion and hatred among the nations and ultimately culminated in the first world war. But with the advancement of technology the arms became more sophisticated. With this emphasis, arms race shifted from quantity to quality, viz., the states started acquiring more and more sophisticated weapons. In fact, after the second world war there was a mad race between Soviet Union and United States of America to outwit each other in the acquisition and development of more and more sophisticated weapons. Arms trade in recent years has assumed unprecedented proportions and has emerged as an instrument of foreign policy of major powers. There has been a substantial increase in the military expenditures in national budgets of each country as well as the purchase of arms by the developing countries after the Second World War.

In this way we can see how the Soviet Union and the United States emerged as the two powerful ideological blocs. After the Bolshevik revolution of 1917, Russia had emerged as a power to be reckoned with in Europe. But it took a long time for Soviet Union to get recognition from the Western powers. In this way because of mutual distrust and antagonism each bloc tried to strengthen itself. It arose from the ideological incompatibilities. The USA was worried because communist ideology was intent upon converting the entire world into a communist world. The Soviet Union became a powerful ideological bloc which forced Eisenhower to say that "we face a hostile ideology global in scope, atheistic in character ruthless in purpose and insidious in method."[13]

Communism in Eastern Europe

The establishment of Soviet power in Eastern Europe can be seen, historically, as a continuation, perhaps the culmination of a process of westward expansion began long ago under the Czars. Stalin's bargain with Hitler and their subsequent disputes left no doubt about the Soviet Union's interest and ambitions in Eastern Europe—whether for security, or for imperial expansion or for the cause of revolution.[14] With the defeat of Hitler's armies and the creation of a vacuum in the region, it was inevitable that the Soviets would move in. The Western powers were not there and were not prepared to contest.

Stalin's ambitions may have been extensive but his policies did not become fixed at an early date except perhaps in the case of Poland, which he was resolved to control. He knew that control of Poland would give the Soviet Union access to Germany and decisive leverage over Czechoslovakia, where President Benes himself, sensing that what independence his country would be allowed to enjoy depended primarily on Moscow. As for Hungary and the Balkans, Stalin's famous percentage deal with Churchill in 1944 documented his insistence on Soviet primacy in Romania and Bulgaria (in return for British primacy in Greece), while in Yugoslavia and Hungary, where he agreed to a more even division of influence with the West. The lines marking occupation in Germany and Austria were set by international agreement. Soviet forces did not occupy all of Czechoslovakia and withdrew very soon in 1945. They passed through only part of Yugoslavia and did not stay, and did not enter Albania at all.

The decisive events that established Soviet dominance in Eastern Europe were those that marked the seizure of political power by Communist parties. The pace, pattern and degree of Soviet involvement varied from country to country, taking account of local conditions. The Soviets were always prepared to make their own conditions when necessary in order to bring about the desired result. In Yugoslavia and Albania the National Communist parties gained power on their own. In Bulgaria and Romania the Soviet had imposed Communist regimes by the spring of 1945. In Hungary they followed a strategy of gradualism, even permitted a free election (in which the Communists got 17% of the vote), and did not establish full Communist control until 1947.[15] In Czechoslovakia they gave up a powerful lever by withdrawing their forces counting on President Benes's mixed regime, with Communists in key positions to secure their interests; as it turned out, the timing and circumstances of the Communist takeover in February 1948 were determined more by internal factors, including a perceptible decline in Communist popularity than by Moscow although Moscow, made sure of the outcome.

By the spring of 1948 Stalin had succeeded in his primary purpose which was to seal off the entire area from the Arctic to the borders of Greece from the military power and effective political influence of the West. In Finland, a nation with peripheral location and demonstrated will to independence, he had settled for a compromise that met Soviet security interests through limitations on Finland's foreign policy without insisting on Communist domination in domestic affairs.[16]

The Americans took on a global role, in effect organising the non-Soviet world into an anti-Soviet world. Soviet Control of Eastern Europe appeared all the more necessary. The Soviet Empire in Eastern Europe had become a fact of world politics. In the same year there was a coup in Prague which produced a new kind of challenge in Yugoslavia, a revolt from within on the part of a ruling Communist Party. Tito's defiance was a surprise to the Soviets and to the World. Stalin intended to deal with Tito as he had dealt with others, at home or in international movement. Khrushchev reported later, he thought that he had only to lift his little finger and Tito would fall. He tried methods he apparently felt sure would bring about that result like condemnation by loyal Communist states and parties, armed threats and incursions across Yugoslavia's borders, breaking of alliance, treaties, economic boycotts and pressures, intrigues with conformists within Yugoslavia, and constant propaganda. As Western aid and commitments to Yugoslavia increased and world tensions rose with the fighting in Korea, the risks of war were greater. Stalin stayed his hand and Tito withstood all other pressures. It was left for Khrushchev, two years after Stalin's death, to make the friendly gesture of reconciliation with Yugoslavia. The new Soviet policy towards Yugoslavia was adopted primarily because the old one had not worked. In re-establishing normal relations they conferred a certain legitimacy on Tito's heresy.

The New Course of liberalisation and reform begun in Hungary in 1953, putting Imre Nagy, at the head of the government and clipping the Wings of Matyas Rakosi, the old Stalinist. In seeking to maintain a reliable political base in Eastern Europe, Stalin's successors grouped their way towards new relationships, acting to ease tension and to dissociate themselves from unpopular leaders. These events shook the foundations of the system. The Soviets took the necessary decision to protect their vital interests in military control and in the maintenance of Communist rule. In Poland they made sure of their minimum terms through tough negotiations with Wladyslaw Gomulka, the new party leader. In Hungary, negotiations were overtaken by revolution where upon decisions were taken for military intervention and the imposition of a new leader, Janos Kadar, and a reconstituted Communist Party.

Khurshchev's regime was innovative in Eastern Europe as in other aspects of his policy. He knew he had to find substitutes for Stalinist terror and coercion. Khrushchev introduced the concept of socialist commonwealth. The Soviet Union never accepted the concept of multiple centres of authority on ideology and doctrine and asserted the right to determine which policies were correct and which were revisionist.[17] The discussions at the world conferences of communist parties held in Moscow in 1957 and 1960 reflected a determined effort to discipline institutional diversity with ideological conformity, leaving no doubt that the leading role of the Soviet Union was the primary principle that all, including Gomulka's Poland, would have to accept.[18] This was the issue that sealed Yugoslavia's exclusion from the socialist camp, or expressed differently, its choice for independence.

The remarkable thing about Soviet policy in the Khrushchev period was not its striving for unity and control but its unexpected flexibility in tolerating changes that escaped or even challenged Soviet control. For example Gomulka kept the gains of events in Poland to strengthen his position in the party and Kadar took the road of his version of communism and conciliation with non-communists and Khrushchev endorsed it. Albania left the bloc and got away with it. Romania rejected Khrushchev's plan for integrated development through Council for Mutual Economic Assistance and embarked on a series of independent moves in foreign policy. By the time Khrushchev was ousted in 1964, these extraordinary changes had become more or less institutionalised.

The transition to Brezhnev and Kosygin period brought no indications of new departures in policy towards Eastern Europe. Again however, the uncertainty of where power resided in Moscow in the transitional period raised doubts in the minds of East European leaders. In the first years Brezhnev's primacy was not clearly established nor was the position of Kosygin vis-a-vis top Soviet leadership clearly understood. A muted tug-of-war was going on in Moscow among individuals and factions not with a clear division but between neo-Stalinist reformers. It is in this situation that Czech and Hungarian reformers got an opportunity to act independently. The main challenge of the late 1960's came from Czechoslovakia hitherto a relatively docile member of the bloc. A new leadership in January 1968 announced the relaxation of censorship and discipline, the democratisation of Communist Party and the momentum of liberalising forces; but the leadership could not control the new bold steps. This annoyed Soviet leaders who launched not only a political campaign but an actual invasion of the country. They were replaced by a subservient Czech and Slovak leaders.

On the Sino-Soviet ideological front the tension was very severe so much so that the cultivated myths of political and ideological solidarity in the communist world got exposed. The Chinese were contesting Soviet hegemony not only in Asia but also in Eastern Europe—USSR's European backyard. The Soviets naturally intensified their efforts to maintain a primacy and ideological discipline. But one practical effect of the Sino-Soviet dispute was that East European States were given a liberal treatment. Thus Albania could afford to break with Moscow, having China as a model for it. Romania presumed she could seek a diplomatic middle-ground between the two giants.

Soviet Interest in East Europe

The basic Soviet interests in East Europe were of three kinds, i.e, the strategic, ideological and economic. From the very beginning, it was made clear that Eastern Europe was vital to the security of the USSR. To Stalin and his successors, the territory as a glacier providing defensive death and protecting the Soviet Union from invasion not just by some future Hitler but by a pleasant and a powerful America. It could not solve its purpose if the East European states were free to ally themselves with the West or to choose non-alignment as Yugoslavia did. That is the reason why there was a crackdown in Czechoslovakia in 1968. Moreover, Eastern Europe could be used for defensive purposes against Western Europe, if the situation so demanded. The capability for attack however, adds much to the influence of Soviet Union in world affairs.

The Soviet Union's capability was further affirmed by the existence of more than half a million East European soldiers trained by the Soviets and equipped with Soviet weapons and integrated into combined forces under Soviet command. This undoubtedly, contributed to the Soviet security.

Creation and the preservation of the political base of the Soviet power in the Eastern Europe contributed more than just a security requirement, it became an end in itself and an integral part of Soviet leaders conception of USSR as a great power. To maintain this status it is necessary to have other states making up a large part of Europe in the socialist camp. The whole bloc could co-operate more forcefully when supported by ideological considerations. Ideology in Soviet bloc is woven into policy especially into its public aspirations but could be seen in relation to politics in power. East Europe was a tested ground where the world would witness the success of Moscow's defined Marxism-Leninism in lands beyond its country of origin. So they were very cautious that Yugoslavia and Chinese experiments both having set-up counter models were not repeated but subsequently the issue of de-stabilization created uncertainty in both USSR and Eastern Europe. This trend could not be checked and the result was dis-integration.

The economic side of the Soviet policy was meant to maintain the system of military security and political subordination of its satellite states. Originally, Soviet aims were confined to taking East European assets as war-reparations and also to use economic pressure to advance Soviet economic programme such as the rationalisation of industry and collectivization of agriculture and expansion of trade with the USSR at the expense of traditional ties with the West. In the early years, the new regimes with Soviet guidance concentrated on building new industries which would serve as small scale Soviet models. Moreover, some of the industrialised states like Czechoslovakia supplied capital goods for heavy industries in Moscow. Likewise the devastated rural economy of Ukraine was also rehabilitated with the help of East European countries. The CMEA was established in 1949 to match with the west's Marshall plan so that the East European countries would collectively develop their damaged economy. It is only after the death of Stalin it could make name headway.[18]

REFERENCES

1. David Footman, *The Russian Revolution (Men and Events).* Faber and Faber, London, 1962, pp. 29,75,115.
2. Yu Kushukin, *History of USSR, (An Outline Socialist Construction)* Progress Publisher, Moscow, 1981, pp. 15-44.
3. Adams and Others, *Foreign Governments and their Backgrounds,* p. 766.
4. Towster Julian, *Political Power in the USSR,* p.7.
5. K. Gusev and V. Naumov, *The USSR—A Short History,* Progress Publihsers, Moscow, p. 183-272.
6. Prakash Chander, *Studies in International Relations,* Bookhive (Regd.) New Delhi, pp. 113-142.
7. Charles W. Kegley and Eugene R Wittkoff, *World Politics Trends and Transformation,* p. 42.
8. *Strategic Analysis,* Vol. 7, No. 2-2, p. 76.
9. Y. Couart, *Disarmament,* p. 17.
10. Abba Eban, *The New Diplomacy-International Affairs in the Modern Age,* p. 198.
11. Rama S. Melkote and A. Narasimha Rao, *International Relations,* Sterling Publishers Pvt. Ltd., p. 113-130.
12. *Ideological Paanacea,* A Chapter in the Book Political Realities—Contemporary Political Ideas—Dereh Heater, Longman, p. 27.
13. D.W. Brogan and Douglas V. Verney, Political Patterns in Today's World, Harmish Hamilton, London, 1963, p. 148-149.
14. Vojtech Mastney, *Russia Road to the Cold War: Diplomacy, Warfare and the Politics of Communism,* 1941-45, (New York, Columbia University, 1979, pp. 183-228.

15. Stephen D. Kertesz, ed., *The Fate of East Central Europe: Hopes and Failures of American Foreign Policy*, (Notre Dam: University of Notre Dam Press, 1956), pp. 228-31.

16. Paul E. Zinner, *Communist Strategy and Tactics in Czechoslovakia, 1918-1948*, (London: Pall Mall, 1963), pp. 186-218.

17. Zbigniew K. Brezezinski, *The Soviet Bloc; Unity and Conflict, 2nd ed.* Cambridge, Harvard University Press 1967, pp. 292-308.

18. John C. Campbell, *Soviet Policy in Eastern Europe:* An Overview pp 1-31. This chapter is in the book "Soviet Policy in Eastern Europe" ed. Sarah Meikiejohn Terry, Yale University, Press, New Haven, and London, 1984.

5

BREAK-UP OF THE SOVIET UNION: RATIONALE AND CONSEQUENCES

Developments in the socialist world particularly since 1989 have had a tremendous impact on the entire global system. The developments were so quick and fast that they left the political analysts and observers completely confused and bewildered. Starting with Gorbachev's prestroika and glasnost; followed by the signing of the INF treaty and the fall of the socialist regimes in Eastern Europe and the reunification of Germany and on top of all, the disintegration of the mighty Soviet Union, the events moved at such a speed that even before the fall of one was assessed, the other came with a bang.

No social scientist could explain or predict that such total changes were in the offing though there were plenty of sophisticated and empirical frameworks and models. Samuel Huntington, the great philosopher of the concept of political change and decay, wrote in 1984 that the possibility of democratic developments in Eastern Europe were virtually nil.

The survival of the Soviet Union had become a subject of intense discussion in the academic and political circles. But the development leading to its end were so unpredictable that it was not visualised as a certainty till the close of the year 1990. The change could be described either as the fall of the communist ideology or it could be called only the failure of the Soviet style of state system. The process of change has been hailed by many in the West except of course by the Marxists as an ideological victory of the capitalist model of democracy.[1]

These regimes came to symbolise repression, censorship, ethnic chauvinism, militarism, red tapism and economic backwardness. The failure of the economic content of communism which was the most vital aspect of the Marxist-Leninist ideology was believed to have been a bane to these societies which wrought political degeneration leading to instability. The responsibility can also be laid on the shoulders of the ruling elites in those societies. Bureaucracy and their misconceived and ill-administered policies which failed to construct a social order based on justice, individual dignity and freedom contributed a great deal in bringing about a situation in which collapse of the system became inevitable. They were mostly responsible for the loss of confidence among the people in the ideology which was initially upheld as a benefactor of mankind. Besides, in each of these societies there were some unique domestic historical and political factors which also contributed to the rise of inimical forces to which the political and economic institutions fell prey.[2]

Gorbachev's policies of perestroika and glasnost did also contribute in bringing about the change in Europe. Only the extent of contribution to the initiation and activation of the process of decay of communism can be debated. Gorbachev like the rulers in Washington, Bonn, London or Paris did neither seek, nor work for any change that would have disturbed the existing European or world order. Thus, while all of them wanted democracy to win, they only reluctantly supported the change in the status quo. Hence neither the dissolution of the Soviet Union, nor the crisis in Yugoslavia, nor even the split in Czechoslovakia, were envisaged in the Gorbachevian framework of glasnost.

A new global order minus communism, but with one integrated Soviet Union, was indeed a more desirable global system because dealing with only one more Super Power was much simpler than a multi-polar system which was far more complex. Secondly, a bipolar system is more predictable as it is stabler than a volatile global system with many centres of power. Thirdly, in a bipolar system, the Great Powers had got accustomed to shape their policies and strategic responses focussed on the super structure. But in the new system, with Washington left as the sole military Super Power, and with the disappearance of a common perceived centre of security threat, the attitude and responses of both the allies and friends could not be easily assessed or cast in a set mould. Hence, the new realities were not only more complicated but they also posed a challenge to the Great Powers to plan and formulate their policies befitting each situation and even differently. The rationale for a common security language either superimposed on satellites or arrived at after endless debate had gone in the East and contested in the West.[3]

The collapse of the Soviet power in East Central Europe was described as the most significant geopolitical shift since the end of the Second World War. The beginning of the end of Cold War was thus attributed to the launching of perestroika and glasnost and the disintegration of the Soviet Union as the logical culmination of it. However, it does not mean that the collapse of the Soviet Union was inevitable in the process even though Gorbachev's new thinking acted as a catalytic agent all through. In brief the end of cold war need not have coincided with the end of the post war global system.[4]

In this context a query arises as to how Marxism met its fate and was there any possibility of its regeneration? The USA perhaps did not wish for the disintegration of the Soviet Union even though Washington would have welcomed the co-Super Power into the overall Western dominant global system. If such a hypothesis was acceptable the Americans would not have worked consciously for the collapse of Soviet Union. As a matter of fact American strategists were arguing that there was good reason to believe that a declining Soviet Union buffeted from within by almost uncontrollable centrifugal forces would have a highly destabilising impact on the world politics.[5] Therefore, before the end of the Soviet Union, the US State Department was still toying with the idea of a stable and integrated Soviet Union, which was much more in the interest of the United States. Washington indeed wished for a detente that ended the cold war but wanted the predictable post war period to continue.

Systematic Change and Systematic Collapse

The attempt to reform the Soviet system led to its collapse. The revolution from above initiated secessionism from below. The search of real socialism led to the demise of 'barrack' socialism. Did the system break down because of the kind of reforms initiated by Gorbachev or the manner in which they were implemented or was the break down due to long term weaknesses of the Soviet system? A brief analysis of the reforms and the processes which emerged as their consequences, would show that it was the conjunction of the objective and subjective contradictions—the long term accumulation of weaknesses and short term methods of their resolution, which broke the Soviet Union into 15 independent republics.[6]

Gorbachev, the key factor in this historic drama, emerged out of the highly unified network of the Soviet political structure. He was installed to power as the Central Committee felt that a younger and dynamic leader was necessary for stopping the gradual Soviet decline. Trends from the late Brezhnev period pointed to economic stagnation, falling growth rates and increasing technological gaps vis-a-vis the west. The Soviet system was running into problems in meeting the requirements of a modern industrial state with super power status.

Controversies surrounded the method of Gorbachev's reforms of perestroika and glasnost. Gorbachev's reforms were not evolutionary or systematic but the system was attacked from all sides and a number of issues were raised simultaneously. Gorbachev needed the support of bureaucracy. He convinced the party apparatus that without reforms the very survival of the system was at stake. Since the party lacked their own thought out programme, they fell in line with Gorbachev's proposal. Gorbachev was also convinced that the public should be well informed. This was done through the policy of "openness" which he felt would help mobilise people for reforms and initiate a communication revolution in the Soviet Union. With this policy, resolution of basic human problems were exposed. Press censorship was lifted. The gaps between the socialist theory and practice were revealed. These measures were meant to encourage discussions on the reforms and evolving changes. But it led to the initiation of delegitimizing the communist party—the very basis of the Soviet system.

Gorbachev criticized the bureaucratic control and blamed the bureaucracy for blocking the reforms and sabotaging the economy. The bureaucracy comprised 18 million people with functions at every level of organised life. They functioned like a grid in Soviet society and proved too widespread a phenomenon to root out. Gorbachev attacked individual manifestations of this system. The reformers did not possess the cadres necessary for a reforming regime. The bureaucracy got split into pro-reformers and anti-reformers. The bureaucracy they attacked, was the bureaucracy they continued to rely upon. The reforms were thus not only restricted by the apparatus but also constrained by it.

The reforms brought the ethnic problems to the forefront. The elements from the Baltics and their demand for independence was the most serious issue, promising to put an end to perestroika. The demand for independence was not restricted to the Baltics, but Moldova, Georgia, Armenia and Ukraine also voiced this demand. This was followed by popular movements and election of leaders proposing this issue. A referendum on the Union proposed by Gorbachev in March 1991 was backed essentially by the Russians and the Muslim central Asian states. But the Baltics and others refused to participate. Perestroika offered no solution to this issue.

As regards the economic policies of Gorbachev his main object was to accelerate the economic growth by tackling stagnation and over centralisation. Decrees were issued for autonomy of enterprises and collectives. Anti-alcohol campaigns and a struggle against unearned incomes were launched. These initiatives were abruptly stopped, since they led to a decline in government revenues and proved unpopular. Decrees on cooperative and autonomy helped little and remained workable only on paper. Shortages increased. The domestic consumer demand in 1990-91 fell short by 70 billion roubles. Official statistics revealed for the first time that 28 per cent of the population lived below the official poverty line of 100 roubles a month. Gorbachev shifted from one economic strategy to another. He abandoned one programme and used another programme with no concrete results coming out of them. Likewise the 500 days plan which was supported by the radical liberals also failed to achieve any success. Clearly the system itself was blocking out the changes necessary to modernise it.

Gorbachev and his team were convinced that military overstretch had led to deep internal crisis of the Soviet system. Soviet control over East Europe, the necessity of maintaining an ideological wall vis-a-vis the west, sustenance of a system of alliances in the crisis-ridden third world, and conservation of super-power status had led to a spiralling arms race with disasterous effects. The Soviet economy had become lop sided with a very high defence account. Upto 40 per cent of the budget was linked to defence expenditure. Technological upgradation was concentrated in the defence sector. The consumer sector was continually neglected. Moreover, as Gorbachev stressed, the consciousness of the Soviet people had got militarised.

To resolve this, Gorbachev advocated deideologization, disarmament and confidence-building with the west. The ensuing result of this policy was Soviet withdrawal from Afghanistan, East European revolutions, and new bridges with the west and other hostile states. These changes which transformed the basis of international relations, were criticised by the conservatives at home because of the loss of super power status which had for long sustained the internal bureaucracy. These changes did not substantially improve the internal economic situation. This was because large parts of the army in East Europe had to be demobilised and reorganised within the Soviet Union. Though a cut in defence expenditure was planned, this was not systematic. Conversion of the military sector to the consumer takes time and is not necessarily viable. The Soviets temporarily lost markets and trade with East Europe. However, on the whole Gorbachev's foreign policy successes, thus helped his image internally only for a limited period of time.

Gorbachev and his team had inherited a highly integrated political structure. The party apparatus had for over 70 years controlled all key institutions. In this process these institutions had lost their identity. The state government administration and civil society were held together by one institution—the party apparatus. Unity of thought and tight control had removed all nuances of flexibility. In fact, this gave the system a false appearance of strength, when actually it was highly brittle.

Gorbachev emphasised the democratisation of the political system as an essential aspect of reform. Electoral reforms, a system of rule of law under the concept of socialist law based state, transfer of power from party bodies to the elected societies and other institutional changes were introduced. An element of choice crept into the local soviet-elections of 1987. Voters at large showed keen interest in the 1989 elections of the Congress of Peoples Deputies, despite the intricate procedure. The results of this election were sensational, especially since a number of leading party and state officials were defeated. All this indicated that an element of pluralism had made inroads into the old indifferentiated system. A nascent civil society began to develop. State guided political culture started giving way to a differentiated and plural one.

Despite the development of some democratic movements, no significant political structures arose at the national level. Workers and miners strikes were spontaneous and their links with the democratic movements were weak. The CPSU continued to dominate political life, though factions developed within it. This lack of non-governmental civil or alternative political institutions, led to the reinforcement of traditional institutions like church and mosque and ethnic and regional loyalties. At the republican level, political parties and popular fronts focussed around sectarian issues. Given the quick delegitimization of the communist party, nationalist groups filled the political space which had been created. In many instances, the Communist ruling leadership realised the shift in political aspirations and the pressure for nationalist demands. Some leaders shifted positions and became leaders of new nationalist political formations.

Perestroika did not encourage the development of a popular mass front. Y. Yakovlev stated that there was no single influential mass movement on which the supporters of Perestroika could rely. Despite political reforms, no political formation appropriate to the political life of the Soviet Union emerged. At the same time the support bases and legitimacy of single structure which held up the Soviet Union was being hacked away by the centrist leadership and by the growing opposition. The reforms led to changes within the CPSU in a direction not envisaged by the reformers.

However, Perestroika launched by Mikhail Gorbachev soon after becoming General Secretary in March 1985, was the last great attempt at communist reform. He believed that the old system remained viable, that it was still a powerful motor that required only some fine tuning. Despite the revolutionary language, this was essentially a reformist programme. His tragic fate was to act as the destroyer rather than the builder. The more he tinkered with the system, the deeper the crisis became. His reform of communism only exacerbated what was already a system in crisis, and worsened the legacy facing the post communist governments. It fell to his successors in Russia and the other republics to rebuild economies and to nourish the fragile shoots of democracy that perestroika had encouraged.

Perestroika passed through four main phases. In the first, lasting from 1985 to 1986, Gorbachev applied traditional methods to improve the Soviet economy. In this phase, known as uskorenie or acceleration, the government led by Nikolai Ryzhkov devoted yet more resources to investment and re-investment, the improvement of old plant and facilities. Imports were cut back and once again the consumer sector was neglected. The emphasis on labour, and social discipline recalled Yurii Andropov's programme of authoritarian reform following Leonid Brezhnev's death in November 1982 before Konstantin Chernenko's brief rule (February 1984 to March 1985) sought to turn the clock back to the comfortable corruption of the Brezhnev years. The misconceived anti-alcohol campaign, inspired by Yagor Ligachev, led to the increased production of bootleg liqour and devastating losses to the budget revenues of central and local authorities. Uskorenie was designed to last a long time and during this period grand programmes were announced such as the promise that every Soviet citizen would have an apartment of their own by the year 2000. How these promises were to be fulfilled were left unclear, and the whole programme of acceleration was caught in the trap of simultaneously trying to modernise industry while pressing for increased production. Growth and reform could not be achieved simultaneously.

The second phase of perestroika, from January 1987 to June 1988, was dominated by the twin concepts of glasnost and demokratizatsiya (democratisation). It was in this period that increasingly bold strategies for the political system were adopted to tap the alleged hidden potential of the Soviet model of development. The plenum of the Central committee (CC) of the CPSU called for the extension of competitive elections in the work place, the Soviets and in the party itself. In June 1987 a further plenum of the CC adopted a plan for the economic transformation of the country which focussed on greater autonomy for enterprises and increased rights of workers to elect their own managers. The revelations made possible by glasnost about the crimes of past and the inadequacies of the present only undermined the legitimacy of the regime as a whole.

The third phase of perestroika, characterized by the attempt to implement programme of reforms, lasted until March 1990. Gorbachev's strategy for the radical reform of the political system was based on the CPSU retaining a leading and directing role. But the attempt to implement his reforms within the framework of the one party system proved unfeasible. The period was characterized by a mass of contradictions, and it soon became obvious that one-party parliamentarianism was self-defeating. A 'socialist' legal state appeared to be an obstacle to the development of a straight forward legal state in which the rights of citizens could be defended by law and in which powers were separated and defined. It appeared that the radical strategy for perestroika was unimplementable.

The fourth phase began with the dissolution of Gorbachev's definition of Perestroika as a party led programme. It was characterised by intensified conflicts over economic policy, national issues and political strategies. Despite a host of difficulties, such as complex registration laws and harassment, numerous parties were established. Gorbachev's 'socialist pluralism of opinions' was now superceded by structured political conflict and the veritable rebirth of politics. The problem soon became one not of the lack of alternatives but the sheer abundance of new parties that failed to coalesce into a coherent force that could challenge the CPSU or provide the basis for viable government.[6]

By 1990 Gorbachev had broadly decided in favour of establishing a market economy, but like most of the population he was unwilling to face the hardships that would accompany the transition. Above all, he feared the political price that would inevitably accompany the change. Gorbachev's failure to support the plan proposed by Stanislav in August 1990, which envisaged a rapid transition to the market economy in '500 days' and which would have devolved great powers to the republics while maintaining a single economic space and currency, was in retrospect probably the moment when the USSR passed the point of no return and could no longer be held together. It appeared that no single economic reform plan could work for all of the USSR, hence each republic had to devise its own. In economic policy this period was even more catastrophic than anything that had come before. In December 1990, Ryzhkov was replaced as Prime Minister by Valentin Pavlov, a man who had earlier been Minister of Finance and had almost single handedly destroyed the rouble by printing money as fast as the budget deficit grew. He now set about destroying the whole economy by his refusal to countenance a rapid advance to the market and by his poorly planned currency reform and price rises.

The attempted coup of 1991 represented an attempt to resolve the crisis power and the struggle of conflicting ideologies. The 'manifesto' of the putschists played down the ideological appeal to communist values. Instead they sought to ground their venture on Soviet nationalism, the attempt to maintain the Soviet Union as a centralised state, and Soviet populism, to gain popular support by denouncing the unpopular cooperatives and other new forms of business activity which had been termed as 'blood-suckers'. The plotters were not reactionaries, realising that the clock could not be turned back to before 1985 and thus were willing to accept some of Gorbachev's reforms, but insisted that the time had come to stop the retreat. They represented a return to Andropov's authoritarian reform and a rejection of Gorbachev's democratising reforms. The attempted coup was therefore a conservative one, trying to preserve the USSR and its political system but ready to accept some necessary changes.

The coup was statist in two senses; in the preservation of the territorial integrity of the Soviet State, and the preservation of the institutions of the Soviet state with or without the communist party. Not only the democrats but the conservatives as well realised that the CPSU had its day, and for the first time since Stalin a major initiative had been launched bypassing the party leadership. While the central committee was not slow in drumming up support for the coup and neither the Politburo nor the CC secretariat defended their own General Secretary imprisoned in Crimea, the coup was as much a defeat for the communist party as it was for Gorbachev personally. The coup was the final act of a cannibalistic regime. The Soviet system had destroyed the old Russian middle class and the cultural intelligentsia; it had destroyed the self-sufficient peasantry and liquidated the Kulaks as a class, and largely as individuals as well. The system had squandered the vast natural resources of the country and the wealth accumulated from the past and in its final act the regime devoured itself.[8]

The communist party was riddled with factions and had lost not only its much prized ideological unity but also its ability to rule. While Gorbachev's achievements in ending the cold war and returning consciousness to the people by lifting the burden of fear ensured him his place in the pantheon of history, his legacy was profoundly flawed. Gorbachev's own policy-making procedures perpetuated the arbitrariness that had always characterised the Soviet system. He played the game of bureaucratic politics with supreme mastery, but his responsiveness to popular aspirations allowed him to modify the Soviet system in a relatively peaceful manner. He was constantly drawing the lines, as in his insistence up to the last moment of the need to keep the Communist Party at the head of the reform process, and then stepping over it when he saw the popular pressure for change. However, by the end Gorbachev's style achieved the maximum confusion for the minimum advantage. Gorbachev should have taken advantage of the stability and popular consensus that existed in the first stage of perestroika, and moved more towards a market economy. The common judgement at the time was that perestroika could only triumph when its exponents had passed from the scene, and this applied particularly to Gorbachev himself.

Politics began to take public and parliamentary form and Gorbachev's mastery of bureaucratic intrigues was no longer relevant. Gorbachev's tragedy was that he was unable to make the transition from party functionary to national leader and the longer he tried to combine the posts of General Secretary of the CPSU and the president of the country, the less effectively was he able to fulfil either. The debate over the Soviet past was to cast a long shadow over the post communist future. Much had been achieved since the revolution in terms of economic and social modernisation, but much of this could be labelled 'mis-development' and 'mismodernisation', achieved at great cost and often in wasteful and superfluous forms. A huge defence sector and machine tools industry produced more and more weapons and machine tools, while the shortage of consumer goods, of international contacts, the regulated cultural and economic systems impoverished daily life. The darkened streets of late communism, the empty shops and frustrated careers, the potholes, the tawdry buildings and the lack of meeting places, all reflected an exhausted ideology and an exhausted society. It was against this background, the new society and the polity struggled to be born.[9]

Gorbachev's attempts to revive socialism appeared increasingly irrelevant. Thinking moved beyond Gorbachev's reform communism towards civil society, liberalism and democracy. The reformers quite simply, it appeared, had lost the philosophical debate. Early excitement about the rehabilitation of Nikolai Bukharin and discussion of Khruschev's reforms gave way to a new interest in the classics of western liberalism like John Stuart Mill and James Madison, and a revived fascination in the Russian religious philosophy at the turn of the century including Nikolai Berdyaev and Vladimir Solovyev, and the social philosophy of Semyon Frank and others. From March 1990 it was clear that Gorbachev's attempts to devise a viable form of late communism, characterised by a high degree of democratic mass participation within a predominantly state-managed economy loyal to Leninist principles of single party dominance, was doomed. From that time the system itself became increasingly deideologised and stopped looking for an over-arching theoretical principle and simply became a system trying to stay in power. The concept of a party guided process of socialist reform known as perestroika was dead, and it was unlikely that the USSR could survive without the communist system that had given it birth.[10]

The absence of a clear demarcation between the Union and Russian institutions gave rise to a dangerous vacuum of authority. Russia in effect suffered from a form of dual power, with two presidents and two parliaments, which gave rise to a type of 'dual powerlessness and a paralysis of government'. As much by necessity as by desire, the Russian authorities engaged in a form of 'Salami tactics' as slice by slice they took over the powers of the Union. Despite the resounding commitment to 'universally recognised norms concerning human rights', no method of implementing these goals was indicated. Article 3 expressed the commitment to the 'preservation and progress of the ethnic, cultural, linguistic and religious identity of national minorities, but stopped short of recognising their right to political self-determination. The agreement attempted to maintain the status quo, and article 5 forcefully committed the member states to recognise and respect the territorial integrity of each other and the inviolability of the existing borders within the Commonwealth, though there was to be free movement of people and information within the Commonwealth. Above all, Article 6 committed the member states to maintain a common military strategic space under joint command, including unified control over nuclear weapons.

The failure of perestroika turned into a catastrophic breakdown of society and economy. All the institutions that maintained Soviet statehood were shattered simultaneously. The main being the communist party, the secret police, the economic apparatus and the state mechanism. All of this was in terrible fulfillment of George Kennan's prediction soon after the Second World War that Soviet power, like the capitalist world of its conception bears within it the seeds of its own decay. He warned that if anything were ever to disrupt the unity and efficacy of the party as a political instrument, Soviet Russia might be changed overnight from one of the strongest to one of the weakest and most pitiable of national societies. This indeed came to pass, and in the space of a mere three years from 1989 Soviet Russia fell from being one of two superpowers to becoming a suppliant at the gates of the West. The psychological and political consequences of such a dramatic fall have yet to work themselves out.[11]

Post-communist Russia had two old regimes against which to measure its achievements, the Tsarist and the Soviet. It was not at all clear whether the factors that had given gist to Bolshevism in the first place had been overcome. What was clear was that the seventy-four years of Soviet power would profoundly influence the post-communist period and that there could be no direct return to the Russia of before the revolution. One of the main themes of post-communist politics must necessarily be the interaction between continuity and change, between the existing conditions in society the economy and politics, and the process of change itself reacting with these historically determined conditions. The fall of the communist regime was a necessary but not a sufficient condition for the triumph of democracy.[12]

For the first forty-eight hours after the Chernobyl nuclear disaster there was silence, but as the west increasingly insisted on having information to determine the extent of the radiation Gorbachev realized that the accident could not be covered up. This was the turning-point of glasnost. The opening up on Chernobyl led to demands for information and action on the whole spectrum of environmental pollution in the Soviet Union. The press began to report other accidents; crime and prison statistics, a long held secret in the Soviet media, were published. Soon Soviet journalists were writing about all the seamy aspects of Soviet life, concentrating with relish on every thing which had long been forbidden. A non-Communist press emerged from the underground. Publishing was the first area where market forces overcame ideology. The voluntary association memorial, revealed the secrets of Stalin's years of tenor even more dramatically than Solzhenitsyn.

Perestroika 'restructuring' started to seem an old fashioned word. The whole system was being destroyed, not rebuilt. At first there was something exhilarating about it. To see public life awakening and people discarding their fear was moving and impressive; only a few ultra conservatives resisted it. But as the destruction continued it became clear that the country lacked architects with a blue print for the structure which should follow. There were grandiose hopes for a new and effective multi-party pluralism, but there was no one with a clear view of how to build it, and very few builders able and willing to do the work. The politics of alternatives did not turn into the politics of creating a social consensus and institutions which could resolve conflicts peacefully. The end of the Soviet control over Eastern Europe and the collapse of Comcon, the old trading system caused a sharp contraction of mutual deliveries between the member states. Within the Soviet Union the drive for autonomy in the republics and later for full political independence produced more cracks in traditional economic links. The abandonment of the old system of state orders to factories and state allocation of raw materials created a free-for-all in which managers reverted to barter. The economic reformers embraced the notion of a market but found it hard to introduce in conditions of declining output and a monopolized economy where a few enterprises controlled key sectors. Privatization turned into the redistribution of state assets without any mechanism for improving efficiency or increasing production.

Gorbachev's main mistakes were in the political field. He launched a programme of political reform, including a reform of the Communist Party, but was never sufficiently consistent. He missed several chances to enlist democratic allies into a broad coalition of forces in favour of perestroika, yet turned a blind eye to its conservative enemies. He knew there was strong resistance to change within the party, but refused to confront the saboteurs or make an open alliance with the reformers. He kept trying to balance between them, partly because of indecision and partly because he refused to contemplate splitting the part.[13]

Even when issues were put before the Politburo, Gorbachev often pre-empted discussion with the rambling but authoritarian style that he later showed publicly when he presided over the Supreme Soviet. People were being asked not to comment but merely approve what had been done already. The relations between a general secretary and the Politburo had always been difficult. In a Western system of government the president or prime minister chooses his cabinet. In the Soviet Union they chose him and then put the matter to the central committee to ratify. There was no tradition of a clean sweep at the top when a new administration came in. General secretaries spent the first two or three years of their power trying to remove opponents they inherited. Gorbachev proved adept at doing this initially but his use of advisers and brain trusts meant that even potential allies in the Politburo felt excluded. By running his reform compaign like a conspiracy behind the Politburo's back he inevitably built up a reservoir of mistrust. It later encouraged his opponents to plot against him.

For all his personal charm and in spite of his repeated diplomatic surrenders, Gorbachev never broke through the barrier of anti-Sovietism among Western leaders, whatever ordinary people felt. He might be a 'good' Communist but he was still the incarnation of the enemy state, and it was not until Boris Yeltsin replaced Gorbachev, burying both the Soviet Union and Communism in Russia, that Western leaders relaxed. This is not to say that Gorbachev's initial strategy of unilateral moves towards arms control and sweeping offers of a non-nuclear world were native. By undermining the Soviet Union's 'enemy-image' he hoped in part to appeal to western public opinion and the peace movements to put pressure on their governments for an end to the arms race and for cuts in military spending. This strategy worked to an extent. The 1987 treaty eliminting the Soviet SS 20 missiles and the American medium-range nuclear weapons which NATO had managed to deploy in Europe only after massive public protests gave both sides an equally balanced success.

At home his popularity continued to slip. The fact that he was feted abroad and visibly enjoyed the applause seemed to increase his negative image in the Soviet Union. Some of his Politburo colleagues saw it as an escapist dereliction of duty. Gorbachev often said he wanted a revolution 'from below' but when it happened he could not accept it. He never seemed to want to be outflanked on the progressive wing, as though only he, as the leader of perestroika, could decide at what pace it should go. The reformers in the informal politcal clubs had proposed a broad-based alliance for reforms. They said this would replace 'authoritarian perestroika' with 'democratic perestroika'. Later they were matched by reformers in the new Soviet parliament and in the Communist party itself. But

Gorbachev would not agree to a coalition for reform which would align non-Communist reformers with progressive forces in the party. It was as though after giving the green light to grassroots activity he did not dare to accept its advocates as his political equals, let alone as allies. His old instincts as a party apparatchik proved to be too strong. When hostile placards appeared at the May Day parade in 1990, he lost his temper and walked off the reviewing stand above the Lenin mousoleum. In 1991 he referred to demonstrators who assembled outside the Kremlin as 'mobs'.

Gorbachev's failure to understand the nationalism of non-Russians stemmed from the same lack of democratic instincts. he had not spent enough time listening to non-Russians. He could not grasp that Baltic peoples had a different conceptions of Russia from his. He believed the Soviet Union was indeed a new kind of state which made nationalism out of date. Even when his fellow Slavs, the Ukrainians, were preparing to vote for independence in December 1991. Gorbachev was unable to believe it. The result shocked him, and even after the vote he continued to argue that Ukrainians had not opted to leave the Union. One problem was that he hardly ever travelled to the other republics, even after nationalist pressures burst into the open. When he visited Lithuania in January 1990 it was the first time he had been there for ten years. His only trip to the Caucasus as leader was a day trip to Armenia after the earthquake. He even had his enormous Zil limousines flown down to Yerevan for the tour, but Nikolai Ryzhkov, the prime minister, persuaded him to leave them at the airport and use a bus.[14] He lost much of the sympathy his visit was meant to arouse when he addressed a crowd with an attack on the Armenian nationalists who were raising the issue of Nagorno-Karabagh. In Kiev in 1985 he referred to being 'in Russia'.

In the autumn of 1989 the Inter-regional Group of Deputies, the main democratic faction in the newly elected Congress of People's Deputies, proposed that the USSR become a confederation instead of the tight federation it had been since 1922. Their plan, which would have given individual republics greater economic and political rights, chimed in with the spirit of decentralization and greater democracy which Gorbachev's perestroika was aiming to develop. Gorbachev rejected it. Later in April 1991 under pressure from Yeltsin, by then Russia's parliamentary leader, Gorbachev came round to the confederative view. But the loss of a year and a half was a vital factor in increasing the political polarization which eventually spelled Gorbachev's doom. It allowed the pro-empire forces in the army and party who mounted the August coup to grow stronger. They saw his confederation as at best weakness, at worst treachery. On the opposite flank it pushed the anti-party democrats in the Russian parliament more firmly into the Yeltsin camp and against Gorbachev. The president was left with minimal support.

Gorbachev's third major error was his mishandling of Boris Yeltsin. It was the most conspicuous example of one of Gorbachev's key weaknesses, his poor judgement of Boris Yeltsin and his inability to make close friends. Gorbachev could be remarkably insensitive to colleagues. he did have a serious character flaw. He could not brook equals. Gorbachev's excessive trust of subordinates and his excessive mistrust of Yeltsin were not in contradiction. As long as a man was in a definite position below him in the hierarchy, he would tolerate him but he could not, if some one tried to go ahead of him even by dint of his virtues.

In any case if a man was in an undefined role especially if he was also pretending to rivalry, Gorbachev was jealous and would go to any extent in disowning him. In the wider interests of the State, he should have set aside these information and should have taken the first step of reconciliation with Yeltsin. There were many opportunities, but he could never bring himself to offer Yeltsin a post of genuine responsibility or a political alliance. He also had awakward moments with dissidents. Gorbachev was the most democratic minded man who had ever ruled Russia, but he was still not democratic enough to see what was happening beneath him. And there were times when he seemed to want to be the only democrat around.

Yeltsin had an unparalleled opportunity to move Russia towards building new democratic institutions. In many ways he had squandered it. He had not set up his own political party to create a lasting basis of support. He did not introduce a new constitution for Russia early in his term, when he still had a majority backing in parliament. He started to undermine the Russian congress of People's Deputies which he had inherited, even though it was the body which first introduced a democratic separation of powers, with an executive presidency and a constitutional court.[15]

Gorbachev and his Reforms

Never in the lives of men and nations had one human being altered the destinies of so many people in so vast a tract of earth and in so short a time as Mikhail Gorbachev had done in Russia. The man who set about the task of providing a human face to communism—through 'glasnost' providing freedom for the people and 'perestroika', seeking to introduce efficiency into the system which eventually obliterated the face of communism itself. It may rightly be argued that Gorbachev was not a product of history, he was its maker.

Such was the elemental force he generated that no one could stop the course of events. The superpowers moved towards the genuine reduction of forces and weapons, freedom of expression reared its head in Eastern Europe, the Berlin wall collapsed, Germany was reunited, the Warsaw pact got dismantled, Soviet troops left Afghanistan, Communist dictators in East Europe fell one after the other, the dreaded KGB and powerful CPSU collapsed and finally the USSR dissipated giving place to Commonwealth.[16] There are lots of doubts about the commonness of the wealth among members of Commonwealth of Independent States but the man who was the architect of this emerging edifice, became its first victim. The people feel no mercy, 'you do good and no one thanks you', says Torboris Godunov in the epic poem by Pushkin.[17] Gorbachev was communist who banished communism, the reformer who was consumed by reforms, the liberater who fettered himself.[18]

In just over five years Gorbachev turned his country upside down. He gave them (people of Soviet Union) back their horrific history which his predecessors had concealed for sixty years. He ended the cold war that had dominated the world politics, and discovered that he had started a revolution he could not control 'a discovery that led to chaos and tragedy'. Gorbachev emerged in March 1985 from the struggle among his polit-bureau colleagues to become Secretary General of CPSU and the effective leader of Soviet state.[19] He grew up in Communist Party of Soviet Union; he was a party man, instantly recognizable as such by other party men. At that time Soviet Union seemed a very weary, yet immensely powerful country. It was decaying economically, but politically still it appeared to be static.[20] The Russians use the word 'partinost' roughly translatable as 'partyness', to signify qualities connected with party office bearers.[21] Even before they took power, however, Gorbachev and his associates realized their country was stagnating, but they termed it as a 'pre-crisis situation.'[22] So, although, they perceived some crises of effectiveness in the regime, they did not yet comprehend its depth. The regime aimed only at needed reforms. Gorbachev was an improviser and a planner. He had a vision and kept his vision to the end. His immovable goals and rigid political attitude became increasingly unrealistic and dangerous to his own power. Leaders in Communist systems 'campaigned' not in order to achieve power but to consolidate it, once installed. The power of leader was derived as much from personality and ability to promote supporters as from the post occupied.[23] In the process of strengthening his power, Gorbachev had to reckon with the large number of senior officials of Brezhnev era, as well as those promoted during the Andropov period.

Gorbachev's Perceptions of Soviet Crisis: The crisis of Soviet system was certainly 'objective' in nature. Gorbachev's perception of Soviet crisis did change as he became conscious of its much greater depth.[24] Yet, in essence his perception characterised Stalinism as, 'the boil on healthy body of Soviet Socialism'. Gorbachev and his associates believed that organism could be cured and healthy Soviet Union could again demonstrate socialism to its true potential.[25] Through all this Gorbachev never hinted at a loss of faith in Communism. The limited perception about the Soviet crisis by successive regimes in Soviet Union can be exemplified by understanding the relationships among its different nationalities. The republics strongly opposed Russian chauvimism and supported human rights of minorities in Russia and other republics. But in the best Marxist tradition, the Gorbachev leadership did not perceive the real dimension of the problems. To a large extent, it thought the issue would fade once the excesses of Stalin's nationality policy were rectified and a new policy of tolerance introduced. A new stress on democracy was the characteristic of Gorbachev's approach to political reforms in Soviet Union. Gorbachev reversed the trend from 'socialism' to a new ascent to democracy. It was felt that without restoring real democracy in all spheres of life-social, economic and political—there could be no progress towards socialism. 'More democracy more socialism' was the new slogan under Gorbachev.[26] In 28th Congress reports, the new slogan put forward was, for a 'democratic human socialism.' Gorbachev intended to liberalize economy and to provide respectable status to citizens of former USSR.

As soon as Gorbachev came to power, it was postulated by the CPSU leader that there must be a new thinking about world affairs to avert the dangers of a devastating nuclear war. His call for new thinking was only the beginning of the procession of abandonment of Marxism itself. The concept of de-ideologisation put forward by CPSU actually called for giving up the class approach in analysing the international situations. Based on new thinking and de-ideologisation the CPSU soon stopped even references to imperialism, and the national liberation movements. Gorbachev was well aware of prevailing conditions of Soviet society. His object in bringing this to the attention of the nation was to demonstrate the underlying discontent with the conduct of party and government and to show that there was no alternative to going for reforms.[27] He never abandoned the socialistic principles while achieving the economic and social objectives with the help of recent revolution which he tried through 'Perestroika' and 'Glasnost'. He was optimistic that the goals of his reforms may be realised under the guise of socialism. He tried to give a viable solution to the socio-economic problems of USSR with the tactics measurable through socialistic standards.

Legacy of Past: The legacy handed over to Gorbachev in 1985, was an enviable one. Not only had Brezhnev's rule witnessed a declining economic growth rate and stagnant economy besides falling standards of living and growing corruption, but also the basic principles on which the Soviet system was based. It appeared that the system needed radical overhaul when Gorbachev was appointed General Secretary in March 1985. The Soviet leadership faced an array of problems, which were more complex than at any time in the post-war era. These were the following:

(i) Soviet Union was beset by political malaise extending back to the final years of Brezhnev period.

(ii) Economic stagnation in much of Eastern Europe, a political unrest in Poland and counter-revolutions in Afghanistan, Angola, Ethiopia and Mozambique, threatened to undermine the stability of Soviet empire and increase the cost of its maintenance.

(iii) Reagan's defence build up and NATO's modernization of its conventional and thereafter nuclear forces threatened military gains of the 1970s.

(iv) The Soviet Union's status as a 'role model economic development' was being more openly called into question by some developing countries. During the 'personality cult' days, the entire function of political system of Soviet Union over the years, handed over powers and functions to ever expanding bureaucratic structures that stifled public opinion and initiative and weakened the role of vigilant socialist activists. Thus an over simplified image of socialist democracy emerged in world's bastion of socialism. Gorbachev wanted to neutralize the personality factor and wanted to make Soviet decision making machinery more representative.[28]

The nature of the system which Gorbachev inherited was going through overall deformation in which Lenin's principles were deformed by successive Soviet leadership. Other legacy inherited by Gorbachev from his predecessors, was organisation of communist party.[29] Growing ideological and political demarcation within the party gave the important manifestation to the crisis. Main trends existing in communist party, which Gorbachev inherited, were as follows:

1. Conservative Stalinist trend which stood for cosmetic repair of party structure and was against any serious change both in party and society.
2. Moderate reformist (centrist) trend, which was for partial changes, so that there was transformation from direct and open party power to indirect wielding of governmental power by the CPSU within the framework of one party system.
3. Radical reformist trend, which was fighting for radical reforms in the CPSU in the direction of modern democratic party of parliamentary type working in conditions of multiparty system. With the advent of over-centralisation, the Communist Party of Soviet Union became undemocratic and perpetually it was losing the public sympathy and legitimacy. Gorbachev himself was one of the modern reformists.

A full hierarchical structure of party of a totalitarian neostalinist type, was extremely centralised and anti-democratic. The main cementing link in the non-democratic character of the party as well as entire political system, happened to be the principle of democratic centralism. The main features of this principle were that:

(a) it did not guarantee real plurality of opinions within the party and with the help of organisational means did not give the possibility to defend these opinions and criticise adopted decisions;

(b) it did not guarantee the protection of the interests of minority, innovative ideas were often smothered and in this way the party was condemned to permanent stagnation;

(c) it did not give the right of decision to those who were directly concerned and on all questions made the lower organisation duty bound, to submit to the higher one;

(d) it forbade formation of horizontal relationship within the party as a result of which party apparatus became all powerful, uncontrolled and capable of manipulating

the opinion of individual communist as well as entire party organisation;

(e) it dictated iron discipline to comply, disallowing creative activity from below;

(f) it did not allow members of CPSU and elected people's deputies to reflect the will of their electors but were controlled by the will of the higher party organs.

There was nothing like democratic, everything was 'centric', public opinion had no meaning. Towards the end of Brezhnev's leadership-the so called 'years of stagnation'—the CPSU leadership got almost completely alienated from the people. Brezhnev's successors—Andropov and Chernenko—died too early to leave a permanent mark.

The very first meeting of CPSU Central Committee held under Gorbachev leadership in April 1985, chalked out the new path of advance. According to Joe Slovo they (proletariat) have always believed that it is indispensable for working class to have an independent political instrument which safeguards its role in the democratic revolution and which leads it towards an eventual classless society.[30] But such leadership must be won rather than imposed. By the time Gorbachev came to power, the kind and nature of party which he inherited can be briefly summarised in the words of Ravi M. Bakya as follows:[31]

1. Gorbachev inherited a huge party organisation which in 1986 had a membership of over 19 million. This vast membership had become the instrument of bureaucratic command—administrative system in which the Politburo decided the most important questions.
2. The party could be distinguished from the state. Not only were all state leaders also party leaders but even at the lowest level of administration the party 'diktats', were supreme. Article 6 of Soviet Constitution rectified the role of communist party of Soviet Union.
3. The party members owned more wealth and property than any other organisation in the USSR, indeed any other political organisation any where in the world. It owned thousands of buildings, sanatoria, hotels, rest-homes and dachas, hospitals, fleets of cars and so on.

4. Gorbachev also inherited a legacy of secrecy, unknown in any ruling party. The ordinary Soviet citizen did not know where the party leaders lived, what kind of people they were and who were their family members.

5. Gorbachev inherited a repressive state machine which sent thousands to prison, to labour camps and even to mental asylums for crimes of political dissent. Ofcourse, the open violations of the law were nothing compared to Stalin's time, but the laws themselves were loaded against the freedom of expression.

System which Gorbachev inherited, needed the reforms not only in political field, but in all aspects of life including economic and social status of Soviet citizens. There was a wide gap between the rulers and the ruled and the leader and the led. Perverted form of 'democratic centralism', incompetent economy with highly centralised characteristics and other various repressive measures of communist party over citizens, were the features of Soviet communist system when Gorbachev took over the power. Another important source of undemocratic character of party was the nomenclature system or deletion and fixing up of personnel everywhere. A class of party-elite had emerged which had its own cooperative interests. The irresponsible overgrowth of elites with inherent privileges, a section of which was closely connected with black economy and organised crime was another evil which had emerged in the pre-reform days,. Through this 'nomenclature system', the one party system in USSR remained secure, although losing all types of illegitimacy.

Basis of Gorbachev's Reforms

Gorbachev, in the historic drama, emerged out of highly unified net-work of the Soviet political structure. He was installed in power because the central committee felt that a younger and dynamic leader was necessary for stopping the gradual Soviet decline. Trends from late Brezhnev period pointed to economic stagnation, falling growth rates, and increasing technological gaps vis-a-vis the West. The Soviet system was running through problems in meeting the requirements of a modern industrial state with super power status. In remarkably brief period and in a dramatic manner, largely unforeseen, the study of Soviet Union has been transformed from a moribund subject into an exciting, revitalized field. As Seweryn Bialer put it, Soviet Union had become the most interesting country in the world. The building of socialism in Russia was not so much a natural-historical process as the consequences of political will of the Bolshevik party and the ability of its leaders to seize the opportunity to stage the October Revolution and to lead the politically inexperienced and semiliterate masses with their utopian faith in the feasibility of creating a paradise on earth within a short time. The situation was exacerbated by a fierce and disasterous civil war and by an 'un-institutionalised' environment unfavourable to Russia.[32] Such was the form of such socialism turned to irreparable consequence in USSR.

By the time Gorbachev came to power in March 1985, the Soviet Union faced a broad spectrum of economic problems. Looking back, since coming to power, Gorbachev had been intending to make Soviet economy dynamic and efficient. In Soviet Union civilian industrial facilities were, to a large extent, old and technologically obsolete. The rapid advances in computers, transistors, and integrated circuit microchips in the past decade which led to the mass production of high tech products in most developed countries. This which Marshal Goldman called the 'third industrial revolution' had neither been well assimilated in Soviet Union nor diffused effectively throughout new economy. The socialist economy was not consumer oriented economy and was not in a position to meet the growing needs of the ordinary people. Therefore, Soviet economy had collapsed by 1988 for which the reform processes were initiated within the system in mid-eighties.[33] Even after the initiation of 'perestroika' no improvement was achieved, rather by 1986 it had been a dismal failure. The systematic dismantling of the socialist economic foundations, was one of the key factors leading to collapse of socialism and beginning of the process of restoration of capitalism in USSR.[34]

Some analysts have visualised the period of Brezhnev as the 'stagnation period' and Gorbachev started the 'perestroika and glasnost' under this background of 'command economy' built up by Brezhnev.[35] Signs of crisis in Soviet economy looked prominent. Aggravated shortages of basic necessities, were the foremost features by which people of Soviet Union got alienated from Communism. But its very nature, a Soviet type economy—in Johns Karnai's words—had become an 'economy of shortages'. The outstanding change that occurred in the mid 1980s was that the perennial imbalances on the domestic Soviet market were sharply aggravated. Fiscal imbalances and administrative stalemates, etc. were other features of the Soviet economy.

In fact, by mid 1970s the Soviet economy showed declining trends in growth rates. During 1976-85 decade the growth rates of, both the national product and industrial production, declined substantially. There were several reasons which led to deterioration of Soviet economy:

(i) The purchasing power of rouble had gone down and hence collective and state farms and farmers did not want to sell to the government.

(ii) Collective farms and not the state farms were preferred so as to use grain exclusively for barter with industrial constructions and other enterprises, which supplied the needs of agriculture inputs such as tractors, chemicals, plant protection, etc.

(iii) There was absence of parity between industrial and agricultural prices and hence this did not boost interest of farmers to increase output and to increase sales to government.

(iv) There was a serious undesirable trend which was observed in the case of many regions to negotiate a reduction in the procurement contracts as the consequence of heavy losses to producing limits.

Besides, the country had been facing serious problems of budgetary deficit, inflation and balance of payment deficit. The shortages of goods had reached epidemic proportions. Ever widening zone of shortages had reached the most basic of all goods—the bread—compelling the country to seek aid from West. Under such grave situations, the economic reforms were the only alternative to bring the Soviet economy to the respectable place at national and international levels.

These deteriorating economic conditions were giving rise to new processes unknown in Soviet Union in the past and these new phenomena, of course, dangers to Soviet Union's stability, were to be checked. Ethnic plurality led to social and political problems in the Soviet Union, including discrimination and other forms of intolerances. Some hostility on the part of minorities towards the majority and predominant Russians, as well as the language (Russian) was clearly perceptible in day-to-day life. The Soviet Union had been undergoing an aging process, which was caused by a natural demographic consequence of declining fertility and continued low mortality. The issue of health of Soviet population and resultant mortality levels of Soviet Union had generated considerable interest.

Pointing to the real causes which led to the mess, the document of communist party, entitled "Developments in Soviet Union and Eastern Europe", stated, that the present mess was the result of basic flaws of the model of socialism constructed in the Soviet Union, which the Gorbachev leadership had inherited. It further stated that, what was built in the Soviet Union was socialism, albeit highly distorted and perverted. In fact, it was socialism with 'anti-democratic and bureaucratic features'. The document enlisted the following political features of Soviet Communist System:

1. It (Party) established State monopoly ownership of the total means of production, exchange and distribution. The working class and working people were alienated from the products of their labour and means of production.

2. A totalitarian political structure from top to bottom was established in which total absence of freedom and democratic rights was there. In earlier years, whenever the question of individual rights was raised, it was suggested that freedom of individual was restricted under the state of the 'dictatorship of the proletariat'—the answer used to be that freedom from 'exploitation

was highest freedom', and the individuals possessed this freedom under the state of 'proletariat'. Thus 'freedom of individual was completely identified with freedom of exploitation'. In the name of freedom of individual, the USSR constitution declared: In confirmity with the interest of working people, and in order to strengthen the Socialist system, the citizens are guaranteed by law; (i) freedom of speech, (ii) freedom of press, (iii) freedom of street procession and demonstration. People were forced to follow the will of the Government and their own ideology had no meaning in the face of Communist ideology. In this context Stalin and post-Stalin excesses over innocent people were examples when the state officials violated the rights for personal gains.

3. The leading role and hegemony of party was imposed on society, which later, in Brezhnev era was constitutionally embodied. This meant that the overwhelming majority of the people, non-party masses and intelligentsia were excluded from participation in governance, in state functions and leading layers of the economy.
4. Inside the party, in the name of democratic centralism, bureaucratic centralism was evolved in the real sense. Absence of democratic choice led to a group of self-perpetuating leaders.
5. Through the party structure and the fusion of state party functions a minority, or even an individual, exercised dictatorship over the overwhelming majority of the party membership.
6. The party state and its bureaucratic substratum, appropriates and disposes the surplus in the economy. At the lower level, the workers individually or collectively did not have any autonomy.

The totality of these negative phenomena in economic, social and political systems of USSR, became an in-built feature of socialism founded in USSR decades back. Further, negative phenomena were putting strains on Soviet Communist System and compelled the Soviet leadership to initiate the reform processes so as to make socialist society viable.

Background of the Reforms

The Gorbachevite reformers were confronted with some of the consequences of the prolonged period of self satisfied drift of Brezhnev period. This period can be understood as the apogee of what has been called the social contract policies of the new Stalinist compromise. This was a system that emerged after Stalin's death in 1953, predicted on the continuation of the Stalinist socio-economic system but stripped of its terroristic features and its most inflexible economic policies. Since World War II, one can distinguish seven attempts of reforms, which can be grouped into three periods. The first period contained first and second waves of reforms. The first wave included changes made during the Malekov period. There was a reduction in and then a revival of industrial ministries in 1953 and 1954, the splitting of GOSPLAN, and establishment of 'Gosekonomkommissiya' in 1955.

The second wave included the Khrushchev era. The second reforms period began after the 22nd party Congress in October 1961. It also included Khrushchev's third wave of reforms. The third reforms period began in July 1979 with Brezhnev's efforts. The reform process in Soviet Union started effectively after the death of Stalin, i.e., by Khrushchev. Khrushchev, until his ousting in 1964, had modified some of Stalin's policies. The vast prison population was reduced and Stalin's 'personality cult' and the purges were condemned in Khrushchev's secret speech at both Congress of February 1956 and again in 1961. At 22nd party Congress, Khrushchev also sought to establish a new balance in Soviet system between coercion and mass participation. He also sought to modify the vast concentration of economic power, in the hands of the ministries based in Moscow. Khrushchev established 'Sovnarkhozy' (regional economic councils) in 1957. Party apparatus was altered to be organised in strict accordance with the production principle and committees on party and state control were announced.

According to some analysts the wage reforms of 1956-61 were perhaps the most important policy change which saw a few amendments under Brezhnev. The system, determining norms and wages, was changed which had remained basically unchanged since long. The reforms raised the basic wage rates, output quotas, and piece workers were switched from progressive piece rates to bonuses.[36]

Brezhnev era began with his accession in September 1964. Brezhnev initiated reforms with 'policy of Stability' in party cadre. In last years of Brezhnev period, Soviet economy was on its way to collapse and Brezhnev observed it clearly and felt the need of the effective reforms in the existing system. Brezhnev's report to 26th CPSU congress mentioned 'glasnost' as an effective means of strengthening the party's ties with masses. As the leadership was not prepared to abandon the old Stalinist administrative command, the reforms could not make much progress.[37]

Under Andropov a new law on work-collectives was adopted and a limited economic reform experiment was launched in five industrial ministries. At June 1983 CPSU Central Committee plenum, Andropov used the phrase-words are never at variance with deeds while stressing the importance of 'glasnost'. Therefore, as Gorbachev came to power in Soviet Union, platform for reforms was already established. In fact, Gorbachev, being the member of politburo, had recognised the need for reforming the Soviet Communist System. On coming to power, Gorbachev still had many options to reform the Soviet system, the most likely of which included:

1. A reversion to the war communism method of economic control.
2. A continuation, without significant change of Soviet-type model inherited from Andropov.
3. An introduction of decentralized variant of the current system, such as Polish WOG reform of the 1970's.
4. A replication of the Hungarian economic model.
5. The implementation of the Yugoslav economic model.

Table: Stages of Economic Reforms in USSR: 1953-86

Reforms period and events	Chronology 1953-61	1961-79	1979-86
(*a*) Announcement of political programme	August 1953	22nd Congress of CPSU	July 1979
(*b*) Announcement of reforms programme	March 1953	November 1962	July 1979
(*c*) Establishment of central management body over planning Council	May 1953 establishment of Gose-konommissiya	1963 establishment of Supreme Council of national economy	
(*d*) Growth of No. of Central Adminis-trative institutions	Increase in number of industrial ministries (18%)	Increase in number of state committees (100% from 16 to 32)	Increase in number of state committees (12 to 18)

Source: Wladyolaw W. JermaKoniez, "Foundations and Prospects for Soviet Economic Reforms" in Ronald D. Liebowitz (ed.), Gorbachev's New Thinking: Prospects for Joint-venture, Ballinger Publishing Company, Cambridge, 1988, p. 119.

Gorbachev's contributions to world lexicon are the two Russian terms-'perestroika' and 'glasnost'—which today have acquired a world wide common currency requiring no translation in any language any more. These concepts suggested two vital comprehensive and inter linked processes of transformation of socialism according to Marxism-Leninism, in the Soviet Union, namely over all socio-economic and political changes in an atmosphere of openness of debate, discussion and decision making.

The 'perestroika' is ambiguous and its two sides are reflected in debate of whether it should be called a reform or revolution. 'Perestroika' was more than a political revolution, led by Gorbachev and his group. The distinctive feature of 'perestroika' is, in Gorbachev's words, a 'revolution within revolution'. Communist reformism was based on the belief that the system of communist power could be humanised and democratised to allow the flowering of human endeavour in arts, sciences and economy. Gorbachev's plan for economic restructuring and political reforms in the early period stressed the party's role in ushering change and socialist renewal. He stated that, 'party must be engine of perestroika' as 'Perestroika' was a multifaceted programme covering several dimensions.[38]

To start with, he said in its politico-legal dimension, it sought to reform state structure, governmental functioning and administrative procedures tried to introduce revised electoral system based upon plurality of choice and to restore the rule of law. In the economic dimension, 'perestroika' entailed the inculcation of management skills and work efficiency, introduction of cost counting culture of self management in the entire process of socialist agricultural development and industrialisation. 'Perestroika' as a social and moral dimension emphasised respect for socio-cultural diversity and autonomy of nationalities and ethnic groups, promotion of creative and innovative spirit in educational, scientific and intellectual activities. At international level 'perestroika' involved radical new thinking in the realm of inter-state diplomacy, bilateral and multilateral relations, security and strategic consideration, trade, UN and other agencies.

Besides the above stated ideals which were to be achieved through 'perestroika', there were three main goals of 'perestroika' which Gorbachev underlined as follows:

1. Radical reforms of management of the economy, in order to bring about qualitative changes in system of economic mechanism which would open up new possibilities for using the advantages of the socialist economic and production system;
2. The aim of accelerating social and economic developments to over-come the lag that had accumulated and deformations that had appeared in various fields of society's comprehensive development; and
3. The first priority items were to be provision of food, housing, consumer goods and services.

Gorbachev tried to adopt Leninist approach to revolutionise whole production machinery of Soviet Union. He related

Perestroika with the pure form of democracy. However, he ignored the widening gap between various communist party factions on one hand and common people on the other, for which he had to repent later on. It was under the banner of 'glasnost' that the reformist spirit of the Gorbachev era was first introduced. The 'glasnost' referred to a policy aimed at increasing access to information, thereby reducing the veil of censorship and 'secrecy' that had long smothered Soviet Society. Glasnost became the word to describe a broad range of policies designed to expose Soviet Society to criticism and self-criticism. Glasnost literally is derived, from the verb 'glasit', meaning 'to say', and, as noun connotes, 'speaking out publicly'.[39]

Major feature of 'glasnost' was the lifting of most restrictions on the circulation of information. Censorship had been relaxed, though not abolished. In the process of 'glasnost', many of intelligentsia understood the risk of political instability but remained within the regime taking up reforms boldly with the result, it allowed the press to look at Soviet reality in a new and more critical manner. 'Glasnost' allowed controversies to be aired publicly. It had opened the doors of interaction between party and government on one hand and mass of Soviet people on the other. Therefore, 'glasnost' was adopted for the supervisory role and for the public participation, in the sense not to control but to supervise over the workings of state apparatuses, somewhat akin to the role envisaged by Lenin for the organs of workers control in factories in 1918. This proves that Gorbachev tried to put communism on the right track on the fundamental principles of Marxism-Leninism. Need of hour in Soviet Union was democratisation of all governmental institutions vis-a-vis communist party of Soviet Union.

In the path of reformation of communist party, two stages were discussed in 28th Congress of CPSU.

1. Transfer of governing power from monopolistic ruling party to the Soviets, and democratization of party; and
2. Transformation of CPSU into a parliamentary party working in conditions of multi-party system and a lawful parliamentary state.

'Perestroika' and 'glasnost' as first stage of renovation, saw gradual and growing criticism of the past and the present of Soviet society, quests for the causes of the ailments and deformations of socialism, and an awakening of social consciousness and political activities at grassroot levels. Ultimate goals of reform processes, that is 'perestroika' and 'glasnost' and criteria of their realization, were all-round democratization of society, the granting of rights to all adult people and people's involvement in policy formulation and decision-making. The task was to dismantle the authoritarian bureaucratic system of the party apparatuses and to restore a civic society.

The overwhelming majority of population accepted and supported the above mentioned aims of the political reforms and opinions on the ways and pace of attaining them remained highly contradictory. As measures, continuously they were tried to prevent the economy of Soviet Union from going beyond the stagnation level. These two objectives were achieved in economic rejuvenation through 'perestroika' and openness of CPSU and democratization of inner party life through 'glasnost'. A move towards multiparty system, sustaining the right to criticism and information, were the measures adopted at grassroot levels, which partially helped in bringing up the latest consequences, i.e. a total demise of USSR. Several critics mentioned that 'glasnost', as a process to open up the Soviet society had certain limitations, due to which Soviet society was deformed.

The first phase of 'glasnost' devoted itself to the hesitant but increasingly bold exposure of past wrongs, present dangers, the years of lies and evils on a stupendous scale. After a few years, however, it became clear that a society cannot live on a diet of exposure alone. It was evident that the analytical process which could expose certain aspects of the past, but was not able to examine their source openly or more accurately was highly unsatisfactory. Richard Sakwa in his studies observed that, even though the language of reforms exposed real internal problems in the system, there were limits to permit criticism. The gulf between permitted criticism and social and political realities was still not fully abridged. The major achievement of 'glasnost' was the reconstitution of intelligentsia as a free thinking and relatively independent groups to act as counter-weight to bureaucracy and administrative system 'Perestroika' helped through transformation of the socio-cultural structure of society.

Why Did Gorbachev Fail?

From 1985 onward, Gorbachev was beset by his own shortcomings. Besides the mass scale support, controversies surfaced against the methods of, Gorbachev's reforms of 'perestroika', 'glasnost' and demokratria. In fact, Gorbachev's reforms were not revolutionary or systematic, they attacked the system from all sides, and a number of issues were raised simultaneously. First and foremost cause which contributed to failure of Gorbachev was shortage of time, i.e., Gorbachev went very fast and wanted to change the whole system quickly. The democratization of the consciousness of masses, was not marked to the point of their revolutionisation, to the point of creating a powerful mass support in favour of reforms.[40]

Other grave mistake made by Gorbachev was the error of assessment and action. Gorbachev was not able to choose right side and associates in the reform mechanism, a serious disability for a political revolutionary, trying to push such a giant nation in a new direction. While the unity of pro-perestroika was not formed, reform movement was poorly organised.[41] Gorbachev should have established a party of pro-perestroika communists and led it into action, so that public support could have been attained and mass of population could have become aware of reform advantages. Prospect of reforms were not made clear to public and Gorbachev got muddled with intra party forces, so much so that no attention was paid in the direction of reforms.

Another major error which Gorbachev committed was that he did not understand the nationality problem properly. Nation-class relationship was seen as a hostile one. Right to information was given at once, without reforming the governing process and maintaining equitable distribution of opportunities in governance among different nationalities. That means, the need of hour was to reform governing mechanism first of all. Gorbachev's inability to drag off any positive economic results, was disasterous for his standing in the country. Because of his failure to produce goods that people wanted, the 'old guard reactionaries' who felt defeated by first year of Gorbachev's rule, came openly and challenged Gorbachev's authority.

In the process of reformation, time and again, he talked about openness but he did not raise any objection when it was sacrificed during troops assault in Lithuania and criticised both by the party and the public. Therefore, Gorbachev's political status and credibility declined tremendously in his own country as well as in the socialist world. He was appreciated abroad and criticised in his own country for the failure of his policy of perestroika. A number of causes can be stated for the failure of Gorbachev, like allowing foreign capitalists to produce goods in USSR, approaching the West by sending his people to the USA and elsewhere to study the market economy, etc., which may be described as part and parcel of reformism. It is a reality that 'perestroika' and 'glasnost' cannot be blamed for the misfortunes in the Soviet Union. It was Soviet Communist System which could not adapt to socialistic revolutions which were desirable and required since the death of Lenin. Reform processes were exhausted because of internal set-up conditions of socialist system which emerged in its over seventy years of existence.

Strains to socialist system were not only internal but external factors also contributed in degradation of socialist system. So-called liberal democratic system of West remained always an opponent to socialist system. Ideological differences isolated the two blocs and gave birth to the cold war. West, which was relatively powerful than East, arose collectively against the socialist system of East. Gorbachev was the lonely example of Soviet leadership, who dared to revolutionise the Soviet system after October Revolution in 1917, which was needed in the early history of communism but unfortunately, instead of reforming the system socialism—as theory of economic development—collapsed. The ultimate reason was that the people who had seen the socialist system could not adapt to the conditions of changing world with desirable speed. 'Glasnost' and democratisation for Gorbachev, was means to an end. The end was improvement of Soviet economic performance. Economic reforms were the central feature of the programme but due to some misunderstanding and misjudgement of conditions, Gorbachev could not succeed. Economic system collapsed in 1988. Thereafter the adoption of 'perestroika' was an utter failure.

Impact of Reforms on Eastern Europe

The wind of 'perestroika' and 'glasnost' had become a hurricane sweeping through Eastern Europe, bringing political revolutions and fore-shadowing the end of Europe's division. Gorbachev initiated systematic change, sought to democratise the USSR and the Communist Eastern Europe, thereby sounding the death-knell for totalitarian communist rule and also knocking out the very basis of ideological divide between the two adversarial blocs. The extra-ordinary significance of this historic event lies in the fact that, the German Democratic Republic (GDR), once it felt relieved of the Soviet ideological hold formed union with West Germany and ended the barriers in Central Europe. Likewise the East European countries gave up the communist authoritarian system and moved towards liberal democratic system existing in Western countries.

Gorbachev made it clear that it was not only the Soviet communist system which had become sick but entire communist Eastern Europe needed the reorientation programmes in all spheres of life. It is noteworthy that Gorbachev did not argue much about the Chinese Communist system. One important reason for that was emergence of Sino-Soviet cold-war. There was almost negligible intimacy between former USSR and China and Eastern Europe was entirely dependent on USSR for over-all development. Therefore, if USSR itself had come under socio-economic crisis, the implications for allied communist bloc were obvious to be disastrous. So far as establishment of communist regimes in East European countries was concerned, the system was relatively newer than that of Soviet communist system as the former came into being only after second world war.[42] The communism came in East Europe, as an imposed hot house plant rather than the natural growth from the soil.

The countries of the region became communist because Stalin claimed them as spoils of war. Communist parties came to power in Russia and then in Eastern Europe and elsewhere, with the promise that scientific socialism would pioneer new dimensions of freedom, eliminate exploitation, vest political power in masses eradicate nationalism and raise standards of living to unprecedented heights. These countries faced almost similar kinds of problem like economic crisis, ethnic and linguistic diversities and above all Stalinism in governing mechanism. West bloc, with which they were engaged in cold war, was more advanced and developed. The principle governing factor defining the relationship between Soviet Union and Eastern Europe was the legacy of nearly fifty years of Soviet domination and occasional resort to brutal force creating a tradition of bitterness and hostility.

The states of Eastern Europe became the allies of one super power. The people of region, meanwhile, were regarded as spiritual allies of the former USSR by the West. There were four issues in policy agenda which determined the relationship between the Soviet Union and the East European countries. These four issues given by Michael Kraus, are as follows:[43]

(i) The opportunity cost of Soviet subsidies to East Europe;

(ii) The quality of East European machinery and goods imported by the Soviet Union;

(iii) Relationship between East European performance, political stability and bloc cohesion; and

(iv) The nexus between economic performance and the requirement of Warsaw pact military planners.

The arms race and security measures in post world war II era made Soviet Union so weak that the domestic industrial production was not capable even to meet the indigenous demands of Soviet society, what to talk about that of East European countries. Under such situations, Soviet Union had no other option but to redefine trade parameters with East European countries. At this point of time, to make communism viable under present circumstances Soviet Union might have helped in bringing up the industrial infrastructure of these countries to a higher level so that these countries could retain comparative self-reliance. Ironically, Western World was economically very powerful and succeeded in sustaining desirable growth rate besides going for arms race. It compelled the communist world to increase the defence budget tremendously, which sidetracked the overall developmental process and investment in productive sector fell substantially. This was one of the major reasons which paralysed whole communist economy except that of China and a few others.

The East European countries achieved the so called independence after their revolutions in 1989 in which Poland was first in early 1989 followed by Czechoslovak revolution and then others. The traditional pattern of economic relations with the Soviet Union changed dramatically. Warsaw Treaty Organisation which was a military alliance and was used as an instrument of political integration, was diluted. In July 1989, at the Warsaw Pact Summit, Gorbachev declared that, each party was totally independent and evoked a looser and more pluralistic communist alliance in which each country was free to pursue its own policies in accordance with national conditions while learning from the experiences of its neighbours.

The change in policy of Soviet leadership towards the Socialist bloc came as a result of 'New Thinking' of Gorbachev in determining the Soviet Foreign Policy. Demilitarizations affected not only international relations but communist policies as a whole. Gorbachev had observed that Eastern Communist world could not run without Western assistance. This was really unfortunate that Gorbachev activated reforms aimed at Western societies and instead of reorganisation of communist forces first, he moved towards West blindly which later on did not prove true friend.[44]

The Soviet leadership had to fight with the incredible legacies of the socialist system; it could not continue the hold on its allied countries and these allied countries became well aware of the problems and crises generated within the socialist system, with the result that critics of communism in East European countries raised their heads. The socialist countries initiated their individual reforms on Hungarian and Yugoslav models, decentralized model of Poland and GDR etc; to reform the socialist system in their respective countries. Since there was no concrete solution to this basic problem of economics, the East European malaise was there to stay in communist system for the foreseeable future.

The emancipatory project initiated by Gorbachev has had wide ranging repercussions within the Socialist World. It inspired and encouraged the people of Eastern Europe to topple the tyrannical regimes led by communist parties in Czechoslovakia, Hungary, Romania and Poland. In China also

Gorbachev's visit during 1989 acted as a catalyst in emboldening students who eventually launched a non-violent protest to enlarge democratic rights in China. As is well known this was severely repressed by Chinese authority leading to massacre of thousands of protesters. Gorbachev relied much on the principles of liberal democracy as compared to Socialist Democracy. Though, he tried to bring revolution to strengthen the scientific socialism through Marxism-Leninism yet he kept quiet when whole of Eastern Europe was sweeping through complete overturn of communism.[45] The socialist regimes, instead of fulfilling the promise of prosperity and modernization managed only to create a 'rough equality of poverty' while maintaining severe controls on the exercise of civil rights.

Therefore, there were chronic social tensions being faced by these socialist countries and reforms within system were indigenous and inevitable need of the system. With Gorbachev's rise to the helm of CPSU in 1985, Soviet Union abandoned its long standing policy of confrontation with the West to seek accommodation and cooperation. In East European countries which were already suffering from unprecedented crises, these changes kindled hopes of greater independence and meaningful social reforms. Gorbachev's leadership had changed the Soviet policy towards East Europe taking into account the widely different local political aid economic circumstances. It is clear that, the programmes of Soviet domestic reforms had legitimized the hope of reforms in East Europe, strengthening the ranks of reform-oriented elements in the region in the process.

Gorbachev turned the Brezhnev doctrine on its head to exert pressure for political and economic change in Eastern Europe, rather than to support liberalization and democratisation. Therefore, the 'perestroika' and 'glasnost' initiated in Soviet Union paved the way for mobilisation of the socialist movements in East Europe which subsequently posed a threat to the whole communist regime after getting out of hand. The turmoil in Eastern Europe also received boost from the winding down of cold war tensions and development of new paradigm of international relations.[46] However, once in motion, the process of change in these countries had been carried forward by its own momentum.

REFERENCES

1. Manorma Kohli, *'Disintegration of the Soviet Union, Implications for India'*, India Quarterly, Vol. XLIX, July-Sept 1993, No. 3, p. 85.
2. Peter M.E. Volten, *'Security Dimensions of Imperial Collapse'*, *Problems of Communism*, Vol. XVI, Jan-April 1992, p. 137.
3. Lleon Wofsy, *'Gorbachev's New Thinking and World Politics'*, Monthly Review (New York), Vol. 40, No. 5.
4. Valamidir G. Khoros, *'Perestroika and the History of Russia'*, Mainstream, Jan 18, 1992.
5. *Ibid.*
6. Anuradha M. Chenoy, *'Systematic Change and Systematic Collapse,* Seminar 393, May 1992, p. 18.
7. Stanley Hoffmann: *Contemporary theory in International Relations,* Englewood Cliffs, New Jersey: Prentice-Hall, 1964.
8. *Ibid.*
9. K.W.Thompson: *Political Realism and the Crisis of World Politics:* An American Approach to Foreign policy.
10. E.H.Carr: *International Relations between Two World Wars, 1919-39,* London: Macmillan, 1952.
11. *Ibid.*
12. K.J.Holsti: *International Politics: A Framework for Analysis,* New Delhi: Prentice-Hall of India, 1978.
13. *Ibid.*
14. Stoessinger: *The Might of Nations: World Politics in Our Time,* New York, 1969.
15. Cecil V. Crabb, Jr.: *Nations in a Multipolar World,* New York: Harper and Row, 1968.
16. V.N. Narayanan, Quoted in, *'Man of History'*, The Tribune, Dec. 8, 1992,
17. *Ibid*
18. Robert G. Keiser, *'Gorbachev: Triumph and Failure', Foreign Affairs,* Vol. 70, No. 2, Spring, 1991, p. 160.
19. Sewergn Bialer, *'Death of Soviet Communism', Foreign Affairs,* Vol. 70, No. 5, Winter 1990-91, p. 166.
20. Robert G. Kaiser, *Op. Cit.*, p. 160.
21. *Ibid.*

22. Richard Sakwa, *"Gorbachev and His Reforms 1985-90'*, Prentice Hall, New York, 1990, p.11.

23. *Ibid*.

24. Mohit Sen, *'The Remaining of Gorbachev'*, Linc News Weekly, Dec. 29, 1991, p. 22.

25. Gennadi Zoleyeve, *'Catalyst of Economic Reforms of USSR'*, *Social Sciences:* Quarterly Review, Vol. 21, No. 4, 1990, p. 34-35.

26. Sunil Maitra, *'Some Aspects of the Historical Experience of Socialism in Soviet Union'*, The Marxists, Vol. 9, (3-4), July-Dec 1991, p. 26.

27. P. Ramachandran, *'Ideology: How the CPSU leadership Abandoned Marxism'*, The Marxist, p. 23.

28. Robert E. Leggett and Robert E. Kellogg, *'The Soviet Union: An Economy in Transition and its Prospects for Eco. Growth'*, Cambridge, 1980, p. 28.

29. Rasheeduddin Khan, *'Perestroika: An Overview'*, World Focus-Monthly Discussion Journal, Vol. 9, 10-11-12, Oct-Nov-Dec, 1988, p.4.

30. Joe Slovo, *'Has Socialism Failed?'* Linc News Weekly, Vol. 35, No. 11, Nov. 1, 1992, p. 37.

31. Ravi M. Bakaya, *'Crisis in CPSU: Causes and Consequences'*, Mainstream, Vol. 29, No. 50, Oct 5, 1991, p. 15.

32. William Smimov, *'Democratisation in the USSR: Its Domestic and Global Aspects'* Social Sciences, Vol. 22, No. 2, 1991, p. 88.

33. S.M.Patil, *'Recent Changes in Theory and Practices in Socialism: A General Survey,'* Indra Quartrly—A Journal of Interntional Affairs, Vol. 48, No. 3, Jan-Sept, 1992, p. 17.

34. R.G. Gidadhubli, *'Uncertain Future of Economy'*, World Focus-Monthly Discussion Journal, Vol. 12, Nos. 9,10 Sept.-Oct. 1991, p. 24.

35. Arun Ghosh, *'End of Socialism'*, Economic and Pol. Weekly, Vol. 25, No. 51, Dec. 22, 1990, p. 2758.

36. Krishenendu Ray and Ravi Sundram, *'Socialism at the End of Century-Reflections of an Epoch Past'*, EPW, Vol. 25, No. 30, July 28, 1990, p. 1658.

37. Devendra Kaushik, *'Political Reforms—A Balance Sheet'*, World Focus: Monthly Discussion Journal Vol. 9, No. 10-11-12 Oct-Nov-Dec. 1988, p. 13.

38. Prakash Karat, *'Gorbachevian Reforms, Dismantling the Communist Party'*, The Marxist, p. 54.
39. Rusel Bova, *'Political Dynamics of the Post-Communist Transition-A Comparative Perspective'*, World Politics—A Quarterly Journal of International Relations, Vol. 44, Oct. 1991, p. 48.
40. Gennadizoleyev, *'Catalyst of Economic Reforms in USSR'*, Social Sciences Quarterly Review, Vol. 21, No. 4, 1991, p. 34-35.
41. Pijush Som, *'Perestroika and After: A Critique of Developments in Soviet Union'*, Mainstream, Vol. 30, No. 24, April 4, 1992, p. 27.
42. K.R. Bombwall, *'Turmoil in Eastern Europe'*, Current Topics, March 1990, p. 149.
43. Michael Kraus, *'Gorbachev's Reform in Eastern Europe'*, Ballinger Publishing Co, Cambridge, 1988, p. 162.
44. Quoted in Bennett Kovrig, *'Housing Time: Emancipation of Eastern Europe'*, Intrnational Journal, Spring 1991, p. 282.
45. Bennett Kovrig, *Op. Cit.*, p. 245.
46. Andre, Gundar Frank, *'East European Revolution in 1989—Lessons of Democratic Social Development*, EPW, Vol 25, No. 5, Feb. 3, 1990, p. 251.

6

CONCLUSION: AN END OR A NEW BEGINNING

The end of cold war marked the end of interstate conflicts that dominated the world since 1945 and at a later stage by the Soviet-US nuclear confrontation. However, two obvious prospective issues were whether this marked an end of great power military rivalry at least for a generation or whether a new pattern of interstate blocs would emerge to replace the old. But one thing appeared certain that major military confrontation or the threat there of was now almost over. As for hegemony, there appeared a situation of great fluidity in which no bloc of states seemed likely to emerge to match the US. All would go well if the US itself would be reluctant to play the unipolar role which the collapse of the USSR had allotted to it. The future seemed to be uncertain and the US may create more problems with consequences which could constitute a threat to peace.

The second dimension of the end of cold war was the end of communism as a political force. But it was a phenomenon confined to Europe; the trends within China indicated a move towards capitalism if not liberalism and the remaining communist states like Cuba, Vietnam, North Korea were unable to provide an international alternative. Two questions arose in this connection, first, what was the future of an alternative to capitalism?, second, what was the historical role of the whole communist experience? As regards the first it seemed that no programme of political challenge to liberal capitalism was visible and the communist revolutionary challenge was exhausted. But it was certain that emergence of social democracy in the wake of the failure of communism did not appear to be a possibility. Perhaps the existing system would get refined and assume a more acceptable form in which both the evils of capitalism and the excesses of socialist system would be non-existent. As regards the role of the communist experience it would remain a matter of historical memory that a situation arose in which communism with all its fallacies was accepted as a means to emancipate the exploited classes. But, ideologies never die and communism may again raise its head if the society continues to suffer from the pangs of social injustice which now the masses could not take lying down. It would continue to be a challenge for the ideology that had replaced communism to continue to adopt mass oriented welfare schemes. In other words it would have to strive to bring about the Marx's exploitationless society which was his ideal.

Factors Responsible for the Collapse of Communism

The collapse of communism was due to many factors like resentment of people against the corrupt dictatorship, misuse of power by the Communist Party leaders and activists, slow rate of economic growth, shortfall of production of consumer goods, people's desire for freedom, democracy and better quality of life and awareness of rosy economic picture in the USA and Western Europe. Socialism and dictatorship went together instead of socialism and democracy in the communist countries. Though communism had abolished to a great extent poverty, unemployment, illiteracy and exploitation yet the people in the communist countries were enamoured by the western life-style in socio-economic and political fields. Rise of a new middle class in these countries led to the craze for economic comforts and political freedom. All these factors contributed to the collapse of communism in the Soviet Union and the Eastern Europe.

Soviet Union: Its Decline and Ideological Fall

After the Second World War, despite a self-imposed conceptual ban, it did not appear that Soviet Union would so soon disintegrate. The Soviet Union was not perceived in the context of other empires which had fallen apart in Europe after the First World War and definitely not in the context of the decolonisation after the Second World War which brought about the end of the British, French, Dutch, Belgian and Portuguese colonial empires. The USSR on the other hand, was recognised as a normal state, a world power with a stable political system. However, its disintegration came about unexpectedly.

In this context two main facts should be emphasised. First, the fall of the USSR was not the result of the last war and, in no way, the consequence of external influences. In this respect, it differed from the collapse of a number of former world empires such as the Roman Empire or Byzantine. The main cause of the end of the Soviet Union was due to the country's internal developments. There was no extensive internal unrest and civil war: indeed the use of force and bloodshed played a secondary role. The causes for the down fall were rooted on the one hand in the designed errors of the Soviet Union and on the other hand in the process of degeneration which had been undermining the stability for decades.

The end of the Soviet Union was the second dissolution of the Russian Empire. It had already fallen apart in 1917 as Czar dictatorship giving place to a new regime which though dictatorship in form professed to practise a new ideology known as communism. In the post 1917 period the new government continued to face several ethnic problems which subsequently became so acute that the communist governments, despite their best efforts could not cope with it and finally succumbed to it. It may be recalled here that in 1991 the non-Russian national movements as throughout Europe-played a major role in the disintegration of the Russian Empire. It is one thing to plead for equal rights being given to the ethnic-linguistic and religious minorities and quite a different matter to allow these groups to dismember nation states and make ethnicity, language and religion the bases of state power. In case of the Soviet Union the political system could not accommodate the grievances of the minorities which later started claiming statehood. If the system had attended to problems of sub-national groups discreetly, the situation would not have become so acute as to challenge the sovereignty of the central government.

Collapse of Soviet Bloc

What happened in the Soviet Union in the late 1980s is of special significance. In a bloc of states dominated by the USSR, which had since the 1940s been engaged in great power competition with the west and which had in the form of the USSR itself been challenging the western world since 1917 the political system collapsed. It occurred without any inter-state war in a very short span of time and without the presence of any form of political vanguards or opposition organisations and without much bloodshed. Moreover, in contrast to other revolutions since 1789, which had to some degree, claimed to defy the international norms or advocate something 'new' those propounding changes in the context of Soviet system did not claim to set up a new world order in place of the existing one. They rather wanted conformity to the old order with rapid and painless transition.

Historians have come to realise that the significance of the event rightly suggests that 1989 brought to the end a period of history that began in 1789 with French Revolution. What was new about the contemporary situation is that in the countries ruled by communist countries (1988: 1.7 billion). There was no certainty as to what kind of government would emerge. It would depend on how the democratic societies react towards these events and helps it to take a course of action which would ultimately be in the interest of the entire mankind. This is going to be a big challenge to the statesmanship of the western world which has to realise how far the post-disintegration situation in Russia had given them what they needed namely the end of cold war and the elimination of the threat of Soviet expansionism.

Assumptions of Marxism

The international developments after Marx clearly suggested that on two counts his predictions had failed. Since Marx wrote, his assumption that the bourgeoisie state would be destroyed by proletarian uprising had proved to be wrong. The rapid speed of industrialisation in European countries had phenomenally raised the living standards of the workers. This had obviated their desire to rise against the exploitation and miseries of the bourgeoisie state thus weakening the strength of the communist movements. Secondly, his belief that the communist revolution would break out in a comparatively developed country turned out to be an illusion as actually it is in the most backward of the European countries that revolution took place. In this context we can say that Russia was an agricultural country and also it was the most religious country in Europe.

Since the end of the Second World War, it is true that a number of communist regimes were established in Eastern Europe and Asia. But all except Yugoslavia, China, Vietnam and Cuba were imposed by the force of Russian arms, they did not emerge out of popular revolution. One of the major features of communism since 1917 has been the substantial control exercised by the Soviet Union, both in terms of ideological orthodoxy as well as in its practical application.

However, this authority has been steadily eroded by a number of events. First, the nationalistic movements had challenged the Soviet Union's position in Eastern Europe on a number of occasions, notably by Yugoslavia, Poland, Hungary and Czechoslovakia. Secondly, Khrushchev's denunciation of Stalin (in 1956) weakened the position of superiority of Soviet leadership and also in Moscow's ideological infallibility. Thirdly, China emerged as an alternative Mecca for the faithfuls and a more realist practitioner in the art of Marxist revolution for the peoples of the under developed countries than the highly industrialised country of the Soviet Union.

Changes in Eastern Europe

Among the changes introduced by Gorbachev in the Soviet politics, his role in the Eastern European affairs was quite significant. Until 1989, the Soviet Union's determination to preserve communism in Eastern Europe was not in doubt. The Soviet Army had intervened in East Germany in 1953, Hungary in 1956 and Czechoslovakia in 1968 to crush challenges to orthodox communist rule under the so called Brezhnev doctrine. Soviet leaders argued that they had both a right and a duty to intervene, whenever the gains of socialism were threatened. But within a few years of taking office Gorbachev reversed the entire direction of Soviet policy and the Brezhnev doctrine became absolete. The notion of a 'socialist commonwealth' which previous Soviet leaders had done their best to uphold, lost its meaning once Gorbachev not only permitted but actually facilitated the collapse of communism in Eastern Europe. This step to end the communist bloc vastly improved the climate for East-West relations (including trade relations) and eliminated the burden that Eastern Europe had long imposed on Soviet Economic and Military resources. It also removed a major impediment to Gorbachev's domestic reform programme.

The revolutions in Eastern Europe in the last months of 1989 had swept away the communist regimes in East Germany, Czechoslovakia, Bulgaria and Romania. Apprehending that this might happen to them also the central committee plenum on 5-7 February 1990 agreed to modify Article 6 of the 1977 Soviet Constitution to remove the constitutional monopoly of CPSU on political power. This was confirmed by the Third (Emergency) Congress of USSR's People's Deputies on 14th March which strengthened Gorbachev's Presidential powers. Thus an era of one-party rule which had in effect begun in October 1917 with the Bolshevik seizure of power came to an end.

To prevent small nations from exercising their right to self-determination, communist ideologues throughout the East and Central Europe renamed them as 'nationalities'. In Marxist-Leninist terminology a nationality is a cultural group in a 'pre-national' state of development. It refers to people who, for whatever reasons, have not yet achieved the more respectable status of nationhood. It also signifies a cultural group that lives outside an existing nation-state in which the majority of its nationals live. While the Soviet constitution of 1977, at least, in theory explicitly allowed for nations in the fifteen republics to exercise their right to self-determination up to secession, most ethnic groups were effectively denied this right simply by their being declared as nationalities.

Baltic States

Soviet Union resorted to military intervention in January 1999 in the Baltic states of Lithuania, Latvia and Estonia. The crackdown started on 7th January 1991, when the USSR Defence Ministry ordered paratroopers to enter the three Baltic Republics as well as into Armenia, Georgia, Maldovia and parts of Ukraine to enforce conscription and round up deserters. Tension between the Republican leadership and the Soviet military had arisen over conscription and the stationing of Soviet troops in the republic. Both the Lithuanian and Latvian leadership had renewed calls for a red army withdrawal and the Latvian Supreme Council had authorised cutting of food and power supplies to Soviet military bases.

What was striking in the Russian political development during the period of 1989-92 was the extent to which the concept of sovereignty of small states was accepted at the expense of Russia's historically imperial vocation. President Boris Yeltsin consented to Baltic independence in January 1991, ratifying Lithuanian independence by treaty in July 1991. Similarly, a newly independent Russian Federation gladly consented to independence to more than 50 million Turkish Muslims of former Soviet Central Asia (1/6th of the Soviet population by 1989) and was agreed to live with an independent Ukraine considered even by many Russian liberals to be part and parcel of the Russian patrimony.

Lithuania

The Lithuanian republic was the first republic to declare its independence from the Soviet Union in March 1990. Election in February 1990 to the Supreme Soviet had resulted in the majority of seats going to the Nationalist Movement. In a referendum that followed in the same month 90.47 per cent voters favoured independence following Soviet military intervention in January 1990. Ethnically Lithuania had a 79.6 per cent Lithuanian population with only 9.4 per cent Russians and 7 per cent Poles. On 5 September, 1991, the Lithuanian Parliament dissolved 3 local councils in Polis and Russian dominated areas for allegedly supporting August coup in the USSR and imposed direct rule of the central government.

Latvia

On 4 May 1990, the Latvian Supreme Soviet declared the independent republic of Latvia by announcing that, 'now onwards all the Soviet laws would be superseded by the Latvian laws'. However, the announcement was subject to the ratification by a national refrendum in which all adults would vote. The referendum was held in March 1991 in which almost the entire population eligible to vote gave its verdict. In the announcement made in this connection it was declared that 73.68 per cent of voters favoured independence. Those who dissented were citizens of Russian origin and some other sub-national groups. The verdict of the people was made effective from 21st August 1991.

Estonia

In November 1989, the Estonian Supreme Soviet declared the republic to be sovereign and the Soviet laws enforced so far would be subject to approval of Estonian Supreme Soviet. In March 1990, the newly elected Supreme Soviet inaugurated a period of transition to independence and in May, five key articles of independent republics of the 1938 constitution were reinstated. Following a referendum on 3 March, 1991 in which 77.83 per cent of voters favoured full independence from the Soviet Union. This became effective from 20 August, 1991.

End of Warsaw Pact

It may be recalled that the Warsaw treaty concluded in 1955 stood disbanded on 25 February 1991, when foreign and defence ministers from Bulgaria, Czechoslovakia, Hungary, Poland, Armenia and the Soviet Union unanimously approved and signed a protocol cancelling the validity of all military agreements, organs and structures of the Warsaw treaty with effect from 31st March. Albania had already withdrawn in 1968 and East Germany ceased to exist on its unification with West Germany in October 1990. The dissatisfaction with the working of the alliance was quite clear at the Warsaw Pact Summit meeting in June 1990. A meeting of military experts of the pact in January 1991 also supported the view but the remarkable effect was that the Soviet President Mikhail Gorbachev himself had suggested to the leaders of the member states recommending the liquidation of Warsaw pact—military structure.

Disintegration

Despite the best efforts made by Gorbachev to hold the country together in December 1991, the Soviet Union formally dissolved into 15 independent states. This occurred partly because of the reluctance of Gorbachev and other central authorities to lose their control over the republics, despite the rapid change in the politics of the republics brought about by the 1990 elections.

Those leaders of the republics who claimed independence were called as separatists who were working against the true interests of the people. In making this remark Gorbachev and his friends ignored the fact that in many republics the drive for independence enjoyed broad popular support. The political future of leaders in these republics would have been in danger if they compromised with the cessation question. In the end concessions offered by Gorbachev to preserve the Union were inadequate and the failure of the coup of August 1991 accelerated the process of disintegration by further discrediting central institutions.

The Soviet system while formally federal constituting of 15 republics was actually an improved form of an extremely centralised military state. But the provisions of some dispersal of powers among the constituents and incorporation of some features of federal form was meant to convey the idea that the Soviet system was in keeping with the spirit of federation of the western concept. The element of tight centralism and a unitary state were brought to the system by a number of institutions, the chief one being the CPSU which while divided into 14 republic organisations retained a centralised structure. The shortcomings of federalism were most apparent in the economic field, where effective control and de jure ownership of the chief elements of the economy was maintained through the central ministries and the USSR state committees. Central control was specially prevalent in high priority sectors of the soviet economy such as heavy industry and the closely related defence industries. Nearly 30 per cent of local capital was invested outside Russia, in rail, air and sea transportation and power generation, but they were controlled by the central authorities located in Moscow. The extent of central control was greatest in the sensitive areas of defence and internal security. The Soviet military was a highly centralised structure with a central command in the form of a General staff that exercised control over all units of the military. The KGB while it had republic level organisations was also tightly monitored by the centre and served the centre almost exclusively.

Limited control over the administration of the economy and security were given to the republics in the form of republican ministries or jointly controlled union-republican ministry. These ministries were typically in areas considered of secondary importance in the Soviet economic system, such as consumer goods services, education and health care. Nevertheless, republic level leaders were not inclined to suggest that considerable power in matter of economic policies be shifted to the republics. The Soviet republics were far from uniform in the way they were governed and republic leaders could negotiate with centre for greater freedom of action. However, during the Brezhnev era, the economic and social policies varied greatly from republic to republic and reflected political culture as well as different styles of leadership.

Post-Disintegration Problems

After the dissolution of the USSR in December 1991, Russia became one of the founding members of the Commonwealth of Independent States. Boris Yeltsin was elected President in June 1991. A period of confrontation in 1992-93 between President Yeltsin and Parliament culminated on 21 September on a Presidential decree on "gradual constitutional reforms" which suspended the operations of Parliament, called new parliamentary elections for December, and assumed emergency executive powers. Parliament and the constitutional court rejected this action and parliament proclaimed Vice-President Rutskoi acting President.

This created a constitutional crisis in which the entire membership of the parliament was involved. Many deputies refused to leave the parliament building which was cordoned off by pro-Yeltsin forces. Public demonstrations and counter demonstration began on 26th September. After a week in which deputies remained in the Parliament building, some thousands of armed anti-Yeltsin demonstrators assembled on 3rd October and marched to seize the Kremlin and television centre. Shots were fired and there were fatal casualties. On 4th October, troops took the Parliament building by storm and in a ten-hour assault 140 people died. Vice-President Rutskoi and Speaker Khasbulatov were stripped off their offices and arrested.

Commonwealth of Independent States (CIS)

In order to prevent the splitting apart of the slav republics in the wake of Soviet disintegration, the Soviet Union was on 21 December 1991 replaced by Commonwealth of Independent States (CIS) grouping 11 of the former constituent republics of the union, but not Georgia, in loose alliance without central governing bodies. The CIS was formerly established at a meeting in Alma Ata where assurances were given to the world community that single control would be maintained over the nuclear weapons on former Soviet territory and that the treaty obligations of the Soviet Union would be respected towards the newly independent states. Some observers believed that the new formation should not be viewed as a permanent body but rather as a means for the republics to escape the central powers exercised by the Soviet Union. However, disputes between the CIS members became apparent immediately especially over economic issues and control of armed forces.

Communist Party

As earlier observed, one of the institutions that played the decisive role in keeping the system togther was of course the Communist Party. The political changes unleashed by Gorbachev affected the role of the Communist Party perhaps more than any Soviet institution. The pressures created by the democratisation led to strengthening the influence of republic level Communist Party organisations. This undermined the potential for the party to play a centralising role and it also failed to reduce the level of conflict between central and republic interests. The first communist party to defect to the side of nationalists was the Communist Party of Lithuania which was followed by others.

The period of six and a half years between the launching of the reforms programme in April 1985 and the aftermath of the abortive coup of August 1991 had seen CPSU transformed from the dominant institution within the political system to one which had been denied a place in the post coup political arrangements. A dream period remained in the party during the period of Gorbachev when he wanted to give a new life to the party. Gorbachev had assumed that the party would maintain its leadership in society. With the assistance of reformist allies in the party's ranks, Gorbachev introduced a series of reforms designed to improve the party but even these reforms did not succeed in their operations.

Legalisation of Political Parties

Since the CPSU had renounced its constitutionally 'guaranteed leading role' in March 1990, the USSR Supreme Soviet passed on 9 October 1990 a law on public associations which set up a multi-party system. New political parties and other types of public associations such as trade unions could be set up by as few as ten people. They were required to adopt statutes at a Constituent Congress and to register them with the ministry of justice or the equivalent republican ministry in case of republic-wise parties. All political parties would have the same legal standing as regards the permission to seek recruitment to the army forces and police; the law stated that such individuals, would be guided in their activity by the requirements of the law and were not bound by the decision of parties and public organisations to which they belonged.

A host of new political parties had already been formed in various parts of the Soviet Union and in the Baltic states also. A party seeking to appeal across republican boundaries and to challenge the CPSU on an all union basis had yet to emerge. However, the social democratic party of Russia and the democratic party of Russia were the two parties that had emerged on the political scene of the country. Later Democratic Party of Russia (DPR) was among nine fledgling political parties and 18 other groups which on 20 October 1990 constituted an opposition coalition called Democratic Russia.

Switch to Market Economy

An outline programme to create a market economic system was finally approved by the USSR Supreme Soviet on 19 October 1990. The programme was the product of three week's intensive work by President Gorbachev and his advisers to produce a compromise between radical proposals and more cautious plan proposed by the two sections of economic leaderships. A resolution called on the President in the Government to formulate detailed legislation to implement the programme.

The programme entitled 'Main Directions for Stabilisation of the National Economy and Transmission to a Market Economy' listed the following conditions for the creation of a market economy: (i) maximum freedom of economic activity (ii) full responsibility of organisations, entrepreneurs and workers for the results of their economic activity based on equality of all forms of property, (iii) competition between producers as a vital factor in stimulating economic activity, requiring an end to monopolies, (iv) price freedom based on supply and demand, (v) abandonment of direct state participation in economic activity with the exception of certain specific sectors, (vi) extension of market relations to those spheres where they were more effective than administrative forms of regulation, (vii) an open economy and its progressive integration with the world economic system (viii) a straight social security system.

The programme was conspicuously short on details as it omitted to take into account how its implementation would affect the republics. The republics were to decide for themselves policies in such key areas as private property and land ownership. They were also supposed to 'voluntarily delegate' to the central authorities control over financial credit and exchange policies to ensure protection of union-wide market. Gorbachev used his emergency presidential powers to issue in the month of October 1990 four decrees, marking critical steps towards market economy (i) liberalisation of wholesale prices (ii) rouble commercial exchange rate (iii) foreign ownership enterprises (iv) personal savings. The Supreme Soviet on 31 October 1990 adopted legislation cracking down on black market trading and their period of transition to a market economy. It covered speculative abuse of position by the trade workers such as the unauthorised sale of goods from depots and warehouses and private price fixing by groups or individuals with access to scare goods.

A very important landmark in the contemporary history of the USSR was its initiative to meet leaders of the G-7 Group of industrialised countries in London in July 1991 to discuss plans for Soviet economic reforms. This was made clear that the Soviet reforms would achieve some results if the government could obtain large scale technical and financial assistance tied to a five-year plan to create a market economy. The official indication that the Soviet Union was seeking large scale western aid was available through several government statements issued with a specific purpose to inform the public opinion abroad about how Russia was going to change its economic pattern.

Religion and Church

After Leonid Brezhnev became the leader of the country in the autumn of 1964, the church entered a new phase of its life. Though much of the ideological antagonism of the Khrushchev period survived, it became weaker and weaker as the Brezhnev years piled up. One reason for the weakening enthusiasm for the persecution of the church was that Brezhnev needed its support and participation in the world under peace movement which was sustained at Moscow's initiative. The church also gained because many of the intellectuals—political dissidents felt inclined to the church activities in so far as they promoted the idea of peace and welfare of the people. The Nobel Prize winning writer Alexander Solzhenitesyan declared himself as belonging to the church but protested against the passive acceptance of state control over the church. At the same time many opposition groups began to question publicly the interference by state bodies in the church and religious life of the people through occasional protests. This helped church to improve its position and began to acquire a new stature with the public.

The preceding discussion gives a clear picture of how far reaching changes have been made in the Soviet pattern of society which the leaders of Gorbachev's generation had inherited as a political legacy. The changes were overdue and the Soviet system could not afford to survive in the midst of fierce competition from other ideologies without effecting a radical change in its political and economic set up. All the changes were motivated by pragmatic considerations and not out of any desire to replace the old ideology with a new one. The approach was realistic and the efforts made were with the sole object of avoiding any ideological rigidity so that the society may take to new changes without being subject to any upheaval. However, change is a natural nemesis which in due course overtakes one and all and ideology can by no stretch of imagination be beyond its grip.

In this context a question arises: Was Marxism given a final good bye? Or was there any possibility of its regeneration? Marx and Engels put forward the concept of a classless formation of communist society with socialism as its beginning. For them this was a beginning of a new era which would bring about human society on a stable bases obviating the need of its replacement by a new order. But the history responded in a different way. In the process of formation of societies and regimes socialism in the Soviet Union was a stage in the march of events and so was its dissolution. The former marked the emergence of industrial revolution which witnesses the exploitation of man-by-man in the worst form and its mission was to liberate in its own way the exploited from the barbarity of exploiters. The latter announced that the industrial society had completed its mission and its was on the way to exit. Now in the new dispensation fresh relationships had to be introduced in which the evils of capitalist society would not be tolerated and the excesses of the socialist pattern would be totally discarded.

BIBLIOGRAPHY

Abercrombie N., Hill S., and Turner B.S.: *Dominant Ideology Thesis,* Allan and Unwin, London, 1980.

Adams and Others: *Foreign Governments and their Backgrounds,* p. 766.

Aiken, Henrey D.: *The Age of Ideology,* pp. 16-17.

Albig William, *Public Opinion,* New York, 1939, 12.

Andre, Gundar Frank: *Lessons of Democratic Social Development,* EPW, Vol 25, No. 5, Feb. 3, 1990, p. 251.

Althusser, L.: *Lenin and Philosophy,* New Left Books, London,1971.

Armstrong, John A., *"Ideology, Politics, and Government in the Soviet Union: An Introduction",* Frederick A. Praeger, New York, Publishers, New York, 1967.

Armstrong, John A. *Ukrainian Nationalism.* New York: Columbia University Press, 1956.

Ball, Allan R.: *Modern Politics and Government,* New York, Macmillian, 1973, p. 260.

Baykov, Alexander. *The Development of the Soviet Economic System.* New York: The Macmillan Company, 1947.

Becker, C.L.: *The Heavenly City of the 18th Century Philosophers,* New Heaven, 1932, 5.

Beetham, D: *Marxists face Fascism,* Manchester, Manchester, University Press, 1983.

Bell, D.: *The End of Ideology,* New York, Free Press, 1962, pp. 402-3.

Bell, D: *The End of Ideology,* New York, Free Press, 1960.

Bernstein: *The Preconditions of Socialism.*

Bomwall: *Major Contemporary Constitution System,* Ambala Cantt., Modern Publications, 1986, pp. 324-386.

Bramwell, Anna: *Ecology in the 20th Century,* Yale University, New Haven and London, 1989.

Brezezinski, Zbigniew K.: *The Soviet Bloc; Unity and Conflict,* 2nd ed., Cambridge, Harvard University Press, 1967, pp. 292-308.

Brezinski and Friedrich, C.J.: *Totalitarianism, Dictatorship and Autocracy,* New York, Praeger, 1961.

Campbell, John C.: *Soviet Policy in Eastern Europe: An Overview,* New Haven and London, Yale University Press, 1984.

Carver, Terrell: *Marx's Social Theory, Oxford,* Oxford University Press, Oxford, 1982, p. 44.

Chander, Prakash: *Studies in International Relations,* New Delhi, Bookhive (Regd.), pp. 113-142.

Charques, R.D.: *A Short History of Russia,* New York, E.P. Dutton and Company; Everyone Paper back, 1956.

Chatterjee, Partho: *Thinking About Ideology in Search of an Analytical Framework,* Radiand Publishers, 1980, p. 94.

Consequest Robert: *Russia After Khrushchev,* New York, Frederich A. Praeger, 1965.

Couart, Y.: *Disarmament,* p. 17.

Crabb, Cecilv.: *Nations in a Multi-polar World,* New York, Harper and Row, 1968.

Dunlop, Tohn B.: *The Rise and Fall of the Soviet Empire.*

Durkheim, Emile: *The Rules of Sociological Methods,* Chicago, 1937.

Egan, David R.: *V.I. Lenin (Biography)*

Ellison, Herbert J.: *History of Russia,* New York, Holt, Rinehart & Winston, 964.

Ferguson, Moira: *First Feminist British Women Writers 1578-1799,* Bloomington, Indian University Press, 1985.

Fukuyama, F.: *The End of the History and the Last Man,* London, Hamish Hamilton, 1992.

Fyodorov, Aleksei: *The Underground R.C. Carries On Moscow,* Foreign Languages Publishing House, 1952.

Gailbrith, J.K.: *The New Industrial State,* London, 1967.

Geertz, Clifford: *Ideology as a Cultural System,* New York, Free Press, 1964.

Gellner, E.: *Nations and Nationalism*, Oxford, Blackwell, 198, p. 125.

Gill, Graeme: *The Collapse of a Single Party System.*

Gould, Peter C.: *Early Green Politics: Back to Nature, Back to the Land and Socialism in Britain*, Brighton and New York, Harvester and St. Martin's Press, 1988.

Gusev, K. and Naumov, N.: *The USSR: A Short History.*

Hazard, John.: *Law and Social Change in the USSR*, London, Stevens and Sons, 1953.

Heater, Derck,: *Political Realties—Contemporary Political*, Longman, p. 26.

Hobhouse: *Liberalism and Other Writings.*

Hoffmann, Stanley: *Contemporary Theory in International Relations*, Englewood Cliffs, New Jersey, Prentice-Hall, 1964.

Hunt, Robert N.C.: *The Theory and Practice of Communism*, New York, The Macmillan Company, 1954.

Imam, Jafer: *Soviet Foreign Policy.*

Kegley, Charles W. and Wittkoff, Eugene R: *World Politics Trends and Transformation*, p. 42.

Kertesz, Stephen D.: *The Fate of East Central Europe—Hopes and Failures of American Foreign Policy*, Notre Dam, University of Notre Dam Press, 1956, pp. 228-31.

Kraus, Michael: *Gorbachev's Reform in Eastern Europe*, Cambridge, Ballinger Publishing Co., 1988, p. 162.

Kushukin, Yu: *History of USSR, Moscow*, Progress Publisher, 1981, pp. 15-44.

Laski: *The Social and Political Ideas of Some Representative Thinkers of Victorian Age*, Chapter V, p. 100.

Leggett, Robert E. and Kellogg, Robert E: *The Soviet Union—An Economy in Transition and its Prospects for Eco. Growth*, Cambridge, 1980, p. 28.

Lenin, V.I.: *Imperialism and State and Revolution*, New York, The Vanguard Press, 1929.

Lipset, S.M.: *Political Man*, Double Days and Company Inc.

Lukacs, George: *History and Class Consciousness*, London, Muslim Press, 1971.

Marcuse, Herbert: Soviet Marxist: *A Critical Analysis London*, Routladge and Kegan Paul.

Marcuse, Herbert: *One Dimensional Man*, London, Routladge and Kagan Paul, 1964.

Marx, Karl & Engels, Friedrich: *The German Ideology*, London, Lawrence. and Wishart, 1974, p. 64.

Marx Karl and Engels, Friedrich: *Selected Works in One Volume*, London, Lawrence and Wishart, 1984, p. 183.

Mannheim, Karl: *Ideology and Utopia*, London, Routledge and Kegan Paul, 1936.

Mastney, Vojtech: *Russia Road to the Cold War: Diplomacy, Warfare and the Politics of Communism*, New York, Columbia University, 1979, pp. 183-228.

McGovern, W.H.: *From Luther to Hitler*, Boston, 1941, Chapter IX.

Melkote, Rama S. and Rao, A. Narasimha: *International Relations*, Sterling Publishers Pvt. Ltd., p. 113-130.

Meyer, Alfred G.: *The Soviet Political System—An Interpretation*, New York, Random Hose, 1965.

Monnerot, Jules: *Sociology and Psychology of Communism*, Boston, Beacon Press, 1953.

Moskvichov, L.N.: *The End of Ideology Theory—Illusion and Reality*, Moscow, 1964, p. 115.

Oelschlaeger, Max: *The Idea of Wilderness From Pre-history to the Age of Ecology*, New Haven and London, Yale University Press, 1991, ch. 1.

Parekh, Bhikhu and Pantham, Thomas: *Political Discourse: Exploration in Indian and Western Political Thought*.

Plamentz, John: *Ideology*, London, Pall Mall, 1970, p. 11.

Piere, R.T. La, *Collective Behaviour*, New York, 1938, 56 and 57.

Pistrak, Lazar: *The Grand Tactician*, New York, Frederick A. Praeger, 1961.

Popper, K.: *The Open Society and its Enemies*, Vol. 2, London, Routledge and Kegan Paul, 1961.

Rakowska, Teresa, Harnstone and Gyorgy: *Communism in Eastern Europe*.

Ray, Amal and Battacharya, Mohit: *Political Theory—Ideas and Institutions*, The World Press Pvt. Ltd., p. 602.

Roucek, Joseph S., *A History of the Concept of Ideology*.

Rush, Myron: *Political Succession in the USSR*, New York, Columbia University Press, 1961.

Sakwa, Richard: *Gorbachev and his Reforms 1985-90*, New York, Prentice Hall, 1990, p. 11.

Sartori, G.: *Democratic Theory*, Calcutta, 1965, p. 364.

Scruton, R.: *In Defence of the Nation*, in Britain, London, Macmillian, 1990, pp. 58-9.

Seliger, H.: *Ideology and Politics*, London, Allen and Unwin, 1976, p. 13.

Singh, Gopal and Bharadwaj, Prem: *Soviet Disintegration*.

Smith, A: *The Ethnic Origin of Nations*, Oxford, Basil Blackwell, 1986.

Sorokin, P.A.: *Mutual Convergence of the United States and the USSR to the Mixed Socio-Cultural Type*, Mexico, 1961.

Stalin Joseph V.: *The History of the Communist Party of the Soviet Union (Bolsheviks)*, New York, International Publishers, 1939.

Steele, Jonathan: *Eternal Russia*.

Stoessinger: *The Might of Nations: World Politics in Our Time*, New York, 1969.

Strong, Douglas H.: *Dreamers and Defenders: American Conversationists*, London, University of Nebraska Press, 1988.

Sullivan, N.O.: *The Structure of Modern Ideology*, Elgas, Aldershot, 1989.

Towster, Julian: *Political Power in the USSR*, p. 50, p. 7.

Vyshinsky, Aa.V.: *The Law of the Soviet State*, pp. 152.

Watkins, F.M.: *The Age of Ideology—Political Thought, 1750 to Present*, New Delhi, Prentice Hall of India, Pvt. Ltd., 1968.

Waxman, C.I.: *The End of Ideology Debate*.

Watter, Gustav A.: *Dialectical Materialism*, New York, Frederick A. Praeger, 1959.

White, Stephen: *Political Culture and Soviet Politics*, London, The Macmillian Press, 1979, p. 64.

Wirth, Louis: *Introduction to Ideology and Utopia*, New York, 1938.

Wiseman, H.V.: *Political System,* London, Routlege and Kegan Paul, 1966.

Wright, Quincy: *A Study of International Relations,* New York, Appleton, Century—Crofts, 1955.

Yakovlev, Alexander: *The Fate of Marxism in Russia.*

Young, Oran R: *Systems of Political Science,* Englewood Cliffs, N.J.: Prentice Hall, Inc. 1968.

Young, Ronald: *Approaches to the Study of Politics,* Evanston, RII, Northwestern University Press, 1958.

Zimmes, Paul E.: *Communist Strategy and Tactics in Czechoslovakia, 1918-1948,* London, Pall Hall, 1963.

Zoll, D.A.: *Twentieth Century Political Philosophy,* Prentice Hall, Inc., Engelwood Cliffs, New Jersey, 1974.

PERIODICALS

Banerjee, Arup: *Privatisation in the Russian Federation,* Economic and Political Weekly, Dec. 18, 1993.

Benegal, Som: *Meeting the Soviet Crisis,* Mainstream, Nov. 30, 1991.

Bose, Arun: *The fate of USSR,* Seminar 389, Jan. 1992.

Buzgalin, Alexander and Kolganov, Andrei: *Right Suffers Powerful Moral Defeat,* Mainstream, Jan. 6, 1996.

Chakravartty, Sumit: *Russia's Changing Scene,* Mainstream, March 16, 1996.

Chandra, Nirmal Kumar: *Dimensions of Social and Economical Crisis in Russia Today,* Economic and Political Weekly, May 1, 1996.

Chenoy, Anuradha M.: *Systematic Change and Systematic Collapse,* Seminar 393, May 1992.

Clairmont, Frederic F.: *Russia: Countdown to What?* Economic and Political Weekly, June 29, 1996.

Drobizheva, Leokadia: *Russian Ethnic Attitudes in Changing Political Situation,* Economic and Political Weekly, Dec. 18, 1993.

Gill, Ashim: *Ideological Considerations—Impact of Various Ideologies Down The Age,* The Hindustan Times, New Delhi, Feb. 17, 1996.

Gonsalves, Eric: *Lessons from the Soviet Revolution,* Mainstream, Annual 1991.

Gujral, I.K. USSR: *The Contemporary Scene,* Mainstream, Annual 1991.

Huntington, Samuel: *Will More Countries Become Domocratic*, Political Science Quarterly, Vol. 99, Summer, 1984.

India Today, Vol. XVII, No. 18, Sept. 16-30, 1992 pp. 124-25.

Keesing: *Record of World Events, 1990, 1991, 1992.*

Kohli, Manorama: *Disintegration of Soviet Union: Implications for India,* Quarterly, Vol. XLIX, July-Sept., 93, No. 3, p. 85.

Khoros, Vladimir G.: *Perestroika and the History of Russia,* Mainstream, January 18, 1992.

Karun, Timur: Not Out of Power: *The Elements of Surprise in the East European Revolution of 1989,* World Politics, Vol. 44, Oct. 1991, p. 26.

Lowenthal, Richard: *A World Adrift, Encounter.*

Munirka, Dev: *Religion in Russia Today,* Economic and Political Weekly, Dec. 18, 1993.

Mutton, R.K. and Mannheim, Karl: *Journal of Liberal Religion*, Winter 1941.

Narayanan, K.R.: *Soviet Changes: Multi-Dimensional Impact,* Mainstream, Annual 1991.

Parekh, Bhikhu: *Superior People,* Commentary, Feb. 25. 1994.

Palombara Joseph La: *Decline of Ideology: A Dissent And An Interpretation,* The American Political Science Review, Yale University, Vol. LX, March 1966.

Rai Lajpat: *Reflections on Soviet Events,* Mainstream, February 4, 1992.

Ramachandran, P.: Ideology: *How the CPSU Leadership Abandoned Marxism,* The Marxist, pg. 23.

Roucek, Joseph S.: *A History of The Concept of Ideology,* Notes and Documents.

Schopflin, George: *The End of Communism in Eastern Europe,* International Affairs, Vol. 66, No. 1, pg. 3-6.

Sen. Mohit: *The Soviet Crisis and India,* Seminar 389, January 1992.

Shebarshin, Leonid: *Reflections on the KGB in Russia,* Economic and Political Weekly, December 18, 1993.

Slovo, Joe, *Has Socialism Failed?* Linc News Weekly, Nov. 1, 1992.

Som, Pijush: *Perestroika and After: A Critique of Developments in Former Soviet Union, Mainstream,* April 4, 1992,

Special Report, Time, Sept. 5, 1950.

Times of India, New Delhi, Sept. 4, 1992.

Tisshkov, Valerii: *Women in Russian Politics*, Economic and Political Weekly, December 18, 1993.

Vasudevan, Hari: *Russia's Presidency*, Economic and Political Weekly, December 18, 1993.

Weir, Fred: *Russian Parliamentary Poll: Yeltsin's Greatest Accomplishment*, Mainstream, January 13, 1996.

Weir, Fred: *Russian Communists Plan Broadbased Opposition Movement*, Mainstream, July 27, 1996.

Weir, Fred: *Russia's Descent into Latin America*, Economic and Political Weekly, December 18, 1993.

Wofsy, Leon: *Gorbachev's New Thinking and World Politics*, Monthly Review (New York), Vol. 40, No. 5, p. 20.

APPENDIX

CHRONOLOGY OF ETHNIC UNREST IN THE USSR 1986-1991

This chronology was compiled from various sources including Report on the USSR, FBIS Daily Report, The New York Times, Nationalities Papers, and The Economist.

June 1986: Ethnic tensions between Russians and Yakutsin city of Yakutsk.

December 1986: Dinmukhamed Kunaev replaced as party leader of Kazakhstan by Gennadii Kolbin, an ethnic Russian. Riots in Alma-Ata.

August 1987: Demonstrators turn out in all three Baltic capitals to mark the 48th anniversary of the Nazi-Soviet pact which resulted in their incorporation into the USSR.

January 1988: A petition is signed by 75,000 Armenians demanding the annexation of Nagorno-Karabakh by the Armeinian Republic.

February 1988: One million Armenians participate in protests and strikes in the Armenian capital of Erevan. Clashes in Sumgait, Azerbaijan, result in the deaths of at least thirty-one people.

Police and civilian auxiliary officers prevent demonstrations to mark Lithuania's twenty years of independence.

April 1988: Estonia forms a Popular Front. Latvia and Lithuania soon follow suit.

July 1988: 100,000 Lithuanians attend a rally in Vilnius to hear a report from Lithuanian participants in the party conference.

November 1988: The Estonian Supreme Soviet declares its right to veto all-union laws passed in Moscow by a vote of 258-1 (with several abstentions). Gorbachev assails this decision.

January 1989: A rally in Lithuania calls for the removal of all Soviet troops from the Baltic. Estonia and Lithuania make Estonian and Lithuanian their official state languages. Latvia and Moldavia prepare for similar action.

March 1989: 20,000 demonstrate in Riga against the Latvian Party Central Committee's condemnation of "anti-Soviet and separatist" currents in the republic.

April 1989: Nineteen demonstrators are killed and 200 are wounded in clashes with Soviet troops at a pro-independence rally in Tbilisi. Attempts are made to distance Gorbachev from the massacre, leading to the replacement of Georgia's party secretary and premier.

Soviet troops pour into Tashkent, the capital of Uzbekistan, following a nationalist meeting.

Soviet tanks roll into the Estonian cities of Tallinn and Tartu and the Latvian capital of Riga.

2,000 members of the Democratic Union rally in Moscow to protest the killings in Tbilisi; forty-seven are arrested.

May 1989: The Estonian Supreme Soviet votes for an economic autonomy programme. The Lithuanian Supreme Soviet votes for constitutional amendments, granting Lithuania the right to veto Soviet laws.

June 1989: 70,000-80,000 demonstrators participate in a rally by the Popular Front of Moldavia to protest the 1940 annexation of Moldavia by the USSR.

Rioting breaks out in the Fergana region of Uzbekistan between Uzbeks and Meskhetian Turks. Seventy-nine are killed and 800 injured.

July 1989: Ethnic riots break out in Tajikistan, Uzbekistan, and Kazakhastan, as well as in Abkhazia, Georgia. In Abkhazia, eighteen are killed and 239 injured.

Gorbachev warns the Union in a television broadcast that ethnic conflict poses a great threat to continued state stability.

20,000 Georgians march for independence in Tbilisi.

August 1989: Approximately one million demonstrators in the Baltics participate in a human chain of protest against the 50th anniversary of the Nazi-Soviet pact. Lithuania declares that the 1940 annexation to the USSR is invalid.

Estonia passes a voter-registration law.

Representatives of several pro-independence groups gather at Riga Conference to make radical demands.

Moldavians rally to make Moldavian the official language of the republic.

Thousands of Russian factory and shipyard workers in Tallinn walk off their jobs in protest against perceived discrimination. Language and residency requirements are cited.

September 1989: Founding Conference of the Ukrainian Popular Front for Perestroika (Rukh) in Kiev.

Ukraine announces that Ukrainian will become the Republic's official language.

Azerbaijan passes an extensive sovereignty law.

October 1989: The Latvian Popular Front declares a goal of "complete independence" at their 2nd Congress.

November 1989: Lithuania moves to have a popular referendum on the question of secession.

December 1989: The Lithuanian Communist Party secedes from the USSR Communist Party. The Lithuanian legislature votes 243-1 to abolish the clause in its constitution which grants the Communist Party a monopoly on power.

The Armenian Supreme Soviet votes to unite with Nagorno-Karabagh region.

Nationalist and Popular Front movements achieve victory in Latvian and Estonian elections.

January 1990: Fierce fighting breaks out between Armenians and Azerbaijanis. Sixty-six are killed and 220 injured. 10,000 Armenians and many Russians are evacuated from Azerbaijan. Soviet troops attack Baku, using artillery, tank, and naal gunfire to break a blockade of Baku's port and raid the offices of the Azerbaijani Popular Front.

Ukrainian Popular Front mobilizes 400,000 to form a human chain from Lviv to Kiev

February 1990: Thousands participate in riots in the Tajik capital of Dushanbe. Thirty-seven are killed and eighty wounded. The clashes are provoked by false rumours that thousands of Armenians were to be given preference for apartments in the capital.

Lithuania requests talks with Moscow to discuss ending all constitutional ties to the Soviet Union.

Ethnic violence occurs in Samarkand, Uzbekistan after 10,000 people demonstrate to demand an end to persecution of Uzbek Popular Front members.

March 1990: The Lithuanian Supreme Soviet declares Lithuania to be an independent state by a vote of 124-0 (with six abstentions). A non-communist, Vytautas Landsbergis, is elected president, Gorbachev claims acts are "illegal and invalid." Soviet tanks and personnel carriers rumble thorugh the streets of Vilnius. Lithuania appeals for international recognition.

Tens of thousands of Ukrainians defy a ban by the Kiev authorities and answer a call by Rukh for mass meetings in support of Lithuanian independence.

Estonia declares its independence.

April 1990: Moscow imposes severe economic sanctions on Lithuania, implementing embargoes of oil and gas supplies. Estonia supports Lithuanian independence in a resolution.

200,000 rally in Tbilisi to press for independence and to protest the April 1989 massacre.

May 1990: Latvia declares its independence.

The Baltics decide to coordinate independence movement policies.

Commission on Tatars adopts a programme to return Tatars to their historical homeland in the Crimea between 1991 and 1996.

More ethnic violence occurs in Armenia while tens of thousands demonstrate demanding formal political ties with Nagorno-Karabakh.

June 1990: The RSFSR Congress of people's Deputies votes overwhelmingly for sovereignty.

Uzbekistan declares sovereignty.

139 people are killed in inter-ethnic violence over a land dispute between Uzbeks and Kyrghyz in Kyrghyzan's Osh oblast.

July 1990: Ukraine declares sovereignty and rejects the "deployment, production, and use of nuclear weapons on its territory."

Ethnic violence continues in Osh, Kyreyzstan.

Belarus declares sovereignty.

August 1990: Karelia becomes the first ASSR to declare its sovereignty.

Komi and Tataria soon follow.

3,000 people flee Tuva because of conflict between ethnic Russians and locals.

September 1990: "Dniester-Soviet" and Gagauz leaders proclaim secession from Moldavia and recognize each other.

A state of emergency is declared in Mordvinia banning all rallies, meetings, and city and rayon soviet sessions in response to mounting public movement against the republican leadership.

Turkmenistan Parliament declares sovereignty.

75,000 to 100,000 rally in Kiev for greater independence from Moscow.

October 1990: Ukrainian students declare a hunger strike in Kiev, demanding rejection of the new union treaty, full sovereignty and independence, an end to Communist party domination, and radical social and economic reforms. Ukrainian prime minister Masol tenders his resignation Yakutia, Chukchi, Chuvash, Mari, Khanty-Mansil, Yamal-Nenets, and Udmurtia move to declare sovereignty.

November 1990: Following the proclamation of an independent Dniester Republic, the Moldovan militi clashes with an "internationalist detachment" of Russian workers. Six are killed, thirty injured.

December 1990: Lithuania and Estonia boycott the Federation Council Meeting.

North Ossetia declares itself a union republic.

January 1991: Attempting to take control of local radio and television stations in Vilnius, Soviet troops kill fourteen Lithuanians. Gorbachev claims he did not order the violence.

200,000 rally in Moscow to protest Lithuanian crack-down and call for Gorbachev to resign.

Ten are killed in ethnic conflict in Nagorno-Karabakh.

Six Georgian policemen are killed in a South Ossetia shootout.

Moldova revokes a Soviet conscription law declaring Moldova's youth are not obliged to serve in Soviet armed forces.

Moldovan Popular Front decides to boycott the all-Union referendum to be held in March.

Georgia boycotts the March referendum. The Georgian Supreme Soviet moves to create a National Guard.

February 1991: Lithuanians vote 9:1 in favour of a "democrtic and independent state of Lithuania."

Ukraine discusses the possibility of an independent army.

North Ossetia requests presidential rule.

Ukraine Supreme Soveit supports Crimean Independence. A national referendum is slated on the question.

Lviv, Ivano-Frankovsk, and Termopol oblasts decide to hold separate ballots.

Turkmenistan makes plans to crerate foreign consulates.

Gagauz opens its own university.

500,000 rally in Nagorno-Karabakh for a transfer of Nagorno-Karabakh to Armenian control. Two are killed there in continuing ethnic violence.

Shooting occurs among national militias in Tskhinvali, South Ossetia.

March 1991: Latvians and Estonians turn out for a referendum on independence. Both have large majorities in favour.

Armenia decides to hold a referendum on independence, 98 per cent vote for secession.

Moldova creates a presidential style government.

Chechen-Ingushetia ASSR issues a statement that they will not participate in the referendum.

Ethnic Germans in the USSR hold a conference to request the re-creation of a German ASSR on the Volga. South Ossetian extremists burn four Georgians to death.

Latvia approves a law to protect minorities in the republic.

Ukraine approves private land ownership.

Armenians attack the village Kheyrimli, Azerbaijan; casualties result.

April 1991: The Georgian government demands that Gorbachev withdraw troops from South Ossetia and in a unanimous vote declares full secession from the Union.

Soviet troops and Azerbaijani militia begin a crackdown on Armenian insurgents in Western Azerbaijan. Thirty-five Armenians are killed by Soviet troops and Azerbaijani police during an attack on the village of Getasen in Azerbaijan.

Armenia, Estonia, Latvia, Lithuania, Georgia, and Moldova propose cooperation in independence efforts.

The Kyrghyz Supreme Soviet refuses to sign the Union Treaty.

Communist Party property in Armenia is nationalized.

100,000 workers strike in Belarus asserting political demands.

The Peoples' Front of Latvia drafts a plan for a transition period in the move toward Latvian independence.

Eight are killed and sixteen wounded in ethnic clashes between Checken-Ingush and Cossaks in Cossak settlement 80 km. from Grozny in the Checheno-Ingushetia ASSR.

May 1991: Armed Georgians kill seven in South Ossetia, secession conflicts are cited.

200,000 rally for Lithuanian independence in Vilnius.

The New Ukrainian Constitution draft is published. An independence referendum is planned for Ukraine.

Checheno-Ingushetia declares a National "Justice Day" for the rehabilitation of repressed peoples.

The Congress of People's Deputies of Dagestan declares the autonomus republic to be the Sovereign Dagestan SSR.

1,500 Armenians are forcibly deported from Nagorno-Karabakh by Azerbaijanis; 1,200 more are forced to leave their homes and live in tents.

Anti-election protests in Tatarstan. Protestors do not want the RSFSR presidential elections to take place as scheduled for June 12.

Independence-seeking republics set up a coordinating body. Six republics are involved: Moldavia, Lithuania, Latvia, Estonia, Georgia, and Armenia.

June 1991: Soviet troops set up checkpoints in Vilnius. Lithuanians hold a vigil around the parliament building in Vilnius to help prevent an army attack.

Moldova founds a National Bank, separate from the Union.

The Congress of the Chechen People reaffirms the decision to rename Checheno-Ingushetia the Chechen Republic of Nakhnichichi, to exist within historical boundaries.

President of Georgia, Zviad Gamsakhurdia, states that Georgia wants membership in the European Community.

The RSFSR Supreme Soviet approves a draft law "On the Languages of the Peoples of the RSFSR."

Crimean Tatars vote for sovereignty.

A Ukrainian Worekers' Union is formed. During a protest in Kiev demonstrators demand that Ukraine reject the proposed Union Treaty.

An German National Raion is created in Altai Krai.

July 1991: An opinion poll in Lithuania shows that 85 per cent of the population supports independence, with only 4 per cent opposed. A similar poll conducted in Armenia indicates that 80 per cent of Armenians support secession from the USSR.

Troops order the inhabitants of three Armenian villages in the Geranboi region to leave their homes.

Several Russian democratic groups within the RSFSR oppose Azerbaijan's signing of the Union Treaty because of human rights violations in the republic. They demand guarantees of minority Russian rights within Azerbaijan as a pre-condition to Azerbaijan's participation in the new union.

Crimean ASSR drafts a constitution which is adopted by the Crimean Supreme Soviet.

Uzbeks set up an International Association, El, to develop cultural and economic cooperation between Soviet Uzbeks and Uzbek diasporas.

1,000 Meskhetians, Muslim ethnic Georgians who were deported by Stalin, demonstrate outside the Kremlin.

August 1991: The National Independence Front is formed in Lithuania.

The International Israeli Organization opens a branch in Kiev to promote Jewish culture, tradition, and customs in Ukraine.

A proposal to create a Siberian Soviet Federal Republic is published in Narodnaya Tribuna.

The self-styled "Dniester SSR" moves to separate all enterprises and institutions from Moldova.

"Gang of Eight" Soviet hardliners stage a coup, detaining President Gorbachev in the Crimea. Coup fails to gain popular and military support.

Baltic governments in exile are planned in case the elected governments are unable to function after the coup. Lithuania demands removal of Soviet forces from the republic. Latvia asserts that the coupleaderw have no authority in the Latvian Republic. Estonia condemns the coup and declares independence.

Moldova issues a statement condemning the coup and calls for independence.

Anti-coup protests are organized in Ukraine, and the Ukrainian parliament declares independence.

Turkmen President Niyazov declares coup authority in Turkmenistan.

Uzbek President Karimov declares coup initiatives invalid.

Yeltsin issues a decree recognizing Estonia's and Latvia's independence.

September 1991: Belarus declares independence and decides to form its own defense system.

Uzbekistan movers to break away from the Union. Later both Uzbekistan and Kyrgystan declare independence.

Demonistrators in Azerbaijan call for independence. The Azerbaijani Supreme Soviet votes to restore the independent status the republic had in 1918-1920. Nagarno-Karabakh declares independence from Azerbaijan. Azerbaijan Popular Front demonstrations in Baku call for dissolution of the republic's Supreme Soviet.

Lithuania demands that the Soviet army withdraw completely from its territory. Estonia nationalizes all Soviet property. Baltic states are recognized internationally, and the Council of Europe grants all three guest status.

Moldova proclaims independence and receives diplomatic recognition from Romania and Georgia.

Ukraine seeks diplomatic ties with the United States, Canada, Israel, and all states with which it shares a border. Demonstrations occur in Western Ukraine in support of Ukrainian independence. Ukrainian nationalists also protest against the proposed economic union.

Ukraine calls for its own army.

Tajikistan declares economic sovereignty and later declares independence.

Armenia nationalizes all Communist Party property and votes for secession. 95 per cent of the electorate participates in referendum on secession.

The self-proclaimed Gagauz Republic declares independence.

The Georgian parliament breaks ties with the USSR.

Turkmenistan decides to hold a referendum on independence.

October 1991: The Baltic council, comprised the leaders of Lithuania, Latvia, and Estonia, issue a joint statement demanding the withdrawal of Soviet troops from their respective territories to begin immediately. The Baltic states join UNESCO. Later they are admitted as associate members of the North Atlantic Assembly. Lithuania declares it does not intend to take on USSR debts.

The Ukrainian Parliament passes a law on citizenship requirements. Ukraine insists on having its own armed forces.

Northern Ingush Republic is proclaimed.

An overwhelming majority in Azerbaijan votes against signing an interrepublican economic treaty.

The Supreme Soviet of Tatarstan adopts a resolution on state independence. A national referendum is called on the status of the republic.

In Turkmenistan 94 per cent vote for independence in a referendum.

The Belarus Supreme Soviet prepares a draft proposal for a republican national guard.

Uzbek Popular Front proclaims itself an official political party. Uzbeks try to retrieve the throne of the Khans in the Hermitage in St. Petersburg, claiming it belongs to the Uzbek people.

The Kazakh government derives a plan to issue its own currency in the republic.

The Georgian Supreme Soviet rejects Georgian participation in the new treaty on economic union.

November 1991: The Moldovan First Deputy Prime Minister and Economics Minister asserts that Moldova intends to cancel her initial adherence to a proposed Treaty on the Economic Community of Sovereign States. The Moldovan Popular Front calls for reunification with Romania.

Moldova takes over Soviet army property and establishments in Moldovan soil and moves to form a professional army.

Parliamentary elections occur in Checheno-Ingushetia.

Parliament decides to nationalize all enterprises, departments, and associations of Checheno-Ingushetia.

An Independent Association of Ukrainian Officers is formed. Ukraine moves to place military units in its territory under under the republic's control. A Ukrainian independence poll indicate, a majority of people support the August declaration of independence.

Uzbekistan nationalizes all gold mines within the republic.

Magadan Oblast opposes move by Chukchi Autonomous Okrug to secede.

Lithuania and Latvia introduce national currencies.

Latvia claims property occupied by the Soviet army.

Estonia adopts a citizenship law which is in essence a re-adoption of the 1938 citizenship law and tightens border controls by restricting crossings. Lithuania establishes diplomatic links with NATO.

Belarus makes initiatives for a separate currency and establishes a defense ministry.

Balkar Republic is proclaimed by Balkar people in Nalchuk, the capital of Kalbarden-Balkar Republic in the North Caucasus. A Confederation of Mountain Peoples of Caucasus is proclaimed.

Azerbaijan tries to abolish the Autonomous state of Nagorno-Karabakh.

December 1991: Ukraine votes 9:1 for independence.

Kravchuk becomes the first president of independent Ukraine receiving 61 per cent of the popular vote. Kravchuk declares he will not sign a Union Treaty, economic or otherwise. Crimea supports an independent Ukraine with 51 per cent in favour. Poland, Hungary, and Canada recognize independent Ukraine.

Leader of the three Slav republics, Russia, Belarus, and Ukraine, declare a new Commonwealth of Independent States. Minsk is chosen capital of this new Commonwealth. The agreement of the three republics states that the Soviet Union no longer exists. Gorbachev resists dissolution of the Union.

Announcements are made that on December 31, 1991 the Soviet flag will be lowered from atop the Kremlin, Gorbachev says he is prepared to resign.

Five Asian republics, Kyrghyzstan, Kazakhstan, Turkmenia, Uzbekistan, and Tajikistan, join the plan for a Commonwealth.

Russia, Belarus, and Ukraine ask the United States for recognition. Yeltsin declares Russia wants to join NATO.

Eleven states, all of the former republics except the Baltics and Georgia, formally establish the Commonwealth of Independent States.

Russia assumes the Soviet seat of the United Nations Security Council.

Ethnic violence erupts in Georgia as Georgian nationalists demand resignation of President Gamsakhurdia.

Gorbachev resigns marking the formal dissolution of the Soviet Union.

Note:

This Appendix was compiled by

Siobhan Fisher.

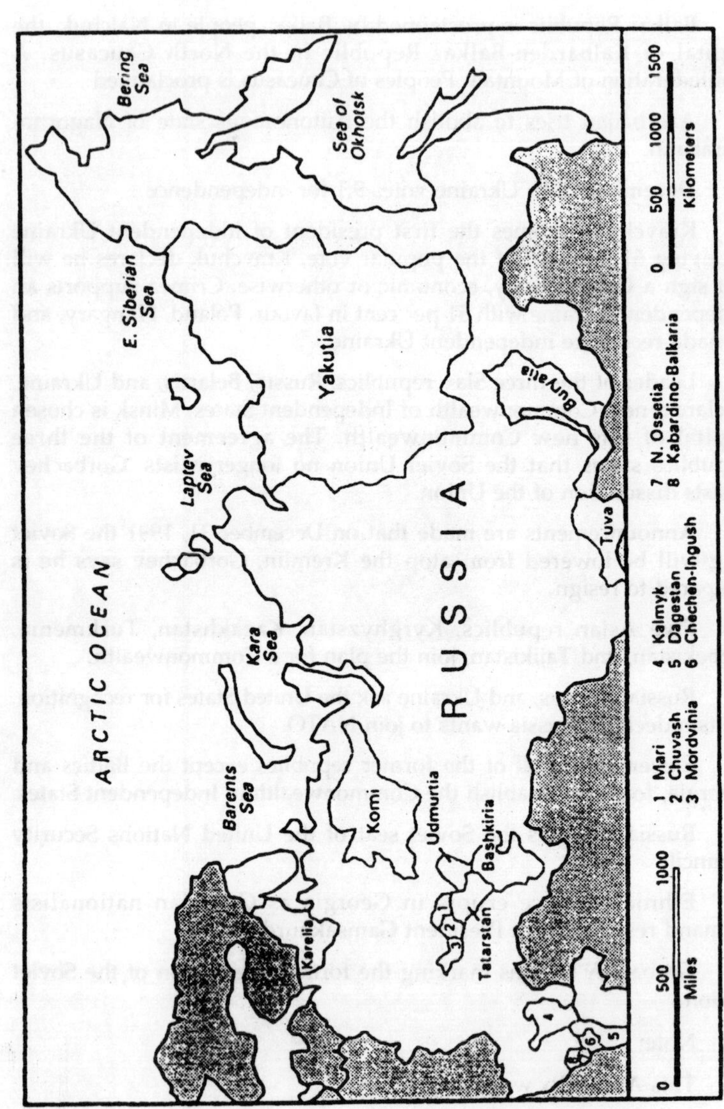
ARCTIC OCEAN
Barents Sea
Kara Sea
Laptev Sea
E. Siberian Sea
Bering Sea
Sea of Okhotsk
RUSSIA
Karelia
Komi
Udmurtia
Tatarstan
Bashkiria
Yakutia
Buryatia
Tuva
1 Mari
2 Chuvash
3 Mordvinia
4 Kalmyk
5 Dagestan
6 Chechen-Ingush
7 N. Ossetia
8 Kabardino-Balkaria
0 500 1000 Miles
0 500 1000 1500 Kilometers

Russia

The Caucasus

Area of Detail
Gulf of Finland
Narva
Rakvere
Ahtme
TALINN
BALTIC SEA
ESTONIA
Tartu
Parnu
Viljandi
Valga
Gulf of Riga
LATVIA
Ventspils
RIGA
Jurmala
Daugava R
Daugavapils
Liepaja
Jelgava
LITHUANIA
Taurage
Kaunas
VILNIUS
Alytus
0 25 50 75 100
Kilometers
0 25 50 75
Miles

The Baltics

Table—1.1. Russian Population Distribution in the Soviet Republics by 1989 (in thousands of persons)

Republic	Total population	Russian population	Russian percentage of total population
Russian Federation	147,000	119,865	81.5
Ukraine	51,452	11,356	22.1
Kazakhstan	16,463	6,228	37.8
Uzbekistan	19,810	1,652	8.3
Belorussia	10,152	1,342	13.2
Kirgizia	4,258	917	21.5
Latvia	2,667	906	34.0
Moldavia	4,335	562	13.0
Estonia	1,565	475	30.3
Azerbaijan	7,021	392	5.6
Tadjikistan	5,093	388	7.6
Lithuania	3,675	344	9.4
Georgia	5,401	341	6.3
Turkmenistan	3,523	334	9.5
Armenia	3,305	52	1.6

Source: 1989 population census.

Percentage Distribution of Population in Latvia and Estonia, by Ethnic, Group, 1959-1989

	1959	1970	1979	1989
Latvia				
Latvians	62.0	56.8	53.7	52.0
Russians	26.6	29.8	32.8	34.0
Belorussians	2.9	4.0	4.5	4.5
Ukrainians	1.4	2.3	2.7	3.5
Others	7.1	7.1	6.3	6.0
Estonia				
Estonians	74.6	68.2	64.7	61.5
Russians	20.1	24.7	27.9	30.3
Ukrainians	1.3	2.1	2.5	3.1
Belorussians	0.9	1.4	1.6	1.8
Others	3.1	3.6	3.3	3.3

Source: Population census for the years shown.

Index